The Quran With Tafsir Ibn Kathir
Part 18 of 30:
Al Muminum 001 To Al Furqan 020

The Quran With Tafsir Ibn Kathir Part 18 of 30: Al Muminum 001 To Al Furqan 020

With
Arabic Script, Transliteration of Arabic, Meaning in English and Ibn Kathir's Abridged Tafsir (Explanation)

Muhammad Saed Abdul-Rahman

BSc, DipHE

© Muhammad Saed Abdul-Rahman, 2012
ISBN 978-1-86179-879-4

All Rights reserved

British Library Cataloguing in Publication Data. A Catalogue record for this book is available from the British Library

Designed, Typeset and produced by:
MSA Publication Limited, 4 Bello Close, Herne Hill,
London SE24 9BW
United Kingdom

Cover design: Houriyah Abdul-Rahman

TABLE OF CONTENTS

- TABLE OF CONTENTS V
- PRELUDE XI
  - OPENING SERMAN XI
  - OUR MISSION XII
  - BIOGRAPHY OF HAFIZ IBN KATHIR (701 H - 774 H) XII
    - Ibn Kathir's Teachers xii
    - Ibn Kathir's Students xiii
    - Ibn Kathir's Books xiii
    - Ibn Kathir's Death xiv
- PREFACE XIV
  - ABOUT THIS BOOK XIV
  - PERFORMING PROSTRATION WHILE READING THE QUR'AN XIV
- PART 18 FULL ARABIC TEXT 1
- CHAPTER (SURAH) 23: AL-MU'MINUN (THE BELIEVERS), VERSES 001 – 118 13
  - *Surah: 23 Ayah: 1, Ayah: 2, Ayah: 3, Ayah: 4, Ayah: 5, Ayah: 6, Ayah: 7, Ayah: 8, Ayah: 9, Ayah: 10 & Ayah: 11* 13
    - Tafsir Ibn Kathir 14
      - The Success is for the believers whose qualities are described here 14
  - *Surah: 23 Ayah: 12, Ayah: 13, Ayah: 14, Ayah: 15 & Ayah: 16* 17
    - Tafsir Ibn Kathir 18
      - The Sign of Allah in the progressive creation of Man from Clay then from Nutfah and thereafter 18
  - *Surah: 23 Ayah: 17* 21
    - Tafsir Ibn Kathir 21
      - His Sign in the creation of the Heavens 21
  - *Surah: 23 Ayah: 18, Ayah: 19, Ayah: 20, Ayah: 21 & Ayah: 22* 22
    - Tafsir Ibn Kathir 23
      - Allah's Signs and Blessings in the Rain, Vegetation, Trees and Cattle 23
  - *Surah: 23 Ayah: 23, Ayah: 24 & Ayah: 25* 24
    - Tafsir Ibn Kathir 25
      - The Story of Nuh, Peace be upon Him; and his people 25
  - *Surah: 23 Ayah: 26, Ayah: 27, Ayah: 28, Ayah: 29 & Ayah: 30* 25
    - Tafsir Ibn Kathir 27
      - Allah tells us that Nuh, peace be upon him, invoked his Lord to help him against his people, ... 27
  - *Surah: 23 Ayah: 31, Ayah: 32, Ayah: 33, Ayah: 34, Ayah: 35, Ayah: 36, Ayah: 37, Ayah: 38, Ayah: 39, Ayah: 40 & Ayah: 41* 28
    - Tafsir Ibn Kathir 29
      - The Story of `Ad or Thamud 29

- Surah: 23 Ayah: 42, Ayah: 43 & Ayah: 44 ... 30
  - Tafsir Ibn Kathir ... 31
    - Mention of Other Nations Allah says: ... 31
- Surah: 23 Ayah: 45, Ayah: 46, Ayah: 47, Ayah: 48 & Ayah: 49 ... 31
  - Tafsir Ibn Kathir ... 32
    - The Story of Musa, Peace be upon Him; and Fir`awn ... 32
- Surah: 23 Ayah: 50 ... 32
  - Tafsir Ibn Kathir ... 33
    - `Isa and Maryam ... 33
- Surah: 23 Ayah: 51, Ayah: 52, Ayah: 53, Ayah: 54, Ayah: 55 & Ayah: 56 ... 34
  - Tafsir Ibn Kathir ... 35
    - The Command to eat Lawful Food and to do Righteous Deeds ... 35
    - The Religion of all the Prophets is Tawhid; and the Warning against splitting into different Groups ... 36
- Surah: 23 Ayah: 57, Ayah: 58, Ayah: 59, Ayah: 60 & Ayah: 61 ... 38
  - Tafsir Ibn Kathir ... 38
    - Description of the People of Good Deeds ... 38
- Surah: 23 Ayah: 62, Ayah: 63, Ayah: 64, Ayah: 65, Ayah: 66 & Ayah: 67 ... 40
  - Tafsir Ibn Kathir ... 41
    - The Justice of Allah and the Frivolity of the Idolators ... 41
- Surah: 23 Ayah: 68, Ayah: 69, Ayah: 70, Ayah: 71, Ayah: 72, Ayah: 73, Ayah: 74 & Ayah: 75 ... 42
  - Tafsir Ibn Kathir ... 44
    - Refutation and Condemnation of the Idolators ... 44
    - Truth does not follow Whims and Desires ... 44
    - The Prophet does not ask for any payment, and he calls to the straight path ... 45
    - The Situation of the Disbelievers ... 46
- Surah: 23 Ayah: 76, Ayah: 77, Ayah: 78, Ayah: 79, Ayah: 80, Ayah: 81, Ayah: 82 & Ayah: 83 ... 46
  - Tafsir Ibn Kathir ... 47
    - A reminder of the Blessings of Allah and His immense Power ... 48
    - The Idolators thought that Resurrection after Death was very unlikely ... 49
- Surah: 23 Ayah: 84, Ayah: 85, Ayah: 86, Ayah: 87, Ayah: 88, Ayah: 89 & Ayah: 90 ... 49
  - Tafsir Ibn Kathir ... 50
    - The Idolators believe in Tawhid Ar-Rububiyyah, which requires them to believe in Tawhid Al-Uluhiyyah ... 50
- Surah: 23 Ayah: 91 & Ayah: 92 ... 52
  - Tafsir Ibn Kathir ... 53
    - Allah has no Partner or Associate ... 53
- Surah: 23 Ayah: 93, Ayah: 94, Ayah: 95, Ayah: 96, Ayah: 97 & Ayah: 98 ... 54
  - Tafsir Ibn Kathir ... 55
    - The Command to call on Allah when Calamity strikes, to repel Evil with that which is better, and to seek refuge with Allah ... 55
- Surah: 23 Ayah: 99 & Ayah: 100 ... 56

Table of Contents

Tafsir Ibn Kathir 56
    The Disbelievers' Hope when death approaches 56
    (And warn mankind of the Day when the torment will come unto them) 57
    Barzakh and Punishment therein 58

Surah: 23 Ayah: 101, Ayah: 102, Ayah: 103 & Ayah: 104. 58
    Tafsir Ibn Kathir 59

Surah: 23 Ayah: 105, Ayah: 106 & Ayah: 107 60
    Tafsir Ibn Kathir 60
    Rebuking the People of Hell, their admission of Their Wretchedness and their Request to be brought out of Hell 60

Surah: 23 Ayah: 108, Ayah: 109, Ayah: 110 & Ayah: 111. 61
    Tafsir Ibn Kathir 62
    Allah's Response and Rejection of the Disbelievers 62

Surah: 23 Ayah: 112, Ayah: 113, Ayah: 114, Ayah: 115 & Ayah: 116 63
    Tafsir Ibn Kathir 64
    Allah tells them how much they wasted in their short lives in this world by failing to obey Allah and worship Him Alone. 64
    Allah did not create His Servants in vain 64

Surah: 23 Ayah: 117 & Ayah: 118 65
    Tafsir Ibn Kathir 65
    Shirk is the Worst form of Wrong, its Practitioner shall never succeed. 65

CHAPTER (SURAH) 24: AN-NOOR (THE LIGHT), VERSES 001–064 .... **65**

Surah: 24 Ayah: 1 & Ayah: 2 66
    Tafsir Ibn Kathir 66
    The Importance of Surat An-Nur 66
    The Explanation of the Prescribed Punishment for Zina (Illicit Sex) 67
    Do not feel pity for Them when carrying out the Prescribed Punishment 68
    Carry out the Prescribed Punishment in Public 68

Surah: 24 Ayah: 3 69
    Tafsir Ibn Kathir 69

Surah: 24 Ayah: 4 & Ayah: 5 70
    Tafsir Ibn Kathir 70
    The Prescribed Punishment for slandering Chaste Women 70
    Explaining the Repentance of the One Who makes a False Accusation 71

Surah: 24 Ayah: 6, Ayah: 7, Ayah: 9, Ayah: 9 & Ayah: 10 71
    Tafsir Ibn Kathir 72
    Details of Al-Li`an 72
    The Reason why the Ayah of Li`an was revealed 73

Surah: 24 Ayah: 11 76
    Tafsir Ibn Kathir 77
    Al-Ifk (the Slander) 77

Surah: 24 Ayah: 12 & Ayah: 13 82
    Tafsir Ibn Kathir 82
    Disciplining the Believers for spreading the Slander 82

Surah: 24 Ayah: 14 & Ayah: 15 84
   Tafsir Ibn Kathir 84
      The Grace of Allah towards the People of the Slander by giving Them the Opportunity to repent 84
Surah: 24 Ayah: 16, Ayah: 17 & Ayah: 18 85
   Tafsir Ibn Kathir 86
      Further Discipline 86
Surah: 24 Ayah: 19 87
   Tafsir Ibn Kathir 87
      Disciplining Those Who like that Illegal Sexual Intercourse should be circulated among the Believers 87
Surah: 24 Ayah: 20 & Ayah: 21 88
   Tafsir Ibn Kathir 88
      A Reminder of the Grace of Allah and a Warning against following the Footsteps of Shaytan 88
   Tafsir Ibn Kathir 89
      Urging Those Who have been blessed with Wealth to give and to be tolerant 89
Surah: 24 Ayah: 23, Ayah: 24 & Ayah: 25 90
   Tafsir Ibn Kathir 91
      A Threat to Those who accuse Chaste Women, Who never even think of anything touching their Chastity and are Good Believers 91
Surah: 24 Ayah: 26 93
   Tafsir Ibn Kathir 93
      The Goodness of `A'ishah because She is married to the best of Mankind 93
Surah: 24 Ayah: 27, Ayah: 28 & Ayah: 29 94
   Tafsir Ibn Kathir 94
      Seeking Permission and the Etiquette of entering Houses 94
Surah: 24 Ayah: 30 98
   Tafsir Ibn Kathir 98
      The Command to lower the Gaze 98
Surah: 24 Ayah: 31 100
   Tafsir Ibn Kathir 101
      The Rulings of Hijab 101
      The Etiquette of Women walking in the Street 104
Surah: 24 Ayah: 32, Ayah: 33 & Ayah: 34 105
   Tafsir Ibn Kathir 106
      The Command to marry 106
      The Command to keep Oneself Chaste if One is not able to get married 107
      The Command to grant Slaves a Contract of Emancipation 108
      The Prohibition of forcing One's Slave-Girls to commit Zina 108
      Reports narrated on this Topic 109
Surah: 24 Ayah: 35 110
   Tafsir Ibn Kathir 110
      The Parable of the Light of Allah 110
Surah: 24 Ayah: 36, Ayah: 37 & Ayah: 38 114

Table of Contents

    Tafsir Ibn Kathir 114
        The Virtues of the Masjids, the Correct Etiquette, and the Virtues of Those who take care of them 114

Surah: 24 Ayah: 39 & Ayah: 40 119
    Tafsir Ibn Kathir 120
        Two Examples of two kinds of Disbelievers 120

Surah: 24 Ayah: 41 & Ayah: 42 121
    Tafsir Ibn Kathir 122
        Everything glorifies Allah, may He be exalted, and to Him belongs the Sovereignty 122

Surah: 24 Ayah: 43 & Ayah: 44 122
    Tafsir Ibn Kathir 123
        The Power of Allah to create the Clouds and that which comes from Them 123

Surah: 24 Ayah: 45 124
    Tafsir Ibn Kathir 125
        Allah's Power in His creation of the Animals 125

Surah: 24 Ayah: 46 125
    Tafsir Ibn Kathir 125

Surah: 24 Ayah: 47, Ayah: 48, Ayah: 49, Ayah: 50, Ayah: 51 & Ayah: 52 125
    Tafsir Ibn Kathir 127
        The Treachery of the Hypocrites and the Attitude of the Believers 127

Surah: 24 Ayah: 53 & Ayah: 54 128
    Tafsir Ibn Kathir 129

Surah: 24 Ayah: 55 130
    Tafsir Ibn Kathir 130
        Allah's Promise to the Believers that He would grant them Succession 130

Surah: 24 Ayah: 56 & Ayah: 57 135
    Tafsir Ibn Kathir 135
        The Command to pray, give the Zakah and obey the Messenger ; the inability of the Disbelievers to escape, and the ultimate Destiny 135

Surah: 24 Ayah: 58, Ayah: 59 & Ayah: 60 136
    Tafsir Ibn Kathir 137
        The Times when Servants and Young Children should seek Permission to enter 137
        There is no Sin on Elderly Women if They do not wear a Cloak 138

Surah: 24 Ayah: 61 139
    Tafsir Ibn Kathir 139
        Eating from One's Relatives' Houses 139

Surah: 24 Ayah: 62 142
    Tafsir Ibn Kathir 142
        Asking Permission to leave when They are doing something together 142

Surah: 24 Ayah: 63 143
    Tafsir Ibn Kathir 143
        The Etiquette of addressing the Prophet 143
        The Prohibition of going against the Messenger's Commandment 144

Surah: 24 Ayah: 64 145

- Tafsir Ibn Kathir 145
  - Allah knows your Condition 145

CHAPTER (SURAH) 25: AL-FURQAN (THE CRITERION, THE STANDARD), VERSES 001- 020 .. 146

- *Surah: 25 Ayah: 1 & Ayah: 2 .... 147*
  - Tafsir Ibn Kathir 147
    - Blessed be Allah 147
- *Surah: 25 Ayah: 3 .... 149*
  - Tafsir Ibn Kathir 149
    - The Foolishness of the Idolators 149
- *Surah: 25 Ayah: 4, Ayah: 5 & Ayah: 6 .... 150*
  - Tafsir Ibn Kathir 150
    - What the Disbelievers said about the Qur'an 150
- *Surah: 25 Ayah: 7, Ayah: 8, Ayah: 9, Ayah: 10, Ayah: 11, Ayah: 12, Ayah: 13 & Ayah: 14 .... 152*
  - Tafsir Ibn Kathir 153
    - What the Disbelievers said about the Messenger , refutation of Their Words, and Their ultimate Destiny 153
- *Surah: 25 Ayah: 15 & Ayah: 16 .... 155*
  - Tafsir Ibn Kathir 155
    - Is the Fire better, or Paradise 155
- *Surah: 25 Ayah: 17, Ayah: 18 & Ayah: 19 .... 156*
  - Tafsir Ibn Kathir 157
    - The gods of the Idolators will disown Them on the Day of Resurrection 157
- *Surah: 25 Ayah: 20 .... 158*
  - Tafsir Ibn Kathir 159
    - All of the Previous Messengers were Human 159

PRELUDE

Opening Serman

Indeed, all praise is due to Allah. We praise Him and seek His help and forgiveness. We seek refuge with Allah from our soul's evil and our wrong doings. He whom Allah guides, no one can misguide; and he whom He misguides, no one can guide

I bear witness that there is no (true) god except Allah – alone without a partner, and I bear witness that Muhammad (peace and blessings of Allah be upon him) is His 'abd (servant) and messenger.

يَٰٓأَيُّهَا ٱلَّذِينَ ءَامَنُوا۟ ٱتَّقُوا۟ ٱللَّهَ حَقَّ تُقَاتِهِۦ وَلَا تَمُوتُنَّ إِلَّا وَأَنتُم مُّسْلِمُونَ ﴿١٠٢﴾

O you who believe! Fear Allâh (by doing all that He has ordered and by abstaining from all that He has forbidden) as He should be feared. (Obey Him, be thankful to Him, and remember Him always), and die not except in a state of Islâm (as Muslims (with complete submission to Allâh)).

يَٰٓأَيُّهَا ٱلنَّاسُ ٱتَّقُوا۟ رَبَّكُمُ ٱلَّذِى خَلَقَكُم مِّن نَّفْسٍ وَٰحِدَةٍ وَخَلَقَ مِنْهَا زَوْجَهَا وَبَثَّ مِنْهُمَا رِجَالًا كَثِيرًا وَنِسَآءً ۚ وَٱتَّقُوا۟ ٱللَّهَ ٱلَّذِى تَسَآءَلُونَ بِهِۦ وَٱلْأَرْحَامَ ۚ إِنَّ ٱللَّهَ كَانَ عَلَيْكُمْ رَقِيبًا ﴿١﴾

O mankind! Be dutiful to your Lord, Who created you from a single person (Adam), and from him (Adam) He created his wife (Hawwâ (Eve)) and from them both He created many men and women; and fear Allâh through Whom you demand (your mutual rights), and (do not cut the relations of) the wombs (kinship). Surely, Allâh is Ever an All-Watcher over you.

يُصْلِحْ لَكُمْ أَعْمَٰلَكُمْ وَيَغْفِرْ لَكُمْ ذُنُوبَكُمْ ۗ وَمَن يُطِعِ ٱللَّهَ وَرَسُولَهُۥ فَقَدْ فَازَ فَوْزًا عَظِيمًا ﴿٧١﴾

He will direct you to do righteous good deeds and will forgive you your sins. And whosoever obeys Allâh and His Messenger (peace be upon him), he has indeed achieved a great achievement (i.e. he will be saved from the Hell-fire and will be admitted to Paradise).

Indeed, the best speech is Allah's Book and the best guidance is Muhammad's () guidance. The worst affairs (of religion) are those innovated (by people), for every such innovation is an act of misguidance leading to the Fire

Our Mission

Our mission is to gather in one place, for the English-speaking public, all relevant information needed to make the Qur'an more understandable and easier to study. This book tries to do this by providing the following:

1. The Arabic Text for those who are able to read Arabic
2. Transliteration of the Arabic text for those who are unable to read the Arabic script. This will give them a sample of the sound of the Qur'an, which they could not otherwise comprehend from reading the English meaning.
3. The meaning of the qur'an (translated by Dr. Muhammad Taqi-ud-Din Al-Hilali, Ph.D. and Dr. Muhammad Muhsin Khan)
4. Explanation (abridged Tafsir) by Ibn Kathir (translated by Safi-ur-Rahman al-Mubarakpuri)

We hope that by doing this an ordinary English-speaker will be able to pick up a copy of this book and study and comprehend The Glorious Qur'an in a way that is acceptable to the understanding of the Rightly-guided Muslim Ummah (Community).

Biography of Hafiz Ibn Kathir (701 H - 774 H)

By the Honored Shaykh `Abdul-Qadir Al-Arna'ut, may Allah protect him.

He is the respected Imam, Abu Al-Fida', `Imad Ad-Din Isma il bin 'Umar bin Kathir Al-Qurashi Al-Busrawi - Busraian in origin; Dimashqi in training, learning and residence.

Ibn Kathir was born in the city of Busra in 701 H. His father was the Friday speaker of the village, but he died while Ibn Kathir was only four years old. Ibn Kathir's brother, Shaykh Abdul-Wahhab, reared him and taught him until he moved to Damascus in 706 H., when he was five years old.

Ibn Kathir's Teachers

Ibn Kathir studied Fiqh - Islamic jurisprudence - with Burhan Ad-Din, Ibrahim bin `Abdur-Rahman Al-Fizari, known as Ibn Al-Firkah (who died in 729 H). Ibn Kathir heard Hadiths from `Isa bin Al-Mutim, Ahmad bin Abi Talib, (Ibn Ash-Shahnah) (who died in 730 H), Ibn Al-Hajjar, (who died in 730 H), and the Hadith narrator of Ash-Sham (modern day Syria and surrounding areas); Baha Ad-Din Al-Qasim bin Muzaffar bin `Asakir (who died in 723 H), and Ibn Ash-Shirdzi, Ishaq bin Yahya Al-Ammuddi, also known as `Afif Ad-Din, the Zahiriyyah Shaykh who died in 725 H, and Muhammad bin Zarrad. He remained with Jamal Ad-Din, Yusuf bin Az-Zaki AlMizzi who died in 724 H, he benefited from his knowledge and also married his daughter. He also read with Shaykh Al-Islam, Taqi Ad-Din Ahmad bin `Abdul-Halim bin `Abdus-Salam bin Taymiyyah who died in 728 H. He also read with the Imam Hafiz and historian Shams Ad-Din, Muhammad bin Ahmad bin Uthman bin Qaymaz Adh-Dhahabi, who died in 748 H. Also, Abu Musa Al-Qarafai, Abu Al-Fath Ad-Dabbusi and

'Ali bin `Umar As-Suwani and others who gave him permission to transmit the knowledge he learned with them in Egypt.

In his book, Al-Mu jam Al-Mukhtas, Al-Hafiz Adh-Dhaliabi wrote that Ibn Kathir was, "The Imam, scholar of jurisprudence, skillful scholar of Hadith, renowned Faqih and scholar of Tafsir who wrote several beneficial books."

Further, in Ad-Durar Al-Kdminah, Al-Hafiz Ibn Hajar AlAsqalani said, "Ibn Kathir worked on the subject of the Hadith in the areas of texts and chains of narrators. He had a good memory, his books became popular during his lifetime, and people benefited from them after his death."

Also, the renowned historian Abu Al-Mahasin, Jamal Ad-Din Yusuf bin Sayf Ad-Din (Ibn Taghri Bardi), said in his book, AlManhal As-Safi, "He is the Shaykh, the Imam, the great scholar `Imad Ad-Din Abu Al-Fida'. He learned extensively and was very active in collecting knowledge and writing. He was excellent in the areas of Fiqh, Tafsfr and Hadith. He collected knowledge, authored (books), taught, narrated Hadith and wrote. He had immense knowledge in the fields of Hadith, Tafsir, Fiqh, the Arabic language, and so forth. He gave Fatawa (religious verdicts) and taught until he died, may Allah grant him mercy. He was known for his precision and vast knowledge, and as a scholar of history, Hadith and Tafsir."

Ibn Kathir's Students

Ibn Hajji was one of Ibn Kathir's students, and he described Ibn Kathir: "He had the best memory of the Hadith texts. He also had the most knowledge concerning the narrators and authenticity, his contemporaries and teachers admitted to these qualities. Every time I met him I gained some benefit from him."

Also, Ibn Al-`Imad Al-Hanbali said in his book, Shadhardt Adh-Dhahab, "He is the renowned Hafiz `Imad Ad-Din, whose memory was excellent, whose forgetfulness was miniscule, whose understanding was adequate, and who had good knowledge in the Arabic language." Also, Ibn Habib said about Ibn Kathir, "He heard knowledge and collected it and wrote various books. He brought comfort to the ears with his Fatwas and narrated Hadith and brought benefit to other people. The papers that contained his Fatwas were transmitted to the various (Islamic) provinces. Further, he was known for his precision and encompassing knowledge."

Ibn Kathir's Books

1 - One of the greatest books that Ibn Kathir wrote was his Tafsir of the Noble Qur'an, which is one of the best Tafsir that rely on narrations [of Ahadith, the Tafsir of the Companions, etc.]. The Tafsir by Ibn Kathir was printed many times and several scholars have summarized it.

2- The History Collection known as Al-Biddyah, which was printed in 14 volumes under the name Al-Bidayah wanNihdyah, and contained the stories of the Prophets and previous nations, the Prophet's Seerah (life story) and Islamic history until his time. He also added a book Al-Fitan, about the Signs of the Last Hour.

3- At-Takmil ft Ma`rifat Ath-Thiqat wa Ad-Du'afa wal Majdhil which Ibn Kathir collected from the books of his two Shaykhs Al-Mizzi and Adh-Dhahabi; Al-Kdmal and Mizan Al-Ftiddl. He added several benefits regarding the subject of Al-Jarh and AtT'adil.

4- Al-Hadi was-Sunan ft Ahadith Al-Masdnfd was-Sunan which is also known by, Jami` Al-Masdnfd. In this book, Ibn Kathir collected the narrations of Imams Ahmad bin Hanbal, Al-Bazzar, Abu Ya`la Al-Mawsili, Ibn Abi Shaybah and from the six collections of Hadith: the Two Sahihs [Al-Bukhari and Muslim] and the Four Sunan [Abu Dawud, At-Tirmidhi, AnNasa and Ibn Majah]. Ibn Kathir divided this book according to areas of Fiqh.

5-Tabaqat Ash-Shaf iyah which also contains the virtues of Imam Ash-Shafi.

6- Ibn Kathir wrote references for the Ahadith of Adillat AtTanbfh, from the Shafi school of Fiqh.

7- Ibn Kathir began an explanation of Sahih Al-Bukhari, but he did not finish it.

8- He started writing a large volume on the Ahkam (Laws), but finished only up to the Hajj rituals.

9- He summarized Al-Bayhaqi's 'Al-Madkhal. Many of these books were not printed.

10- He summarized `Ulum Al-Hadith, by Abu `Amr bin AsSalah and called it Mukhtasar `Ulum Al-Hadith. Shaykh Ahmad Shakir, the Egyptian Muhaddith, printed this book along with his commentary on it and called it Al-Ba'th Al-Hathfth fi Sharh Mukhtasar `Ulum Al-Hadith.

11- As-Sfrah An-Nabawiyyah, which is contained in his book Al-Biddyah, and both of these books are in print.

12- A research on Jihad called Al-Ijtihad ft Talabi Al-Jihad, which was printed several times.

Ibn Kathir's Death

Al-Hafiz Ibn Hajar Al-Asgalani said, "Ibn Kathir lost his sight just before his life ended. He died in Damascus in 774 H." May Allah grant mercy upon Ibn Kathir and make him among the residents of His Paradise.

PREFACE

In the name of Allah, Most Gracious, Most Merciful.

About this book

The previous publication of this book included some background information to the chapters of the Qur'an by an Islamic scholar known as Abul Ala Maududi. This information was used to shed more light on the chapters by giving a summery of why each chapter was given its name, It's period of revelation and the circumstances surrounding its revelatiom. However, some Muslims objected to the inclusion of the contributions of Maududi.

In this new publication of Tafsir Ibn Kathir, we have removed all traces of the contribution of Abul Ala Maududi. Personally, I do not know the reasons for the objections to Maududi, but this work concerns only the tafsir of Ibn Kathir, so we have not included anything from Maududi in it. We have also corrected all the typing and formatting errors found in the previous publication. We have not alter the structure of the book. The reader is still able to read the full Arabic Text of the thirty Parts of the Qur'an and follow its meanings in the English language. The transliteration of the Arabic text should also give the reader a taste of the sound of the original Arabic.

May Almighty Allah accept this effort from us, and make it a source of blessings for us in this world and in the next. I bear witness that there is none worthy of worship but Allah and I bear witness that Muhammad (may the peace and blessings of Allah be upon him) is the slave and messenger of Allah.

Performing Prostration While Reading the Qur'an

Question:

Could you please give a list of the Qur'anic verses when a prostration is recommended? What happens if we read these verses and not perform a prostration?

A. Jalil

Answer:

There are 15 verses in the Qur'an that mention prostration before God Almighty as a good action by God-fearing believers. Therefore, it is strongly recommended to perform such a prostration when we read or listen to any of these verses, whether during prayer or in any situation.

Some scholars are of the view that even if one has not performed ablution, one should prostrate oneself. These verses are given here, starting with the Arabic title of the surah which is followed by two numbers, the first indicating the surah, and the second indicating the verse,: Al-Araf 7: 206; Al-Raad 13: 15; Al-Nahl 16: 50; Al-Isra 17: 109; Maryam 19: 58; Al-Hajj 22: 18 & 22: 77; Al-Furqan 25: 60; Al-Naml 27: 26;

Al-Sajdah 32: 15; Saad 38: 25; Fussilat 41: 38; Al-Najm 53: 62; Al-Inshiqaq 84: 21 and Al-Alaq 96: 19.

If you do not perform a prostration when you read or listen to any of these verses, you have done badly because you miss out on the reward of performing a prostration for God. You incur no sin and violate no divine order.

Reference:
http://archive.arabnews.com/?page=5&section=0&article=97811&d=1&m=7&y=2007

The Glorious Qur'an Juz' 18 (Part 18): Chapter (Surah) 23: Al-Mu'minun (The Believers) 001 To Chapter (Surah) 25: Al-Furqan (The Criterion, The Standard) 020

PART 18 FULL ARABIC TEXT

Chapter (Surah) 23: Al-Mu'minun 001-118

بِسْمِ ٱللَّهِ ٱلرَّحْمَٰنِ ٱلرَّحِيمِ

﴿ قَدْ أَفْلَحَ ٱلْمُؤْمِنُونَ ۝ ٱلَّذِينَ هُمْ فِى صَلَاتِهِمْ خَٰشِعُونَ ۝ وَٱلَّذِينَ هُمْ عَنِ ٱللَّغْوِ مُعْرِضُونَ ۝ وَٱلَّذِينَ هُمْ لِلزَّكَوٰةِ فَٰعِلُونَ ۝ وَٱلَّذِينَ هُمْ لِفُرُوجِهِمْ حَٰفِظُونَ ۝ إِلَّا عَلَىٰٓ أَزْوَٰجِهِمْ أَوْ مَا مَلَكَتْ أَيْمَٰنُهُمْ فَإِنَّهُمْ غَيْرُ مَلُومِينَ ۝ فَمَنِ ٱبْتَغَىٰ وَرَآءَ ذَٰلِكَ فَأُو۟لَٰٓئِكَ هُمُ ٱلْعَادُونَ ۝ وَٱلَّذِينَ هُمْ لِأَمَٰنَٰتِهِمْ وَعَهْدِهِمْ رَٰعُونَ ۝ وَٱلَّذِينَ هُمْ عَلَىٰ صَلَوَٰتِهِمْ يُحَافِظُونَ ۝ أُو۟لَٰٓئِكَ هُمُ ٱلْوَٰرِثُونَ ۝ ٱلَّذِينَ يَرِثُونَ ٱلْفِرْدَوْسَ هُمْ فِيهَا خَٰلِدُونَ ۝ وَلَقَدْ خَلَقْنَا ٱلْإِنسَٰنَ مِن سُلَٰلَةٍ مِّن طِينٍ ۝ ثُمَّ جَعَلْنَٰهُ نُطْفَةً فِى قَرَارٍ مَّكِينٍ ۝ ثُمَّ خَلَقْنَا ٱلنُّطْفَةَ عَلَقَةً فَخَلَقْنَا ٱلْعَلَقَةَ مُضْغَةً فَخَلَقْنَا ٱلْمُضْغَةَ عِظَٰمًا فَكَسَوْنَا ٱلْعِظَٰمَ لَحْمًا ثُمَّ أَنشَأْنَٰهُ خَلْقًا ءَاخَرَ ۚ فَتَبَارَكَ ٱللَّهُ أَحْسَنُ ٱلْخَٰلِقِينَ ۝ ثُمَّ إِنَّكُم بَعْدَ ذَٰلِكَ لَمَيِّتُونَ ۝ ثُمَّ إِنَّكُمْ يَوْمَ ٱلْقِيَٰمَةِ تُبْعَثُونَ ۝ وَلَقَدْ خَلَقْنَا فَوْقَكُمْ سَبْعَ طَرَآئِقَ وَمَا كُنَّا عَنِ ٱلْخَلْقِ غَٰفِلِينَ ۝ وَأَنزَلْنَا مِنَ ٱلسَّمَآءِ مَآءً بِقَدَرٍ فَأَسْكَنَّٰهُ فِى ٱلْأَرْضِ ۖ وَإِنَّا عَلَىٰ ذَهَابٍۭ بِهِۦ لَقَٰدِرُونَ ۝ فَأَنشَأْنَا لَكُم بِهِۦ جَنَّٰتٍ مِّن نَّخِيلٍ وَأَعْنَٰبٍ لَّكُمْ فِيهَا فَوَٰكِهُ كَثِيرَةٌ وَمِنْهَا تَأْكُلُونَ ۝ وَشَجَرَةً تَخْرُجُ مِن طُورِ سَيْنَآءَ تَنۢبُتُ بِٱلدُّهْنِ وَصِبْغٍ لِّلْءَاكِلِينَ ۝ وَإِنَّ

لَكُمْ فِى ٱلْأَنْعَمِ لَعِبْرَةً نُّسْقِيكُم مِّمَّا فِى بُطُونِهَا وَلَكُمْ فِيهَا مَنَفِعُ كَثِيرَةٌ وَمِنْهَا تَأْكُلُونَ ۝ وَعَلَيْهَا وَعَلَى ٱلْفُلْكِ تُحْمَلُونَ ۝ وَلَقَدْ أَرْسَلْنَا نُوحًا إِلَىٰ قَوْمِهِ فَقَالَ يَـٰقَوْمِ ٱعْبُدُوا۟ ٱللَّهَ مَا لَكُم مِّنْ إِلَـٰهٍ غَيْرُهُ أَفَلَا تَتَّقُونَ ۝ فَقَالَ ٱلْمَلَؤُا۟ ٱلَّذِينَ كَفَرُوا۟ مِن قَوْمِهِ مَا هَـٰذَآ إِلَّا بَشَرٌ مِّثْلُكُمْ يُرِيدُ أَن يَتَفَضَّلَ عَلَيْكُمْ وَلَوْ شَآءَ ٱللَّهُ لَأَنزَلَ مَلَـٰٓئِكَةً مَّا سَمِعْنَا بِهَـٰذَا فِىٓ ءَابَآئِنَا ٱلْأَوَّلِينَ ۝ إِنْ هُوَ إِلَّا رَجُلٌ بِهِۦ جِنَّةٌ فَتَرَبَّصُوا۟ بِهِۦ حَتَّىٰ حِينٍ ۝ قَالَ رَبِّ ٱنصُرْنِى بِمَا كَذَّبُونِ ۝ فَأَوْحَيْنَآ إِلَيْهِ أَنِ ٱصْنَعِ ٱلْفُلْكَ بِأَعْيُنِنَا وَوَحْيِنَا فَإِذَا جَآءَ أَمْرُنَا وَفَارَ ٱلتَّنُّورُ فَٱسْلُكْ فِيهَا مِن كُلٍّ زَوْجَيْنِ ٱثْنَيْنِ وَأَهْلَكَ إِلَّا مَن سَبَقَ عَلَيْهِ ٱلْقَوْلُ مِنْهُمْ وَلَا تُخَـٰطِبْنِى فِى ٱلَّذِينَ ظَلَمُوٓا۟ إِنَّهُم مُّغْرَقُونَ ۝ فَإِذَا ٱسْتَوَيْتَ أَنتَ وَمَن مَّعَكَ عَلَى ٱلْفُلْكِ فَقُلِ ٱلْحَمْدُ لِلَّهِ ٱلَّذِى نَجَّىٰنَا مِنَ ٱلْقَوْمِ ٱلظَّـٰلِمِينَ ۝ وَقُل رَّبِّ أَنزِلْنِى مُنزَلًا مُّبَارَكًا وَأَنتَ خَيْرُ ٱلْمُنزِلِينَ ۝ إِنَّ فِى ذَٰلِكَ لَأَيَـٰتٍ وَإِن كُنَّا لَمُبْتَلِينَ ۝ ثُمَّ أَنشَأْنَا مِنۢ بَعْدِهِمْ قَرْنًا ءَاخَرِينَ ۝ فَأَرْسَلْنَا فِيهِمْ رَسُولًا مِّنْهُمْ أَنِ ٱعْبُدُوا۟ ٱللَّهَ مَا لَكُم مِّنْ إِلَـٰهٍ غَيْرُهُۥ أَفَلَا تَتَّقُونَ ۝ وَقَالَ ٱلْمَلَأُ مِن قَوْمِهِ ٱلَّذِينَ كَفَرُوا۟ وَكَذَّبُوا۟ بِلِقَآءِ ٱلْءَاخِرَةِ وَأَتْرَفْنَـٰهُمْ فِى ٱلْحَيَوٰةِ ٱلدُّنْيَا مَا هَـٰذَآ إِلَّا بَشَرٌ مِّثْلُكُمْ يَأْكُلُ مِمَّا تَأْكُلُونَ مِنْهُ وَيَشْرَبُ مِمَّا تَشْرَبُونَ ۝ وَلَئِنْ أَطَعْتُم بَشَرًا مِّثْلَكُمْ إِنَّكُمْ إِذًا لَّخَـٰسِرُونَ ۝ أَيَعِدُكُمْ أَنَّكُمْ إِذَا مِتُّمْ وَكُنتُمْ تُرَابًا وَعِظَـٰمًا أَنَّكُم مُّخْرَجُونَ ۝ ۞ هَيْهَاتَ هَيْهَاتَ لِمَا تُوعَدُونَ ۝ إِنْ هِىَ إِلَّا حَيَاتُنَا ٱلدُّنْيَا نَمُوتُ وَنَحْيَا وَمَا نَحْنُ بِمَبْعُوثِينَ ۝ إِنْ هُوَ إِلَّا رَجُلٌ ٱفْتَرَىٰ عَلَى ٱللَّهِ كَذِبًا وَمَا نَحْنُ لَهُۥ بِمُؤْمِنِينَ ۝ قَالَ رَبِّ ٱنصُرْنِى بِمَا كَذَّبُونِ ۝ قَالَ عَمَّا قَلِيلٍ لَّيُصْبِحُنَّ نَـٰدِمِينَ ۝ فَأَخَذَتْهُمُ ٱلصَّيْحَةُ بِٱلْحَقِّ فَجَعَلْنَـٰهُمْ غُثَآءً فَبُعْدًا لِّلْقَوْمِ ٱلظَّـٰلِمِينَ ۝ ثُمَّ

أَنشَأْنَا مِنۢ بَعْدِهِمْ قُرُونًا ءَاخَرِينَ ۝ مَا تَسْبِقُ مِنْ أُمَّةٍ أَجَلَهَا وَمَا يَسْتَـْٔخِرُونَ ۝ ثُمَّ أَرْسَلْنَا رُسُلَنَا تَتْرَا ۖ كُلَّ مَا جَاءَ أُمَّةً رَّسُولُهَا كَذَّبُوهُ ۚ فَأَتْبَعْنَا بَعْضَهُم بَعْضًا وَجَعَلْنَـٰهُمْ أَحَادِيثَ ۚ فَبُعْدًا لِّقَوْمٍ لَّا يُؤْمِنُونَ ۝ ثُمَّ أَرْسَلْنَا مُوسَىٰ وَأَخَاهُ هَـٰرُونَ بِـَٔايَـٰتِنَا وَسُلْطَـٰنٍ مُّبِينٍ ۝ إِلَىٰ فِرْعَوْنَ وَمَلَإِيْهِۦ فَٱسْتَكْبَرُوا۟ وَكَانُوا۟ قَوْمًا عَالِينَ ۝ فَقَالُوٓا۟ أَنُؤْمِنُ لِبَشَرَيْنِ مِثْلِنَا وَقَوْمُهُمَا لَنَا عَـٰبِدُونَ ۝ فَكَذَّبُوهُمَا فَكَانُوا۟ مِنَ ٱلْمُهْلَكِينَ ۝ وَلَقَدْ ءَاتَيْنَا مُوسَى ٱلْكِتَـٰبَ لَعَلَّهُمْ يَهْتَدُونَ ۝ وَجَعَلْنَا ٱبْنَ مَرْيَمَ وَأُمَّهُۥٓ ءَايَةً وَءَاوَيْنَـٰهُمَآ إِلَىٰ رَبْوَةٍ ذَاتِ قَرَارٍ وَمَعِينٍ ۝ يَـٰٓأَيُّهَا ٱلرُّسُلُ كُلُوا۟ مِنَ ٱلطَّيِّبَـٰتِ وَٱعْمَلُوا۟ صَـٰلِحًا ۖ إِنِّى بِمَا تَعْمَلُونَ عَلِيمٌ ۝ وَإِنَّ هَـٰذِهِۦٓ أُمَّتُكُمْ أُمَّةً وَٰحِدَةً وَأَنَا۠ رَبُّكُمْ فَٱتَّقُونِ ۝ فَتَقَطَّعُوٓا۟ أَمْرَهُم بَيْنَهُمْ زُبُرًا ۖ كُلُّ حِزْبٍۭ بِمَا لَدَيْهِمْ فَرِحُونَ ۝ فَذَرْهُمْ فِى غَمْرَتِهِمْ حَتَّىٰ حِينٍ ۝ أَيَحْسَبُونَ أَنَّمَا نُمِدُّهُم بِهِۦ مِن مَّالٍ وَبَنِينَ ۝ نُسَارِعُ لَهُمْ فِى ٱلْخَيْرَٰتِ ۚ بَل لَّا يَشْعُرُونَ ۝ إِنَّ ٱلَّذِينَ هُم مِّنْ خَشْيَةِ رَبِّهِم مُّشْفِقُونَ ۝ وَٱلَّذِينَ هُم بِـَٔايَـٰتِ رَبِّهِمْ يُؤْمِنُونَ ۝ وَٱلَّذِينَ هُم بِرَبِّهِمْ لَا يُشْرِكُونَ ۝ وَٱلَّذِينَ يُؤْتُونَ مَآ ءَاتَوا۟ وَّقُلُوبُهُمْ وَجِلَةٌ أَنَّهُمْ إِلَىٰ رَبِّهِمْ رَٰجِعُونَ ۝ أُو۟لَـٰٓئِكَ يُسَـٰرِعُونَ فِى ٱلْخَيْرَٰتِ وَهُمْ لَهَا سَـٰبِقُونَ ۝ وَلَا نُكَلِّفُ نَفْسًا إِلَّا وُسْعَهَا ۖ وَلَدَيْنَا كِتَـٰبٌ يَنطِقُ بِٱلْحَقِّ ۚ وَهُمْ لَا يُظْلَمُونَ ۝ بَلْ قُلُوبُهُمْ فِى غَمْرَةٍ مِّنْ هَـٰذَا وَلَهُمْ أَعْمَـٰلٌ مِّن دُونِ ذَٰلِكَ هُمْ لَهَا عَـٰمِلُونَ ۝ حَتَّىٰٓ إِذَآ أَخَذْنَا مُتْرَفِيهِم بِٱلْعَذَابِ إِذَا هُمْ يَجْـَٔرُونَ ۝ لَا تَجْـَٔرُوا۟ ٱلْيَوْمَ ۖ إِنَّكُم مِّنَّا لَا تُنصَرُونَ ۝ قَدْ كَانَتْ ءَايَـٰتِى تُتْلَىٰ عَلَيْكُمْ فَكُنتُمْ عَلَىٰٓ أَعْقَـٰبِكُمْ تَنكِصُونَ ۝ مُسْتَكْبِرِينَ بِهِۦ سَـٰمِرًا تَهْجُرُونَ ۝ أَفَلَمْ يَدَّبَّرُوا۟ ٱلْقَوْلَ أَمْ جَآءَهُم مَّا لَمْ يَأْتِ ءَابَآءَهُمُ ٱلْأَوَّلِينَ ۝ أَمْ لَمْ يَعْرِفُوا۟ رَسُولَهُمْ فَهُمْ لَهُۥ

مُنكِرُونَ ۝ أَمْ يَقُولُونَ بِهِ جِنَّةٌ ۚ بَلْ جَآءَهُم بِٱلْحَقِّ وَأَكْثَرُهُمْ لِلْحَقِّ كَـٰرِهُونَ ۝ وَلَوِ ٱتَّبَعَ ٱلْحَقُّ أَهْوَآءَهُمْ لَفَسَدَتِ ٱلسَّمَـٰوَٰتُ وَٱلْأَرْضُ وَمَن فِيهِنَّ ۚ بَلْ أَتَيْنَـٰهُم بِذِكْرِهِمْ فَهُمْ عَن ذِكْرِهِم مُّعْرِضُونَ ۝ أَمْ تَسْـَٔلُهُمْ خَرْجًا فَخَرَاجُ رَبِّكَ خَيْرٌ ۖ وَهُوَ خَيْرُ ٱلرَّٰزِقِينَ ۝ وَإِنَّكَ لَتَدْعُوهُمْ إِلَىٰ صِرَٰطٍ مُّسْتَقِيمٍ ۝ وَإِنَّ ٱلَّذِينَ لَا يُؤْمِنُونَ بِٱلْـَٔاخِرَةِ عَنِ ٱلصِّرَٰطِ لَنَـٰكِبُونَ ۝ ۞ وَلَوْ رَحِمْنَـٰهُمْ وَكَشَفْنَا مَا بِهِم مِّن ضُرٍّ لَّلَجُّوا۟ فِى طُغْيَـٰنِهِمْ يَعْمَهُونَ ۝ وَلَقَدْ أَخَذْنَـٰهُم بِٱلْعَذَابِ فَمَا ٱسْتَكَانُوا۟ لِرَبِّهِمْ وَمَا يَتَضَرَّعُونَ ۝ حَتَّىٰٓ إِذَا فَتَحْنَا عَلَيْهِم بَابًا ذَا عَذَابٍ شَدِيدٍ إِذَا هُمْ فِيهِ مُبْلِسُونَ ۝ وَهُوَ ٱلَّذِىٓ أَنشَأَ لَكُمُ ٱلسَّمْعَ وَٱلْأَبْصَـٰرَ وَٱلْأَفْـِٔدَةَ ۚ قَلِيلًا مَّا تَشْكُرُونَ ۝ وَهُوَ ٱلَّذِى ذَرَأَكُمْ فِى ٱلْأَرْضِ وَإِلَيْهِ تُحْشَرُونَ ۝ وَهُوَ ٱلَّذِى يُحْىِۦ وَيُمِيتُ وَلَهُ ٱخْتِلَـٰفُ ٱلَّيْلِ وَٱلنَّهَارِ ۚ أَفَلَا تَعْقِلُونَ ۝ بَلْ قَالُوا۟ مِثْلَ مَا قَالَ ٱلْأَوَّلُونَ ۝ قَالُوٓا۟ أَءِذَا مِتْنَا وَكُنَّا تُرَابًا وَعِظَـٰمًا أَءِنَّا لَمَبْعُوثُونَ ۝ لَقَدْ وُعِدْنَا نَحْنُ وَءَابَآؤُنَا هَـٰذَا مِن قَبْلُ إِنْ هَـٰذَآ إِلَّآ أَسَـٰطِيرُ ٱلْأَوَّلِينَ ۝ قُل لِّمَنِ ٱلْأَرْضُ وَمَن فِيهَآ إِن كُنتُمْ تَعْلَمُونَ ۝ سَيَقُولُونَ لِلَّهِ ۚ قُلْ أَفَلَا تَذَكَّرُونَ ۝ قُلْ مَن رَّبُّ ٱلسَّمَـٰوَٰتِ ٱلسَّبْعِ وَرَبُّ ٱلْعَرْشِ ٱلْعَظِيمِ ۝ سَيَقُولُونَ لِلَّهِ ۚ قُلْ أَفَلَا تَتَّقُونَ ۝ قُلْ مَنۢ بِيَدِهِۦ مَلَكُوتُ كُلِّ شَىْءٍ وَهُوَ يُجِيرُ وَلَا يُجَارُ عَلَيْهِ إِن كُنتُمْ تَعْلَمُونَ ۝ سَيَقُولُونَ لِلَّهِ ۚ قُلْ فَأَنَّىٰ تُسْحَرُونَ ۝ بَلْ أَتَيْنَـٰهُم بِٱلْحَقِّ وَإِنَّهُمْ لَكَـٰذِبُونَ ۝ مَا ٱتَّخَذَ ٱللَّهُ مِن وَلَدٍ وَمَا كَانَ مَعَهُۥ مِنْ إِلَـٰهٍ ۚ إِذًا لَّذَهَبَ كُلُّ إِلَـٰهٍۭ بِمَا خَلَقَ وَلَعَلَا بَعْضُهُمْ عَلَىٰ بَعْضٍ ۚ سُبْحَـٰنَ ٱللَّهِ عَمَّا يَصِفُونَ ۝ عَـٰلِمِ ٱلْغَيْبِ وَٱلشَّهَـٰدَةِ فَتَعَـٰلَىٰ عَمَّا يُشْرِكُونَ ۝ قُل رَّبِّ إِمَّا تُرِيَنِّى مَا يُوعَدُونَ

۞ رَبِّ فَلَا تَجْعَلْنِى فِى ٱلْقَوْمِ ٱلظَّٰلِمِينَ ۝ وَإِنَّا عَلَىٰٓ أَن نُّرِيَكَ مَا نَعِدُهُمْ لَقَٰدِرُونَ ۝ ٱدْفَعْ بِٱلَّتِى هِىَ أَحْسَنُ ٱلسَّيِّئَةَ ۚ نَحْنُ أَعْلَمُ بِمَا يَصِفُونَ ۝ وَقُل رَّبِّ أَعُوذُ بِكَ مِنْ هَمَزَٰتِ ٱلشَّيَٰطِينِ ۝ وَأَعُوذُ بِكَ رَبِّ أَن يَحْضُرُونِ ۝ حَتَّىٰٓ إِذَا جَآءَ أَحَدَهُمُ ٱلْمَوْتُ قَالَ رَبِّ ٱرْجِعُونِ ۝ لَعَلِّىٓ أَعْمَلُ صَٰلِحًا فِيمَا تَرَكْتُ ۚ كَلَّآ ۚ إِنَّهَا كَلِمَةٌ هُوَ قَآئِلُهَا ۖ وَمِن وَرَآئِهِم بَرْزَخٌ إِلَىٰ يَوْمِ يُبْعَثُونَ ۝ فَإِذَا نُفِخَ فِى ٱلصُّورِ فَلَآ أَنسَابَ بَيْنَهُمْ يَوْمَئِذٍ وَلَا يَتَسَآءَلُونَ ۝ فَمَن ثَقُلَتْ مَوَٰزِينُهُۥ فَأُو۟لَٰٓئِكَ هُمُ ٱلْمُفْلِحُونَ ۝ وَمَنْ خَفَّتْ مَوَٰزِينُهُۥ فَأُو۟لَٰٓئِكَ ٱلَّذِينَ خَسِرُوٓا۟ أَنفُسَهُمْ فِى جَهَنَّمَ خَٰلِدُونَ ۝ تَلْفَحُ وُجُوهَهُمُ ٱلنَّارُ وَهُمْ فِيهَا كَٰلِحُونَ ۝ أَلَمْ تَكُنْ ءَايَٰتِى تُتْلَىٰ عَلَيْكُمْ فَكُنتُم بِهَا تُكَذِّبُونَ ۝ قَالُوا۟ رَبَّنَا غَلَبَتْ عَلَيْنَا شِقْوَتُنَا وَكُنَّا قَوْمًا ضَآلِّينَ ۝ رَبَّنَآ أَخْرِجْنَا مِنْهَا فَإِنْ عُدْنَا فَإِنَّا ظَٰلِمُونَ ۝ قَالَ ٱخْسَـُٔوا۟ فِيهَا وَلَا تُكَلِّمُونِ ۝ إِنَّهُۥ كَانَ فَرِيقٌ مِّنْ عِبَادِى يَقُولُونَ رَبَّنَآ ءَامَنَّا فَٱغْفِرْ لَنَا وَٱرْحَمْنَا وَأَنتَ خَيْرُ ٱلرَّٰحِمِينَ ۝ فَٱتَّخَذْتُمُوهُمْ سِخْرِيًّا حَتَّىٰٓ أَنسَوْكُمْ ذِكْرِى وَكُنتُم مِّنْهُمْ تَضْحَكُونَ ۝ إِنِّى جَزَيْتُهُمُ ٱلْيَوْمَ بِمَا صَبَرُوٓا۟ أَنَّهُمْ هُمُ ٱلْفَآئِزُونَ ۝ قَٰلَ كَمْ لَبِثْتُمْ فِى ٱلْأَرْضِ عَدَدَ سِنِينَ ۝ قَالُوا۟ لَبِثْنَا يَوْمًا أَوْ بَعْضَ يَوْمٍ فَسْـَٔلِ ٱلْعَآدِّينَ ۝ قَٰلَ إِن لَّبِثْتُمْ إِلَّا قَلِيلًا ۖ لَّوْ أَنَّكُمْ كُنتُمْ تَعْلَمُونَ ۝ أَفَحَسِبْتُمْ أَنَّمَا خَلَقْنَٰكُمْ عَبَثًا وَأَنَّكُمْ إِلَيْنَا لَا تُرْجَعُونَ ۝ فَتَعَٰلَى ٱللَّهُ ٱلْمَلِكُ ٱلْحَقُّ ۖ لَآ إِلَٰهَ إِلَّا هُوَ رَبُّ ٱلْعَرْشِ ٱلْكَرِيمِ ۝ وَمَن يَدْعُ مَعَ ٱللَّهِ إِلَٰهًا ءَاخَرَ لَا بُرْهَٰنَ لَهُۥ بِهِۦ فَإِنَّمَا حِسَابُهُۥ عِندَ رَبِّهِۦٓ ۚ إِنَّهُۥ لَا يُفْلِحُ ٱلْكَٰفِرُونَ ۝ وَقُل رَّبِّ ٱغْفِرْ وَٱرْحَمْ وَأَنتَ خَيْرُ ٱلرَّٰحِمِينَ ۝

(Al-Muminun 001-118)

Chapter (Surah) 24: An-Nur 001-064

بِسْمِ اللَّهِ الرَّحْمَٰنِ الرَّحِيمِ

﴿ سُورَةٌ أَنزَلْنَٰهَا وَفَرَضْنَٰهَا وَأَنزَلْنَا فِيهَآ ءَايَٰتٍۭ بَيِّنَٰتٍ لَّعَلَّكُمْ تَذَكَّرُونَ ۝ ٱلزَّانِيَةُ وَٱلزَّانِى فَٱجْلِدُوا۟ كُلَّ وَٰحِدٍ مِّنْهُمَا مِا۟ئَةَ جَلْدَةٍ ۖ وَلَا تَأْخُذْكُم بِهِمَا رَأْفَةٌ فِى دِينِ ٱللَّهِ إِن كُنتُمْ تُؤْمِنُونَ بِٱللَّهِ وَٱلْيَوْمِ ٱلْءَاخِرِ ۖ وَلْيَشْهَدْ عَذَابَهُمَا طَآئِفَةٌ مِّنَ ٱلْمُؤْمِنِينَ ۝ ٱلزَّانِى لَا يَنكِحُ إِلَّا زَانِيَةً أَوْ مُشْرِكَةً وَٱلزَّانِيَةُ لَا يَنكِحُهَآ إِلَّا زَانٍ أَوْ مُشْرِكٌ ۚ وَحُرِّمَ ذَٰلِكَ عَلَى ٱلْمُؤْمِنِينَ ۝ وَٱلَّذِينَ يَرْمُونَ ٱلْمُحْصَنَٰتِ ثُمَّ لَمْ يَأْتُوا۟ بِأَرْبَعَةِ شُهَدَآءَ فَٱجْلِدُوهُمْ ثَمَٰنِينَ جَلْدَةً وَلَا تَقْبَلُوا۟ لَهُمْ شَهَٰدَةً أَبَدًا ۚ وَأُو۟لَٰٓئِكَ هُمُ ٱلْفَٰسِقُونَ ۝ إِلَّا ٱلَّذِينَ تَابُوا۟ مِنۢ بَعْدِ ذَٰلِكَ وَأَصْلَحُوا۟ فَإِنَّ ٱللَّهَ غَفُورٌ رَّحِيمٌ ۝ وَٱلَّذِينَ يَرْمُونَ أَزْوَٰجَهُمْ وَلَمْ يَكُن لَّهُمْ شُهَدَآءُ إِلَّآ أَنفُسُهُمْ فَشَهَٰدَةُ أَحَدِهِمْ أَرْبَعُ شَهَٰدَٰتٍۭ بِٱللَّهِ ۙ إِنَّهُۥ لَمِنَ ٱلصَّٰدِقِينَ ۝ وَٱلْخَٰمِسَةُ أَنَّ لَعْنَتَ ٱللَّهِ عَلَيْهِ إِن كَانَ مِنَ ٱلْكَٰذِبِينَ ۝ وَيَدْرَؤُا۟ عَنْهَا ٱلْعَذَابَ أَن تَشْهَدَ أَرْبَعَ شَهَٰدَٰتٍۭ بِٱللَّهِ ۙ إِنَّهُۥ لَمِنَ ٱلْكَٰذِبِينَ ۝ وَٱلْخَٰمِسَةَ أَنَّ غَضَبَ ٱللَّهِ عَلَيْهَآ إِن كَانَ مِنَ ٱلصَّٰدِقِينَ ۝ وَلَوْلَا فَضْلُ ٱللَّهِ عَلَيْكُمْ وَرَحْمَتُهُۥ وَأَنَّ ٱللَّهَ تَوَّابٌ حَكِيمٌ ۝ إِنَّ ٱلَّذِينَ جَآءُو بِٱلْإِفْكِ عُصْبَةٌ مِّنكُمْ ۚ لَا تَحْسَبُوهُ شَرًّا لَّكُم ۖ بَلْ هُوَ خَيْرٌ لَّكُمْ ۚ لِكُلِّ ٱمْرِئٍ مِّنْهُم مَّا ٱكْتَسَبَ مِنَ ٱلْإِثْمِ ۚ وَٱلَّذِى تَوَلَّىٰ كِبْرَهُۥ مِنْهُمْ لَهُۥ عَذَابٌ عَظِيمٌ ۝ لَّوْلَآ إِذْ سَمِعْتُمُوهُ ظَنَّ ٱلْمُؤْمِنُونَ وَٱلْمُؤْمِنَٰتُ بِأَنفُسِهِمْ خَيْرًا وَقَالُوا۟ هَٰذَآ إِفْكٌ مُّبِينٌ ۝ لَّوْلَا جَآءُو عَلَيْهِ بِأَرْبَعَةِ شُهَدَآءَ ۚ فَإِذْ لَمْ يَأْتُوا۟ بِٱلشُّهَدَآءِ فَأُو۟لَٰٓئِكَ عِندَ ٱللَّهِ هُمُ ٱلْكَٰذِبُونَ ۝ وَلَوْلَا فَضْلُ ٱللَّهِ عَلَيْكُمْ وَرَحْمَتُهُۥ فِى ٱلدُّنْيَا وَٱلْءَاخِرَةِ لَمَسَّكُمْ فِى مَآ أَفَضْتُمْ فِيهِ عَذَابٌ عَظِيمٌ ۝ إِذْ تَلَقَّوْنَهُۥ بِأَلْسِنَتِكُمْ وَتَقُولُونَ بِأَفْوَاهِكُم مَّا لَيْسَ لَكُم بِهِۦ عِلْمٌ وَتَحْسَبُونَهُۥ هَيِّنًا

وَهُوَ عِندَ ٱللَّهِ عَظِيمٌ ۝ وَلَوْلَآ إِذْ سَمِعْتُمُوهُ قُلْتُم مَّا يَكُونُ لَنَآ أَن نَّتَكَلَّمَ بِهَـٰذَا سُبْحَـٰنَكَ هَـٰذَا بُهْتَـٰنٌ عَظِيمٌ ۝ يَعِظُكُمُ ٱللَّهُ أَن تَعُودُوا۟ لِمِثْلِهِۦٓ أَبَدًا إِن كُنتُم مُّؤْمِنِينَ ۝ وَيُبَيِّنُ ٱللَّهُ لَكُمُ ٱلْـَٔايَـٰتِ ۚ وَٱللَّهُ عَلِيمٌ حَكِيمٌ ۝ إِنَّ ٱلَّذِينَ يُحِبُّونَ أَن تَشِيعَ ٱلْفَـٰحِشَةُ فِى ٱلَّذِينَ ءَامَنُوا۟ لَهُمْ عَذَابٌ أَلِيمٌ فِى ٱلدُّنْيَا وَٱلْـَٔاخِرَةِ ۚ وَٱللَّهُ يَعْلَمُ وَأَنتُمْ لَا تَعْلَمُونَ ۝ وَلَوْلَا فَضْلُ ٱللَّهِ عَلَيْكُمْ وَرَحْمَتُهُۥ وَأَنَّ ٱللَّهَ رَءُوفٌ رَّحِيمٌ ۝ يَـٰٓأَيُّهَا ٱلَّذِينَ ءَامَنُوا۟ لَا تَتَّبِعُوا۟ خُطُوَٰتِ ٱلشَّيْطَـٰنِ ۚ وَمَن يَتَّبِعْ خُطُوَٰتِ ٱلشَّيْطَـٰنِ فَإِنَّهُۥ يَأْمُرُ بِٱلْفَحْشَآءِ وَٱلْمُنكَرِ ۚ وَلَوْلَا فَضْلُ ٱللَّهِ عَلَيْكُمْ وَرَحْمَتُهُۥ مَا زَكَىٰ مِنكُم مِّنْ أَحَدٍ أَبَدًا وَلَـٰكِنَّ ٱللَّهَ يُزَكِّى مَن يَشَآءُ ۗ وَٱللَّهُ سَمِيعٌ عَلِيمٌ ۝ وَلَا يَأْتَلِ أُو۟لُوا۟ ٱلْفَضْلِ مِنكُمْ وَٱلسَّعَةِ أَن يُؤْتُوٓا۟ أُو۟لِى ٱلْقُرْبَىٰ وَٱلْمَسَـٰكِينَ وَٱلْمُهَـٰجِرِينَ فِى سَبِيلِ ٱللَّهِ ۖ وَلْيَعْفُوا۟ وَلْيَصْفَحُوٓا۟ ۗ أَلَا تُحِبُّونَ أَن يَغْفِرَ ٱللَّهُ لَكُمْ ۗ وَٱللَّهُ غَفُورٌ رَّحِيمٌ ۝ إِنَّ ٱلَّذِينَ يَرْمُونَ ٱلْمُحْصَنَـٰتِ ٱلْغَـٰفِلَـٰتِ ٱلْمُؤْمِنَـٰتِ لُعِنُوا۟ فِى ٱلدُّنْيَا وَٱلْـَٔاخِرَةِ وَلَهُمْ عَذَابٌ عَظِيمٌ ۝ يَوْمَ تَشْهَدُ عَلَيْهِمْ أَلْسِنَتُهُمْ وَأَيْدِيهِمْ وَأَرْجُلُهُم بِمَا كَانُوا۟ يَعْمَلُونَ ۝ يَوْمَئِذٍ يُوَفِّيهِمُ ٱللَّهُ دِينَهُمُ ٱلْحَقَّ وَيَعْلَمُونَ أَنَّ ٱللَّهَ هُوَ ٱلْحَقُّ ٱلْمُبِينُ ۝ ٱلْخَبِيثَـٰتُ لِلْخَبِيثِينَ وَٱلْخَبِيثُونَ لِلْخَبِيثَـٰتِ ۖ وَٱلطَّيِّبَـٰتُ لِلطَّيِّبِينَ وَٱلطَّيِّبُونَ لِلطَّيِّبَـٰتِ ۚ أُو۟لَـٰٓئِكَ مُبَرَّءُونَ مِمَّا يَقُولُونَ ۖ لَهُم مَّغْفِرَةٌ وَرِزْقٌ كَرِيمٌ ۝ يَـٰٓأَيُّهَا ٱلَّذِينَ ءَامَنُوا۟ لَا تَدْخُلُوا۟ بُيُوتًا غَيْرَ بُيُوتِكُمْ حَتَّىٰ تَسْتَأْنِسُوا۟ وَتُسَلِّمُوا۟ عَلَىٰٓ أَهْلِهَا ۚ ذَٰلِكُمْ خَيْرٌ لَّكُمْ لَعَلَّكُمْ تَذَكَّرُونَ ۝ فَإِن لَّمْ تَجِدُوا۟ فِيهَآ أَحَدًا فَلَا تَدْخُلُوهَا حَتَّىٰ يُؤْذَنَ لَكُمْ ۖ وَإِن قِيلَ لَكُمُ ٱرْجِعُوا۟ فَٱرْجِعُوا۟ ۖ هُوَ أَزْكَىٰ لَكُمْ ۚ وَٱللَّهُ بِمَا تَعْمَلُونَ عَلِيمٌ ۝ لَّيْسَ عَلَيْكُمْ جُنَاحٌ أَن تَدْخُلُوا۟ بُيُوتًا غَيْرَ مَسْكُونَةٍ فِيهَا مَتَـٰعٌ لَّكُمْ ۚ وَٱللَّهُ يَعْلَمُ مَا تُبْدُونَ وَمَا تَكْتُمُونَ ۝ قُل لِّلْمُؤْمِنِينَ

يَغُضُّوا۟ مِنْ أَبْصَـٰرِهِمْ وَيَحْفَظُوا۟ فُرُوجَهُمْ ۚ ذَٰلِكَ أَزْكَىٰ لَهُمْ ۗ إِنَّ ٱللَّهَ خَبِيرٌۢ بِمَا يَصْنَعُونَ ۝ وَقُل لِّلْمُؤْمِنَـٰتِ يَغْضُضْنَ مِنْ أَبْصَـٰرِهِنَّ وَيَحْفَظْنَ فُرُوجَهُنَّ وَلَا يُبْدِينَ زِينَتَهُنَّ إِلَّا مَا ظَهَرَ مِنْهَا ۖ وَلْيَضْرِبْنَ بِخُمُرِهِنَّ عَلَىٰ جُيُوبِهِنَّ ۖ وَلَا يُبْدِينَ زِينَتَهُنَّ إِلَّا لِبُعُولَتِهِنَّ أَوْ ءَابَآئِهِنَّ أَوْ ءَابَآءِ بُعُولَتِهِنَّ أَوْ أَبْنَآئِهِنَّ أَوْ أَبْنَآءِ بُعُولَتِهِنَّ أَوْ إِخْوَٰنِهِنَّ أَوْ بَنِىٓ إِخْوَٰنِهِنَّ أَوْ بَنِىٓ أَخَوَٰتِهِنَّ أَوْ نِسَآئِهِنَّ أَوْ مَا مَلَكَتْ أَيْمَـٰنُهُنَّ أَوِ ٱلتَّـٰبِعِينَ غَيْرِ أُو۟لِى ٱلْإِرْبَةِ مِنَ ٱلرِّجَالِ أَوِ ٱلطِّفْلِ ٱلَّذِينَ لَمْ يَظْهَرُوا۟ عَلَىٰ عَوْرَٰتِ ٱلنِّسَآءِ ۖ وَلَا يَضْرِبْنَ بِأَرْجُلِهِنَّ لِيُعْلَمَ مَا يُخْفِينَ مِن زِينَتِهِنَّ ۚ وَتُوبُوٓا۟ إِلَى ٱللَّهِ جَمِيعًا أَيُّهَ ٱلْمُؤْمِنُونَ لَعَلَّكُمْ تُفْلِحُونَ ۝ وَأَنكِحُوا۟ ٱلْأَيَـٰمَىٰ مِنكُمْ وَٱلصَّـٰلِحِينَ مِنْ عِبَادِكُمْ وَإِمَآئِكُمْ ۚ إِن يَكُونُوا۟ فُقَرَآءَ يُغْنِهِمُ ٱللَّهُ مِن فَضْلِهِۦ ۗ وَٱللَّهُ وَٰسِعٌ عَلِيمٌ ۝ وَلْيَسْتَعْفِفِ ٱلَّذِينَ لَا يَجِدُونَ نِكَاحًا حَتَّىٰ يُغْنِيَهُمُ ٱللَّهُ مِن فَضْلِهِۦ ۗ وَٱلَّذِينَ يَبْتَغُونَ ٱلْكِتَـٰبَ مِمَّا مَلَكَتْ أَيْمَـٰنُكُمْ فَكَاتِبُوهُمْ إِنْ عَلِمْتُمْ فِيهِمْ خَيْرًا ۖ وَءَاتُوهُم مِّن مَّالِ ٱللَّهِ ٱلَّذِىٓ ءَاتَىٰكُمْ ۚ وَلَا تُكْرِهُوا۟ فَتَيَـٰتِكُمْ عَلَى ٱلْبِغَآءِ إِنْ أَرَدْنَ تَحَصُّنًا لِّتَبْتَغُوا۟ عَرَضَ ٱلْحَيَوٰةِ ٱلدُّنْيَا ۚ وَمَن يُكْرِههُّنَّ فَإِنَّ ٱللَّهَ مِنۢ بَعْدِ إِكْرَٰهِهِنَّ غَفُورٌ رَّحِيمٌ ۝ وَلَقَدْ أَنزَلْنَآ إِلَيْكُمْ ءَايَـٰتٍ مُّبَيِّنَـٰتٍ وَمَثَلًا مِّنَ ٱلَّذِينَ خَلَوْا۟ مِن قَبْلِكُمْ وَمَوْعِظَةً لِّلْمُتَّقِينَ ۝ ٱللَّهُ نُورُ ٱلسَّمَـٰوَٰتِ وَٱلْأَرْضِ ۚ مَثَلُ نُورِهِۦ كَمِشْكَوٰةٍ فِيهَا مِصْبَاحٌ ۖ ٱلْمِصْبَاحُ فِى زُجَاجَةٍ ۖ ٱلزُّجَاجَةُ كَأَنَّهَا كَوْكَبٌ دُرِّىٌّ يُوقَدُ مِن شَجَرَةٍ مُّبَـٰرَكَةٍ زَيْتُونَةٍ لَّا شَرْقِيَّةٍ وَلَا غَرْبِيَّةٍ يَكَادُ زَيْتُهَا يُضِىٓءُ وَلَوْ لَمْ تَمْسَسْهُ نَارٌ ۚ نُّورٌ عَلَىٰ نُورٍ ۗ يَهْدِى ٱللَّهُ لِنُورِهِۦ مَن يَشَآءُ ۚ وَيَضْرِبُ ٱللَّهُ ٱلْأَمْثَـٰلَ لِلنَّاسِ ۗ وَٱللَّهُ بِكُلِّ شَىْءٍ عَلِيمٌ ۝ فِى بُيُوتٍ أَذِنَ ٱللَّهُ أَن تُرْفَعَ وَيُذْكَرَ فِيهَا ٱسْمُهُۥ يُسَبِّحُ لَهُۥ فِيهَا بِٱلْغُدُوِّ وَٱلْـَٔاصَالِ ۝ رِجَالٌ لَّا تُلْهِيهِمْ تِجَـٰرَةٌ وَلَا

بَيْعٌ عَن ذِكْرِ ٱللَّهِ وَإِقَامِ ٱلصَّلَوٰةِ وَإِيتَآءِ ٱلزَّكَوٰةِ ۙ يَخَافُونَ يَوْمًا تَتَقَلَّبُ فِيهِ ٱلْقُلُوبُ وَٱلْأَبْصَـٰرُ ۝٣٧ لِيَجْزِيَهُمُ ٱللَّهُ أَحْسَنَ مَا عَمِلُوا۟ وَيَزِيدَهُم مِّن فَضْلِهِۦ ۗ وَٱللَّهُ يَرْزُقُ مَن يَشَآءُ بِغَيْرِ حِسَابٍ ۝٣٨ وَٱلَّذِينَ كَفَرُوٓا۟ أَعْمَـٰلُهُمْ كَسَرَابٍۭ بِقِيعَةٍ يَحْسَبُهُ ٱلظَّمْـَٔانُ مَآءً حَتَّىٰٓ إِذَا جَآءَهُۥ لَمْ يَجِدْهُ شَيْـًٔا وَوَجَدَ ٱللَّهَ عِندَهُۥ فَوَفَّىٰهُ حِسَابَهُۥ ۗ وَٱللَّهُ سَرِيعُ ٱلْحِسَابِ ۝٣٩ أَوْ كَظُلُمَـٰتٍ فِى بَحْرٍ لُّجِّىٍّ يَغْشَىٰهُ مَوْجٌ مِّن فَوْقِهِۦ مَوْجٌ مِّن فَوْقِهِۦ سَحَابٌ ۚ ظُلُمَـٰتٌۢ بَعْضُهَا فَوْقَ بَعْضٍ إِذَآ أَخْرَجَ يَدَهُۥ لَمْ يَكَدْ يَرَىٰهَا ۗ وَمَن لَّمْ يَجْعَلِ ٱللَّهُ لَهُۥ نُورًا فَمَا لَهُۥ مِن نُّورٍ ۝٤٠ أَلَمْ تَرَ أَنَّ ٱللَّهَ يُسَبِّحُ لَهُۥ مَن فِى ٱلسَّمَـٰوَٰتِ وَٱلْأَرْضِ وَٱلطَّيْرُ صَـٰٓفَّـٰتٍ ۖ كُلٌّ قَدْ عَلِمَ صَلَاتَهُۥ وَتَسْبِيحَهُۥ ۗ وَٱللَّهُ عَلِيمٌۢ بِمَا يَفْعَلُونَ ۝٤١ وَلِلَّهِ مُلْكُ ٱلسَّمَـٰوَٰتِ وَٱلْأَرْضِ ۖ وَإِلَى ٱللَّهِ ٱلْمَصِيرُ ۝٤٢ أَلَمْ تَرَ أَنَّ ٱللَّهَ يُزْجِى سَحَابًا ثُمَّ يُؤَلِّفُ بَيْنَهُۥ ثُمَّ يَجْعَلُهُۥ رُكَامًا فَتَرَى ٱلْوَدْقَ يَخْرُجُ مِنْ خِلَـٰلِهِۦ وَيُنَزِّلُ مِنَ ٱلسَّمَآءِ مِن جِبَالٍ فِيهَا مِنۢ بَرَدٍ فَيُصِيبُ بِهِۦ مَن يَشَآءُ وَيَصْرِفُهُۥ عَن مَّن يَشَآءُ ۖ يَكَادُ سَنَا بَرْقِهِۦ يَذْهَبُ بِٱلْأَبْصَـٰرِ ۝٤٣ يُقَلِّبُ ٱللَّهُ ٱلَّيْلَ وَٱلنَّهَارَ ۚ إِنَّ فِى ذَٰلِكَ لَعِبْرَةً لِّأُو۟لِى ٱلْأَبْصَـٰرِ ۝٤٤ وَٱللَّهُ خَلَقَ كُلَّ دَآبَّةٍ مِّن مَّآءٍ ۖ فَمِنْهُم مَّن يَمْشِى عَلَىٰ بَطْنِهِۦ وَمِنْهُم مَّن يَمْشِى عَلَىٰ رِجْلَيْنِ وَمِنْهُم مَّن يَمْشِى عَلَىٰٓ أَرْبَعٍ ۚ يَخْلُقُ ٱللَّهُ مَا يَشَآءُ ۚ إِنَّ ٱللَّهَ عَلَىٰ كُلِّ شَىْءٍ قَدِيرٌ ۝٤٥ لَّقَدْ أَنزَلْنَآ ءَايَـٰتٍ مُّبَيِّنَـٰتٍ ۚ وَٱللَّهُ يَهْدِى مَن يَشَآءُ إِلَىٰ صِرَٰطٍ مُّسْتَقِيمٍ ۝٤٦ وَيَقُولُونَ ءَامَنَّا بِٱللَّهِ وَبِٱلرَّسُولِ وَأَطَعْنَا ثُمَّ يَتَوَلَّىٰ فَرِيقٌ مِّنْهُم مِّنۢ بَعْدِ ذَٰلِكَ ۚ وَمَآ أُو۟لَـٰٓئِكَ بِٱلْمُؤْمِنِينَ ۝٤٧ وَإِذَا دُعُوٓا۟ إِلَى ٱللَّهِ وَرَسُولِهِۦ لِيَحْكُمَ بَيْنَهُمْ إِذَا فَرِيقٌ مِّنْهُم مُّعْرِضُونَ ۝٤٨ وَإِن يَكُن لَّهُمُ ٱلْحَقُّ يَأْتُوٓا۟ إِلَيْهِ مُذْعِنِينَ ۝٤٩ أَفِى قُلُوبِهِم مَّرَضٌ أَمِ ٱرْتَابُوٓا۟ أَمْ يَخَافُونَ أَن يَحِيفَ ٱللَّهُ عَلَيْهِمْ وَرَسُولُهُۥ ۚ بَلْ أُو۟لَـٰٓئِكَ هُمُ ٱلظَّـٰلِمُونَ ۝٥٠ إِنَّمَا كَانَ قَوْلَ ٱلْمُؤْمِنِينَ إِذَا دُعُوٓا۟

إِلَى ٱللَّهِ وَرَسُولِهِۦ لِيَحْكُمَ بَيْنَهُمْ أَن يَقُولُوا۟ سَمِعْنَا وَأَطَعْنَا ۚ وَأُو۟لَٰٓئِكَ هُمُ ٱلْمُفْلِحُونَ ۝ وَمَن يُطِعِ ٱللَّهَ وَرَسُولَهُۥ وَيَخْشَ ٱللَّهَ وَيَتَّقْهِ فَأُو۟لَٰٓئِكَ هُمُ ٱلْفَآئِزُونَ ۝ ۞ وَأَقْسَمُوا۟ بِٱللَّهِ جَهْدَ أَيْمَٰنِهِمْ لَئِنْ أَمَرْتَهُمْ لَيَخْرُجُنَّ ۖ قُل لَّا تُقْسِمُوا۟ ۖ طَاعَةٌ مَّعْرُوفَةٌ ۚ إِنَّ ٱللَّهَ خَبِيرٌۢ بِمَا تَعْمَلُونَ ۝ قُلْ أَطِيعُوا۟ ٱللَّهَ وَأَطِيعُوا۟ ٱلرَّسُولَ ۖ فَإِن تَوَلَّوْا۟ فَإِنَّمَا عَلَيْهِ مَا حُمِّلَ وَعَلَيْكُم مَّا حُمِّلْتُمْ ۖ وَإِن تُطِيعُوهُ تَهْتَدُوا۟ ۚ وَمَا عَلَى ٱلرَّسُولِ إِلَّا ٱلْبَلَٰغُ ٱلْمُبِينُ ۝ وَعَدَ ٱللَّهُ ٱلَّذِينَ ءَامَنُوا۟ مِنكُمْ وَعَمِلُوا۟ ٱلصَّٰلِحَٰتِ لَيَسْتَخْلِفَنَّهُمْ فِى ٱلْأَرْضِ كَمَا ٱسْتَخْلَفَ ٱلَّذِينَ مِن قَبْلِهِمْ وَلَيُمَكِّنَنَّ لَهُمْ دِينَهُمُ ٱلَّذِى ٱرْتَضَىٰ لَهُمْ وَلَيُبَدِّلَنَّهُم مِّنۢ بَعْدِ خَوْفِهِمْ أَمْنًا ۚ يَعْبُدُونَنِى لَا يُشْرِكُونَ بِى شَيْـًٔا ۚ وَمَن كَفَرَ بَعْدَ ذَٰلِكَ فَأُو۟لَٰٓئِكَ هُمُ ٱلْفَٰسِقُونَ ۝ وَأَقِيمُوا۟ ٱلصَّلَوٰةَ وَءَاتُوا۟ ٱلزَّكَوٰةَ وَأَطِيعُوا۟ ٱلرَّسُولَ لَعَلَّكُمْ تُرْحَمُونَ ۝ لَا تَحْسَبَنَّ ٱلَّذِينَ كَفَرُوا۟ مُعْجِزِينَ فِى ٱلْأَرْضِ ۚ وَمَأْوَىٰهُمُ ٱلنَّارُ ۖ وَلَبِئْسَ ٱلْمَصِيرُ ۝ يَٰٓأَيُّهَا ٱلَّذِينَ ءَامَنُوا۟ لِيَسْتَـْٔذِنكُمُ ٱلَّذِينَ مَلَكَتْ أَيْمَٰنُكُمْ وَٱلَّذِينَ لَمْ يَبْلُغُوا۟ ٱلْحُلُمَ مِنكُمْ ثَلَٰثَ مَرَّٰتٍ ۚ مِّن قَبْلِ صَلَوٰةِ ٱلْفَجْرِ وَحِينَ تَضَعُونَ ثِيَابَكُم مِّنَ ٱلظَّهِيرَةِ وَمِنۢ بَعْدِ صَلَوٰةِ ٱلْعِشَآءِ ۚ ثَلَٰثُ عَوْرَٰتٍ لَّكُمْ ۚ لَيْسَ عَلَيْكُمْ وَلَا عَلَيْهِمْ جُنَاحٌۢ بَعْدَهُنَّ ۚ طَوَّٰفُونَ عَلَيْكُم بَعْضُكُمْ عَلَىٰ بَعْضٍ ۚ كَذَٰلِكَ يُبَيِّنُ ٱللَّهُ لَكُمُ ٱلْـَٔايَٰتِ ۗ وَٱللَّهُ عَلِيمٌ حَكِيمٌ ۝ وَإِذَا بَلَغَ ٱلْأَطْفَٰلُ مِنكُمُ ٱلْحُلُمَ فَلْيَسْتَـْٔذِنُوا۟ كَمَا ٱسْتَـْٔذَنَ ٱلَّذِينَ مِن قَبْلِهِمْ ۚ كَذَٰلِكَ يُبَيِّنُ ٱللَّهُ لَكُمْ ءَايَٰتِهِۦ ۗ وَٱللَّهُ عَلِيمٌ حَكِيمٌ ۝ وَٱلْقَوَٰعِدُ مِنَ ٱلنِّسَآءِ ٱلَّٰتِى لَا يَرْجُونَ نِكَاحًا فَلَيْسَ عَلَيْهِنَّ جُنَاحٌ أَن يَضَعْنَ ثِيَابَهُنَّ غَيْرَ مُتَبَرِّجَٰتٍۭ بِزِينَةٍ ۖ وَأَن يَسْتَعْفِفْنَ خَيْرٌ لَّهُنَّ ۗ وَٱللَّهُ سَمِيعٌ عَلِيمٌ ۝ لَّيْسَ عَلَى ٱلْأَعْمَىٰ حَرَجٌ وَلَا عَلَى ٱلْأَعْرَجِ حَرَجٌ وَلَا عَلَى ٱلْمَرِيضِ حَرَجٌ وَلَا عَلَىٰ

أَنفُسِكُمْ أَن تَأْكُلُوا۟ مِنۢ بُيُوتِكُمْ أَوْ بُيُوتِ ءَابَآئِكُمْ أَوْ بُيُوتِ أُمَّهَٰتِكُمْ أَوْ بُيُوتِ إِخْوَٰنِكُمْ أَوْ بُيُوتِ أَخَوَٰتِكُمْ أَوْ بُيُوتِ أَعْمَٰمِكُمْ أَوْ بُيُوتِ عَمَّٰتِكُمْ أَوْ بُيُوتِ أَخْوَٰلِكُمْ أَوْ بُيُوتِ خَٰلَٰتِكُمْ أَوْ مَا مَلَكْتُم مَّفَاتِحَهُۥٓ أَوْ صَدِيقِكُمْ ۚ لَيْسَ عَلَيْكُمْ جُنَاحٌ أَن تَأْكُلُوا۟ جَمِيعًا أَوْ أَشْتَاتًا ۚ فَإِذَا دَخَلْتُم بُيُوتًا فَسَلِّمُوا۟ عَلَىٰٓ أَنفُسِكُمْ تَحِيَّةً مِّنْ عِندِ ٱللَّهِ مُبَٰرَكَةً طَيِّبَةً ۚ كَذَٰلِكَ يُبَيِّنُ ٱللَّهُ لَكُمُ ٱلْءَايَٰتِ لَعَلَّكُمْ تَعْقِلُونَ ۝ إِنَّمَا ٱلْمُؤْمِنُونَ ٱلَّذِينَ ءَامَنُوا۟ بِٱللَّهِ وَرَسُولِهِۦ وَإِذَا كَانُوا۟ مَعَهُۥ عَلَىٰٓ أَمْرٍ جَامِعٍ لَّمْ يَذْهَبُوا۟ حَتَّىٰ يَسْتَـْٔذِنُوهُ ۚ إِنَّ ٱلَّذِينَ يَسْتَـْٔذِنُونَكَ أُو۟لَٰٓئِكَ ٱلَّذِينَ يُؤْمِنُونَ بِٱللَّهِ وَرَسُولِهِۦ ۚ فَإِذَا ٱسْتَـْٔذَنُوكَ لِبَعْضِ شَأْنِهِمْ فَأْذَن لِّمَن شِئْتَ مِنْهُمْ وَٱسْتَغْفِرْ لَهُمُ ٱللَّهَ ۚ إِنَّ ٱللَّهَ غَفُورٌ رَّحِيمٌ ۝ لَّا تَجْعَلُوا۟ دُعَآءَ ٱلرَّسُولِ بَيْنَكُمْ كَدُعَآءِ بَعْضِكُم بَعْضًا ۚ قَدْ يَعْلَمُ ٱللَّهُ ٱلَّذِينَ يَتَسَلَّلُونَ مِنكُمْ لِوَاذًا ۚ فَلْيَحْذَرِ ٱلَّذِينَ يُخَالِفُونَ عَنْ أَمْرِهِۦٓ أَن تُصِيبَهُمْ فِتْنَةٌ أَوْ يُصِيبَهُمْ عَذَابٌ أَلِيمٌ ۝ أَلَآ إِنَّ لِلَّهِ مَا فِى ٱلسَّمَٰوَٰتِ وَٱلْأَرْضِ ۖ قَدْ يَعْلَمُ مَآ أَنتُمْ عَلَيْهِ وَيَوْمَ يُرْجَعُونَ إِلَيْهِ فَيُنَبِّئُهُم بِمَا عَمِلُوا۟ ۗ وَٱللَّهُ بِكُلِّ شَىْءٍ عَلِيمٌۢ ۝

(An-Nur 001-064)

Chapter (Surah) 25: Al-Furqan 001-020

بِسْمِ ٱللَّهِ ٱلرَّحْمَٰنِ ٱلرَّحِيمِ

﴿ تَبَارَكَ ٱلَّذِى نَزَّلَ ٱلْفُرْقَانَ عَلَىٰ عَبْدِهِۦ لِيَكُونَ لِلْعَٰلَمِينَ نَذِيرًا ۝ ٱلَّذِى لَهُۥ مُلْكُ ٱلسَّمَٰوَٰتِ وَٱلْأَرْضِ وَلَمْ يَتَّخِذْ وَلَدًا وَلَمْ يَكُن لَّهُۥ شَرِيكٌ فِى ٱلْمُلْكِ وَخَلَقَ كُلَّ شَىْءٍ فَقَدَّرَهُۥ تَقْدِيرًا ۝ وَٱتَّخَذُوا۟ مِن دُونِهِۦٓ ءَالِهَةً لَّا يَخْلُقُونَ شَيْـًٔا وَهُمْ يُخْلَقُونَ وَلَا يَمْلِكُونَ لِأَنفُسِهِمْ ضَرًّا وَلَا نَفْعًا وَلَا يَمْلِكُونَ مَوْتًا وَلَا حَيَوٰةً وَلَا نُشُورًا ۝ وَقَالَ ٱلَّذِينَ كَفَرُوٓا۟ إِنْ هَٰذَآ إِلَّآ إِفْكٌ ٱفْتَرَىٰهُ

وَأَعَانَهُۥ عَلَيْهِ قَوْمٌ ءَاخَرُونَ ۖ فَقَدْ جَآءُو ظُلْمًا وَزُورًا ۝ وَقَالُوٓا۟ أَسَٰطِيرُ ٱلْأَوَّلِينَ ٱكْتَتَبَهَا فَهِىَ تُمْلَىٰ عَلَيْهِ بُكْرَةً وَأَصِيلًا ۝ قُلْ أَنزَلَهُ ٱلَّذِى يَعْلَمُ ٱلسِّرَّ فِى ٱلسَّمَٰوَٰتِ وَٱلْأَرْضِ ۚ إِنَّهُۥ كَانَ غَفُورًا رَّحِيمًا ۝ وَقَالُوا۟ مَالِ هَٰذَا ٱلرَّسُولِ يَأْكُلُ ٱلطَّعَامَ وَيَمْشِى فِى ٱلْأَسْوَاقِ ۙ لَوْلَآ أُنزِلَ إِلَيْهِ مَلَكٌ فَيَكُونَ مَعَهُۥ نَذِيرًا ۝ أَوْ يُلْقَىٰٓ إِلَيْهِ كَنزٌ أَوْ تَكُونُ لَهُۥ جَنَّةٌ يَأْكُلُ مِنْهَا ۚ وَقَالَ ٱلظَّٰلِمُونَ إِن تَتَّبِعُونَ إِلَّا رَجُلًا مَّسْحُورًا ۝ ٱنظُرْ كَيْفَ ضَرَبُوا۟ لَكَ ٱلْأَمْثَٰلَ فَضَلُّوا۟ فَلَا يَسْتَطِيعُونَ سَبِيلًا ۝ تَبَارَكَ ٱلَّذِىٓ إِن شَآءَ جَعَلَ لَكَ خَيْرًا مِّن ذَٰلِكَ جَنَّٰتٍ تَجْرِى مِن تَحْتِهَا ٱلْأَنْهَٰرُ وَيَجْعَل لَّكَ قُصُورًۢا ۝ بَلْ كَذَّبُوا۟ بِٱلسَّاعَةِ ۖ وَأَعْتَدْنَا لِمَن كَذَّبَ بِٱلسَّاعَةِ سَعِيرًا ۝ إِذَا رَأَتْهُم مِّن مَّكَانٍۭ بَعِيدٍ سَمِعُوا۟ لَهَا تَغَيُّظًا وَزَفِيرًا ۝ وَإِذَآ أُلْقُوا۟ مِنْهَا مَكَانًا ضَيِّقًا مُّقَرَّنِينَ دَعَوْا۟ هُنَالِكَ ثُبُورًا ۝ لَّا تَدْعُوا۟ ٱلْيَوْمَ ثُبُورًا وَٰحِدًا وَٱدْعُوا۟ ثُبُورًا كَثِيرًا ۝ قُلْ أَذَٰلِكَ خَيْرٌ أَمْ جَنَّةُ ٱلْخُلْدِ ٱلَّتِى وُعِدَ ٱلْمُتَّقُونَ ۚ كَانَتْ لَهُمْ جَزَآءً وَمَصِيرًا ۝ لَّهُمْ فِيهَا مَا يَشَآءُونَ خَٰلِدِينَ ۚ كَانَ عَلَىٰ رَبِّكَ وَعْدًا مَّسْـُٔولًا ۝ وَيَوْمَ يَحْشُرُهُمْ وَمَا يَعْبُدُونَ مِن دُونِ ٱللَّهِ فَيَقُولُ ءَأَنتُمْ أَضْلَلْتُمْ عِبَادِى هَٰٓؤُلَآءِ أَمْ هُمْ ضَلُّوا۟ ٱلسَّبِيلَ ۝ قَالُوا۟ سُبْحَٰنَكَ مَا كَانَ يَنۢبَغِى لَنَآ أَن نَّتَّخِذَ مِن دُونِكَ مِنْ أَوْلِيَآءَ وَلَٰكِن مَّتَّعْتَهُمْ وَءَابَآءَهُمْ حَتَّىٰ نَسُوا۟ ٱلذِّكْرَ وَكَانُوا۟ قَوْمًۢا بُورًا ۝ فَقَدْ كَذَّبُوكُم بِمَا تَقُولُونَ فَمَا تَسْتَطِيعُونَ صَرْفًا وَلَا نَصْرًا ۚ وَمَن يَظْلِم مِّنكُمْ نُذِقْهُ عَذَابًا كَبِيرًا ۝ وَمَآ أَرْسَلْنَا قَبْلَكَ مِنَ ٱلْمُرْسَلِينَ إِلَّآ إِنَّهُمْ لَيَأْكُلُونَ ٱلطَّعَامَ وَيَمْشُونَ فِى ٱلْأَسْوَاقِ ۗ وَجَعَلْنَا بَعْضَكُمْ لِبَعْضٍ فِتْنَةً أَتَصْبِرُونَ ۗ وَكَانَ رَبُّكَ بَصِيرًا ۝

(Al-Furqan 001-020)

CHAPTER (SURAH) 23: AL-MU'MINUN (THE BELIEVERS), VERSES 001 – 118

(بِسْمِ اللَّهِ الرَّحْمَـنِ الرَّحِيمِ)

In the Name of Allah, the Most Gracious, the Most Merciful

Surah: 23 Ayah: 1, Ayah: 2, Ayah: 3, Ayah: 4, Ayah: 5, Ayah: 6, Ayah: 7, Ayah: 8, Ayah: 9, Ayah: 10 & Ayah: 11

قَدْ أَفْلَحَ ٱلْمُؤْمِنُونَ ۝

1. Successful indeed are the believers.

ٱلَّذِينَ هُمْ فِى صَلَاتِهِمْ خَـٰشِعُونَ ۝

2. Those who offer their Salât (prayers) with all solemnity and full submissiveness.

وَٱلَّذِينَ هُمْ عَنِ ٱللَّغْوِ مُعْرِضُونَ ۝

3. And those who turn away from Al-Laghw (dirty, false, evil vain talk, falsehood, and all that Allâh has forbidden).

وَٱلَّذِينَ هُمْ لِلزَّكَوٰةِ فَـٰعِلُونَ ۝

4. And those who pay the Zakât.

وَٱلَّذِينَ هُمْ لِفُرُوجِهِمْ حَـٰفِظُونَ ۝

5. And those who guard their chastity (i.e. private parts, from illegal sexual acts)

إِلَّا عَلَىٰٓ أَزْوَٰجِهِمْ أَوْ مَا مَلَكَتْ أَيْمَـٰنُهُمْ فَإِنَّهُمْ غَيْرُ مَلُومِينَ ۝

6. Except from their wives or (the slaves) that their right hands possess, - for then, they are free from blame;

فَمَنِ ٱبْتَغَىٰ وَرَآءَ ذَٰلِكَ فَأُوْلَـٰٓئِكَ هُمُ ٱلْعَادُونَ ۝

7. But whoever seeks beyond that, then those are the transgressors;

وَٱلَّذِينَ هُمْ لِأَمَـٰنَـٰتِهِمْ وَعَهْدِهِمْ رَٰعُونَ ۝

8. Those who are faithfully true to their Amanât (all the duties which Allâh has ordained, honesty, moral responsibility and trusts) and to their covenants;

وَٱلَّذِينَ هُمْ عَلَىٰ صَلَوَٰتِهِمْ يُحَافِظُونَ ۝

9. And those who strictly guard their (five compulsory congregational) Salawât (prayers) (at their fixed stated hours).

أُو۟لَـٰٓئِكَ هُمُ ٱلْوَٰرِثُونَ ﴿١٠﴾

10. These are indeed the inheritors

ٱلَّذِينَ يَرِثُونَ ٱلْفِرْدَوْسَ هُمْ فِيهَا خَـٰلِدُونَ ﴿١١﴾

11. Who shall inherit the Firdaus (Paradise). They shall dwell therein forever.

Transliteration

1. Qad aflaha almu/minoona 2. Allatheena hum fee salatihim khashiAAoona 3. Waallatheena hum AAani allaghwi muAAridoona 4. Waallatheena hum lilzzakati faAAiloona 5. Waallatheena hum lifuroojihim hafithoona 6. Illa AAala azwajihim aw ma malakat aymanuhum fa-innahum ghayru maloomeena 7. Famani ibtagha waraa thalika faola-ika humu alAAadoona 8. Waallatheena hum li-amanatihim waAAahdihim raAAoona 9. Waallatheena hum AAala salawatihim yuhafithoona 10. Ola-ika humu alwarithoona 11. Allatheena yarithoona alfirdawsa hum feeha khalidoona

Tafsir Ibn Kathir

The Success is for the believers whose qualities are described here

(Successful indeed are the believers) means, they have attained victory and are blessed, for they have succeeded. These are the believers who have the following characteristics:

(Those who with their Salah are Khashi`un.) `Ali bin Abi Talhah reported that Ibn `Abbas said:

"(Khashi`un) means those with fear and with tranquillity." This was also narrated from Mujahid, Al-Hasan, Qatadah and Az-Zuhri. It was reported from `Ali bin Abi Talib, may Allah be pleased with him, that Khushu` means the Khushu` of the heart. This was also the view of Ibrahim An-Nakha`i. Al-Hasan Al-Basri said, "Their Khushu` was in their hearts." So they lowered their gaze and were humble towards others. Khushu` in prayer is only attained by the one who has emptied his heart totally, who does not pay attention to anything else besides it, and who prefers it above all else. At that point it becomes a delight and a joy for eyes, as in the Hadith recorded by Imam Ahmad and An-Nasa'i from Anas, who said that the Messenger of Allah said:

«حُبِّبَ إِلَيَّ الطِّيبُ وَالنِّسَاءُ، وَجُعِلَتْ قُرَّةُ عَيْنِي فِي الصَّلَاة»

(Fragrance and women have been made dear to me, and Salah was made the joy of my eye.)

(And those who turn away from Al-Laghw.) refers to falsehood, which includes Shirk and sin, and any words or deeds that are of no benefit. As Allah says:

(And if they pass by Al-Laghw, they pass by it with dignity)(25:72). Qatadah said: "By Allah, there came to them from Allah that which kept them away from that (evil)."

(And those who pay the Zakah.) Most commentators say that the meaning here is the Zakah that is paid on wealth, even though this Ayah was revealed in Makkah, and Zakah was ordained in Al-Madinah in the year 2 H. The apparent meaning is that the Zakah that was instituted in Al-Madinah is the one based upon the Nusub and the specific amounts, apart from which it seems that the basic principle of Zakah was enjoined in Makkah. As Allah says in Surat Al-An`am, which was also revealed in Makkah:

(but pay the due thereof on the day of their harvest,) (6:141) It could be that what is meant here by Zakah is purification of the soul from Shirk and filth, as in the Ayah:

(Indeed he succeeds who purifies himself (Zakkaha). And indeed he fails who corrupts himself.) (91:9-10) It could be that both meanings are intended, purification of the soul and of one's wealth, because that is part of the purification of the soul, and the true believer is one who pays attention to both matters. And Allah knows best.

(And those who guard their private parts. Except from their wives and their right hand possessions, for then, they are free from blame. But whoever seeks beyond that, then those are the transgressors.) means, those who protect their private parts from unlawful actions and do not do that which Allah has forbidden; fornication and homosexuality, and do not approach anyone except the wives whom Allah has made permissible for them or their right hand possessions from the captives. One who seeks what Allah has made permissible for him is not to be blamed and there is no sin on him. Allah says:

(they are free from blame. But whoever seeks beyond that) meaning, other than a wife or slave girl,

(then those are the transgressors.) meaning , aggressors.

(Those who are faithfully true to their Amanat and to their covenants) When they are entrusted with something, they do not betray that trust, but they fulfill it, and when they make a promise or make a pledge, they are true to their word. This is not like the hypocrites about whom the Messenger of Allah said:

«آيَةُ الْمُنَافِقِ ثَلَاثٌ: إِذَا حَدَّثَ كَذَبَ، وَإِذَا وَعَدَ أَخْلَفَ، وَإِذَا اؤْتُمِنَ خَانَ»

(The signs of the hypocrite are three: when he speaks he lies, when he makes a promise he breaks it, and when he is entrusted with something he betrays that trust.)

(And those who strictly guard their Salawat.) means, they persistently offer their prayers at their appointed times, as Ibn Mas`ud said: "I asked the Messenger of Allah , `O Messenger of Allah, which deed is most beloved to Allah' He said,

«الصَّلَاةُ عَلَى وَقْتِهَا»

(Prayer at the appointed time.) I said, `Then what' He said,

«بِرُّ الْوَالِدَيْنِ»

(Kindness to one's parents.) I said, `Then what' He said,

«الْجِهَادُ فِي سَبِيلِ اللهِ»

(Jihad in the way of Allah.) It was recorded in the Two Sahihs. Qatadah said: "At the fixed times, with the proper bowing and prostration." Allah begins and ends this list of praiseworthy qualities with Salah, which is indicative of its virtue, as the Prophet said:

«اسْتَقِيمُوا وَلَنْ تُحْصُوا، وَاعْلَمُوا أَنَّ خَيْرَ أَعْمَالِكُمُ الصَّلَاةُ، وَلَا يُحَافِظُ عَلَى الْوُضُوءِ إِلَّا مُؤْمِن»

(Adhere to righteousness, you will never be able encompass it all. Know that the best of your deeds is Salah. None will preserve his Wuddu' except the believer.) Having described them with these praiseworthy characteristics and righteous deeds, Allah then says:

(These are indeed the heirs. Who shall inherit Firdaws. They shall dwell therein forever.) It was recorded in the Two Sahihs that the Messenger of Allah said:

«إِذَا سَأَلْتُمُ اللهَ الْجَنَّةَ فَاسْأَلُوهُ الْفِرْدَوْسَ، فَإِنَّهُ أَعْلَى الْجَنَّةِ وَأَوْسَطُ الْجَنَّةِ، وَمِنْهُ تَفَجَّرُ أَنْهَارُ الْجَنَّةِ، وَفَوْقَهُ عَرْشُ الرَّحْمَن»

(If you ask Allah for Paradise, then ask him for Al-Firdaws, for it is the highest part of Paradise, in the middle of Paradise, and from it spring the rivers of Paradise, and above it is the (Mighty) Throne of the Most Merciful.) Ibn Abi Hatim recorded that Abu Hurayrah said, "The Messenger of Allah said:

«مَا مِنْكُمْ مِنْ أَحَدٍ إِلَّا وَلَهُ مَنْزِلَانِ: مَنْزِلٌ فِي الْجَنَّةِ، وَمَنْزِلٌ فِي النَّارِ، فَإِنْ مَاتَ فَدَخَلَ النَّارَ وَرِثَ أَهْلُ الْجَنَّةِ مَنْزِلَهُ، فَذَلِكَ قَوْلُهُ:

Chapter 23: Al-Mu'minun (The Believers), Verses 001-118

$$\text{«(أُولَٰئِكَ هُمُ ٱلْوَٰرِثُونَ)»}$$

(There is not one among you who does not have two homes, a home in Paradise and a home in Hell. If he dies and enters Hell, the people of Paradise will inherit his home, and this is what Allah said: (These are indeed the heirs.) Ibn Jurayj narrated from Layth from Mujahid:

(These are indeed the heirs.) "The believers will inherit the homes of the disbelievers because they were created to worship Allah Alone with no partner or associate. So when these believers did what was enjoined on them of worship, and the disbelievers neglected to do that which they were commanded to do and for which they had been created, the believers gained the share that they would have been given if they had obeyed their Lord. Indeed, they will be given more than that as well." This is what was reported in Sahih Muslim from Abu Burdah, from his father, from the Prophet who said:

$$\text{«يَجِيءُ يَوْمَ الْقِيَامَةِ نَاسٌ مِنَ الْمُسْلِمِينَ بِذُنُوبٍ أَمْثَالِ الْجِبَالِ، فَيَغْفِرُهَا اللهُ لَهُمْ وَيَضَعُهَا عَلَى الْيَهُودِ وَالنَّصَارَى»}$$

(Some of the Muslims will come on the Day of Resurrection with sins like mountains, but Allah will forgive them and put (their burden of sin) on the Jews and Christians.) According to another version: the Messenger of Allah said:

$$\text{«إِذَا كَانَ يَوْمُ الْقِيَامَةِ دَفَعَ اللهُ لِكُلِّ مُسْلِمٍ يَهُودِيًّا أَوْ نَصْرَانِيًّا، فَيُقَالُ: هَذَا فِكَاكُكَ مِنَ النَّارِ»}$$

(When the Day of Resurrection comes, Allah will appoint for every Muslim a Jew or Christian, and it will be said, "This is your ransom from the Fire.") `Umar bin `Abd Al-`Aziz asked Abu Burdah to swear by Allah besides Whom there is no other God, three times, that his father told him that from the Prophet, and he swore that oath. I say: this Ayah is like Allah's saying:

(Such is the Paradise which We shall give as an inheritance to those of Our servants who have had Taqwa.) (19:63)

(This is the Paradise which you have been made to inherit because of your deeds which you used to do.) (43:72)

Surah: 23 Ayah: 12, Ayah: 13, Ayah: 14, Ayah: 15 & Ayah: 16

$$\text{وَلَقَدْ خَلَقْنَا ٱلْإِنسَٰنَ مِن سُلَٰلَةٍ مِّن طِينٍ ۝}$$

12. And indeed We created man (Adam) out of an extract of clay (water and earth).

$$ثُمَّ جَعَلْنَـٰهُ نُطْفَةً فِى قَرَارٍ مَّكِينٍ$$

13. Thereafter We made him (the offspring of Adam) as a Nutfah (mixed drops of the male and female sexual discharge and lodged it) in a safe lodging (womb of the woman).

$$ثُمَّ خَلَقْنَا ٱلنُّطْفَةَ عَلَقَةً فَخَلَقْنَا ٱلْعَلَقَةَ مُضْغَةً فَخَلَقْنَا ٱلْمُضْغَةَ عِظَـٰمًا فَكَسَوْنَا ٱلْعِظَـٰمَ لَحْمًا ثُمَّ أَنشَأْنَـٰهُ خَلْقًا ءَاخَرَ فَتَبَارَكَ ٱللَّهُ أَحْسَنُ ٱلْخَـٰلِقِينَ$$

14. Then We made the Nutfah into a clot (a piece of thick coagulated blood), then We made the clot into a little lump of flesh, then We made out of that little lump of flesh bones, then We clothed the bones with flesh, and then We brought it forth as another creation. So Blessed is Allâh, the Best of creators.

$$ثُمَّ إِنَّكُم بَعْدَ ذَٰلِكَ لَمَيِّتُونَ$$

15. After that, surely, you will die.

$$ثُمَّ إِنَّكُمْ يَوْمَ ٱلْقِيَـٰمَةِ تُبْعَثُونَ$$

16. Then (again), surely, you will be resurrected on the Day of Resurrection.

Transliteration

12. Walaqad khalaqna al-insana min sulalatin min teenin 13. Thumma jaAAalnahu nutfatan fee qararin makeenin 14. Thumma khalaqna alnnutfata AAalaqatan fakhalaqna alAAalaqata mudghatan fakhalaqna almudghata AAithaman fakasawna alAAithama lahman thumma ansha/nahu khalqan akhara fatabaraka Allahu ahsanu alkhaliqeena 15. Thumma innakum baAAda thalika lamayyitoona 16. Thumma innakum yawma alqiyamati tubAAathoona

Tafsir Ibn Kathir

The Sign of Allah in the progressive creation of Man from Clay then from Nutfah and thereafter

Allah tells us how He initially created man from an extract of Tin. This was Adam, peace be upon him, whom Allah created from sounding clay of altered black smooth mud. Ibn Jarir said, "Adam was called Tin because he was created from it." Qatadah said, "Adam was created from Tin." This is the more apparent meaning and is closer to the context, for Adam, upon him be peace, was created from a sticky Tin, which is a sounding clay of altered black smooth mud, and that is created from dust, as Allah says:

(And among His signs is this that He created you (Adam) from dust, and then -- behold you are human beings scattered!) (30:20) Imam Ahmad recorded from Abu Musa that the Prophet said:

«إِنَّ اللهَ خَلَقَ آدَمَ مِنْ قَبْضَةٍ قَبَضَهَا مِنْ جَمِيعِ الْأَرْضِ، فَجَاءَ بَنُو آدَمَ عَلَى قَدْرِ الْأَرْضِ، جَاءَ مِنْهُمُ الْأَحْمَرُ وَالْأَبْيَضُ وَالْأَسْوَدُ وَبَيْنَ ذَلِكَ، وَالْخَبِيثُ وَالطَّيِّبُ وَبَيْنَ ذَلِكَ»

(Allah created Adam from a handful which He picked up from throughout the earth, so the sons of Adam came forth accordingly, red and white and black and in between, evil and good and in between.) Abu Dawud and At-Tirmidhi recorded something similar. At-Tirmidhi said, "It is Sahih Hasan."

(Thereafter We made him a Nutfah.) Here the pronoun refers back to humankind, as in another Ayah:

(and He began the creation of man from clay. Then He made his offspring from semen of despised water.) (32:7,8) meaning, weak, as He says:

(Did We not create you from a despised water Then We placed it in a place of safety.) (77:20-21) meaning the womb, which is prepared and readily equipped for that,

(For a known period. So We did measure; and We are the Best to measure) (77:22-23) meaning, for a known period of time, until it is established and moves from one stage to the next. Allah says here,

(Then We made the Nutfah into a clot,) meaning, `then We made the Nutfah, which is the water gushing forth that comes from the loins of man, i.e., his back, and the ribs of woman, i.e., the bones of her chest, between the clavicle and the breast. Then it becomes a red clot, like an elongated clot.' `Ikrimah said, "This is blood."

(then We made the clot into a little lump of flesh,) which is like a piece of flesh with no shape or features.

(then We made out of that little lump of flesh bones,) meaning, `We gave it shape, with a head, two arms and two legs, with its bones, nerves and veins.'

(then We clothed the bones with flesh,) meaning, `We gave it something to cover it and strengthen it.'

(and then We brought it forth as another creation.) means, `then We breathed the soul into it, and it moved and became a new creature, one that could hear, see, understand and move.

(So Blessed is Allah, the Best of creators.)

(and then We brought it forth as another creation.) Al-`Awfi reported that Ibn `Abbas said, "We change it from one stage to another until it emerges as an infant, then it grows up through the stages of being a child, adolescent, youth, mature man, old man and senile man." Imam Ahmad recorded in his Musnad that `Abdullah -- Ibn Mas`ud -- said, "The Messenger of Allah , the Truthful One, told us:

«إِنَّ أَحَدَكُمْ لَيُجْمَعُ خَلْقُهُ فِي بَطْنِ أُمِّهِ أَرْبَعِينَ يَوْمًا نُطْفَةً، ثُمَّ يَكُونُ عَلَقَةً مِثْلَ ذَلِكَ، ثُمَّ يَكُونُ مُضْغَةً مِثْلَ ذَلِكَ، ثُمَّ يُرْسَلُ إِلَيْهِ الْمَلَكُ فَيَنْفُخُ فِيهِ الرُّوحَ وَيُؤْمَرُ بِأَرْبَعِ كَلِمَاتٍ: رِزْقِهِ، وَأَجَلِهِ، وَعَمَلِهِ، وَهَلْ هُوَ شَقِيٌّ أَوْ سَعِيدٌ، فَوَالَّذِي لَا إِلَهَ غَيْرُهُ إِنَّ أَحَدَكُمْ لَيَعْمَلُ بِعَمَلِ أَهْلِ الْجَنَّةِ حَتَّى مَا يَكُونُ بَيْنَهُ وَبَيْنَهَا إِلَّا ذِرَاعٌ، فَيَسْبِقُ عَلَيْهِ الْكِتَابُ فَيُخْتَمُ لَهُ بِعَمَلِ أَهْلِ النَّارِ فَيَدْخُلُهَا، وَإِنَّ الرَّجُلَ لَيَعْمَلُ بِعَمَلِ أَهْلِ النَّارِ حَتَّى مَا يَكُونُ بَيْنَهُ وَبَيْنَهَا إِلَّا ذِرَاعٌ، فَيَسْبِقُ عَلَيْهِ الْكِتَابُ فَيُخْتَمُ لَهُ بِعَمَلِ أَهْلِ الْجَنَّةِ فَيَدْخُلُهَا»

(The creation of anyone of you is gathered for forty days in his mother's stomach as a Nutfah, then he becomes a clot for a similar period of time, then he becomes a little lump of flesh for a similar length of time. Then the angel is sent to him and he breathes the soul into it, and four things are decreed: his provision, his life-span, his deeds, and whether he will be wretched or blessed. By the One besides Whom there is no other god, one of you may do the deeds of the people of Paradise until there is no more than a forearm's length between him and it, then the decree will overtake him and he will do the deeds of the people of Hell and thus enter Hell. And a man may do the deeds of the people of Hell until there is no more than a forearm's length between him and it, then the decree will overtake him and he will do finally the deeds of the people of Paradise and thus enter Paradise.) This was recorded by Al-Bukhari and Muslim.

(So Blessed is Allah, the Best of creators.) means, when Allah mentions His ability and subtlety in creating this Nutfah and taking it from stage to stage until it takes the shape of a perfectly formed human being, He says,

(So Blessed is Allah, the Best of creators.)

(After that, surely you will die.) means, after first being created from nothing, you will eventually die.

(Then (again), surely you will be resurrected on the Day of Resurrection.) means, you will be created anew.

Chapter 23: Al-Mu'minun (The Believers), Verses 001-118

(and then Allah will bring forth the creation of the Hereafter) (29:20) means, the Day of Return, when the souls will be restored to their bodies and all of creation will be brought to account. Everyone will be rewarded or punished according to his deeds -- if they are good then he will be rewarded, and if they are bad then he will be punished.

Surah: 23 Ayah: 17

وَلَقَدْ خَلَقْنَا فَوْقَكُمْ سَبْعَ طَرَآئِقَ وَمَا كُنَّا عَنِ ٱلْخَلْقِ غَـٰفِلِينَ

17. And indeed We have created above you seven heavens (one over the other), and We are never unaware of the creation.

Transliteration

17. Walaqad khalaqna fawqakum sabAAa tara-iqa wama kunna AAani alkhalqi ghafileena

Tafsir Ibn Kathir

His Sign in the creation of the Heavens

After mentioning the creation of man, Allah then mentions the creation of the seven heavens. Allah often mentions the creation of the heavens and earth alongside the creation of man, as He says elsewhere:

(The creation of the heavens and the earth is indeed greater than the creation of mankind) (40:57). A similar Ayah appears at the beginning of Surat As-Sajdah, which the Messenger of Allah used to recite on Friday mornings. At the beginning it mentions the creation of the heavens and earth, then it says how man was created from semen from clay, and it also discusses the resurrection and rewards and punishments, and other matters.

(seven Tara'iq.) Mujahid said, "This means the seven heavens." This is like the Ayat:

(The seven heavens and the earth and all that is therein, glorify Him) (17:44)

(See you not how Allah has created the seven heavens one above another) (71:15)

(It is Allah Who has created seven heavens and of the earth the like thereof. His command descends between them (heavens and earth), that you may know that Allah has power over all things, and that Allah surrounds all things in (His) knowledge) (65:12) Similarly, Allah says here:

(And indeed We have created above you seven Tara'iq, and We are never unaware of the creation.) meaning, Allah knows what goes into the earth and what comes out of it, what comes down from heaven and what goes up into it. He is with you wherever you are, and Allah sees what you do. No heaven is hidden from Him by another and no earth is hidden from Him by another. There is no mountain but He knows its features, and no sea but He knows what is in its depths. He knows the numbers of what is in the mountains, the hills, the sands, the seas, the landscapes and the trees.

(And not a leaf falls, but He knows it. There is not a grain in the darkness of the earth nor anything fresh or dry, but is written in a Clear Record.) (6:59)

Surah: 23 Ayah: 18, Ayah: 19, Ayah: 20, Ayah: 21 & Ayah: 22

وَأَنزَلْنَا مِنَ ٱلسَّمَآءِ مَآءً بِقَدَرٍ فَأَسْكَنَّـٰهُ فِى ٱلْأَرْضِ ۖ وَإِنَّا عَلَىٰ ذَهَابٍۭ بِهِۦ لَقَـٰدِرُونَ ۝

18. And We sent down from the sky water (rain) in (due) measure, and We gave it lodging in the earth, and verily, We are Able to take it away.

فَأَنشَأْنَا لَكُم بِهِۦ جَنَّـٰتٍ مِّن نَّخِيلٍ وَأَعْنَـٰبٍ لَّكُمْ فِيهَا فَوَٰكِهُ كَثِيرَةٌ وَمِنْهَا تَأْكُلُونَ ۝

19. Then We brought forth for you therewith gardens of date-palms and grapes, wherein is much fruit for you, and whereof you eat.

وَشَجَرَةً تَخْرُجُ مِن طُورِ سَيْنَآءَ تَنۢبُتُ بِٱلدُّهْنِ وَصِبْغٍ لِّلْـَٔاكِلِينَ ۝

20. And a tree (olive) that springs forth from Mount Sinai, that grows (produces) oil, and (it is a) relish for the eaters.

وَإِنَّ لَكُمْ فِى ٱلْأَنْعَـٰمِ لَعِبْرَةً ۖ نُّسْقِيكُم مِّمَّا فِى بُطُونِهَا وَلَكُمْ فِيهَا مَنَـٰفِعُ كَثِيرَةٌ وَمِنْهَا تَأْكُلُونَ ۝

21. And Verily in the cattle there is indeed a lesson for you. We give you to drink (milk) of that which is in their bellies. And there are, in them, numerous (other) benefits for you, and of them you eat.

وَعَلَيْهَا وَعَلَى ٱلْفُلْكِ تُحْمَلُونَ ۝

22. And on them, and on ships you are carried.

Transliteration

18. Waanzalna mina alssama-i maan biqadarin faaskannahu fee al-ardi wa-inna AAala thahabin bihi laqadiroona 19. Faansha/na lakum bihi jannatin min nakheelin waaAAnabin lakum feeha fawakihu katheeratun waminha ta/kuloona 20. Washajaratan takhruju min toori saynaa tanbutu bialdduhni wasibghin lilakileena 21. Wa-inna lakum fee al-anAAami laAAibratan nusqeekum mimma fee butooniha walakum feeha manafiAAu katheeratun waminha ta/kuloona 22. WaAAalayha waAAala alfulki tuhmaloona

Tafsir Ibn Kathir

Allah's Signs and Blessings in the Rain, Vegetation, Trees and Cattle

Allah mentions His innumerable blessings to His servants, whereby He sends down rain in due measure, meaning, according to what is needed, not so much that it damages the lands and buildings, and not so little to be insufficient for crops and fruits, but whatever is needed for irrigation, drinking and other benefits. If there is a land that needs a lot of water for its irrigation but its fertile soil would be carried away if rain fell on it, then Allah sends water to it from another land, as in the case of Egypt, which is said to be a barren land. Allah sends the water of the Nile to it, which brings red soil from Ethiopia when it rains there. The water brings the red soil which is used to irrigate the land of Egypt, and whatever of it is deposited is used for agriculture, because the land of Egypt is infertile, and most of it is sand. Glory be to the Subtle One, the All-Knowing, the Most Merciful, the Forgiving.

(and We gave it lodging in the earth,) means, `when the water comes down from the clouds, We cause it to settle in the earth, and We cause the earth to absorb it and the seeds etc. in the earth to be nourished by it.'

(and verily, We are able to take it away.) means, `if We wanted to cause it not to rain, We could do so; if We wanted to divert it towards the wilderness and wastelands, We could do so; if We wanted to make it salty so that you could not benefit from it for drinking or irrigation, We could do so; if We wanted to cause it not to be absorbed by the earth, but to remain on the surface, We could do so; if We wanted to make it go deep underground where you would not be able to reach it and you could not benefit from it, We could do so.' But by His grace and mercy, He causes sweet, fresh water to fall on you from the clouds, then it settles in the earth and forms springs and rivers, and you use it to irrigate your crops and fruits, and you drink it and give it to your livestock and cattle, and you bathe and purify yourselves with it. To Him is due the praise and thanks.

(Then We brought forth for you therewith gardens of date palms and grapes,) means, `from that which We send down from the sky, We bring forth for you gardens and orchards which look beautiful.'

(of date palms and grapes,) These were the kinds of gardens that were known to the people of the Hijaz, but there is no difference between a thing and its counterpart. The people of each region have fruits which are the blessing of Allah given to them, and for which they cannot properly thank Allah enough.

(wherein is much fruit for you,) means, of all fruits. As Allah says elsewhere:

(With it (the rain) He causes to grow for you the crops, the olives, the date palms, the grapes, and every kind of fruit) (16:11).

(and whereof you eat.) This implies that you look at its beauty, wait for it to ripen, then eat from it.

(And a tree that springs forth from Tur Sinai,) means the olive tree. Tur means a mountain. Some of the scholars said, "It is called Tur if there are trees on it, and if it is bare it is called Jabal, not Tur. And Allah knows best. Mount Sinai is the same as Tur Sinin, and it is the mountain on which Allah spoke to Musa bin `Imran, peace be upon him, and in the surrounding mountains there are olive trees.

(that grows oil,) Some scholars think it (linguistically) means that it brings forth oil. Others say it (linguistically) means "comes forth with oil." Allah said,

(and relish) meaning a condiment. according to Qatadah.

(for the eaters.) means, it contains a beneficial oil and condiment. `Abd bin Humayd recorded in his Musnad and Tafsir from `Umar that the Messenger of Allah said:

(Eat (olive) oil as a condiment and apply it as oil, for it comes from a blessed tree.) It was recorded by At-Tirmidhi and Ibn Majah. Allah's saying;

(And verily, in the cattle there is indeed a lesson for you. We give you to drink of that which is in their bellies. And there are, in them, numerous benefits for you, and of them you eat. And on them and on ships you are carried), Here Allah mentions the benefits He has given to His servants in cattle, for they drink their milk which comes out from between dung and blood, they eat their meat and clothe themselves with their wool and hair, they ride on their backs and carry heavy burdens on them to far away lands, as Allah says:

(And they carry your loads to a land that you could not reach except with great trouble to yourselves. Truly, your Lord is full of kindness, Most Merciful.) (16:7)

(Do they not see that We have created for them of what Our Hands have created, the cattle, so that they are their owners. And We have subdued them unto them so that some of them they have for riding and some they eat. And in them there are benefits for them, and drink. Will they not then be grateful) (36:71-73)

Surah: 23 Ayah: 23, Ayah: 24 & Ayah: 25

وَلَقَدْ أَرْسَلْنَا نُوحًا إِلَىٰ قَوْمِهِۦ فَقَالَ يَٰقَوْمِ ٱعْبُدُوا۟ ٱللَّهَ مَا لَكُم مِّنْ إِلَٰهٍ غَيْرُهُۥٓ أَفَلَا تَتَّقُونَ ۝

23. And indeed We sent Nûh (Noah) to his people, and he said: "O my people! Worship Allâh! You have no other Ilâh (God) but Him (Islâmic Monotheism). Will you not then be afraid (of Him i.e. of His Punishment because of worshipping others besides Him)?"

فَقَالَ ٱلْمَلَؤُا۟ ٱلَّذِينَ كَفَرُوا۟ مِن قَوْمِهِۦ مَا هَٰذَآ إِلَّا بَشَرٌ مِّثْلُكُمْ يُرِيدُ أَن يَتَفَضَّلَ عَلَيْكُمْ وَلَوْ شَآءَ ٱللَّهُ لَأَنزَلَ مَلَٰٓئِكَةً مَّا سَمِعْنَا بِهَٰذَا فِىٓ ءَابَآئِنَا ٱلْأَوَّلِينَ ۝

24. But the chiefs of his people who disbelieved said: "He is no more than a human being like you, he seeks to make himself superior to you. Had Allâh willed, He surely could have sent down angels. Never did we hear such a thing among our fathers of old.

إِنْ هُوَ إِلَّا رَجُلٌ بِهِ جِنَّةٌ فَتَرَبَّصُوا بِهِ حَتَّىٰ حِينٍ ﴿٢٥﴾

25. "He is only a man in whom is madness, so wait for him a while."

Transliteration

23. Walaqad arsalna noohan ila qawmihi faqala ya qawmi oAAbudoo Allaha ma lakum min ilahin ghayruhu afala tattaqoona   24. Faqala almalao allatheena kafaroo min qawmihi ma hatha illa basharun mithlukum yureedu an yatafaddala AAalaykum walaw shaa Allahu laanzala mala-ikatan ma samiAAna bihatha fee aba-ina alawwaleena   25. In huwa illa rajulun bihi jinnatun fatarabbasoo bihi hatta heenin

Tafsir Ibn Kathir

The Story of Nuh, Peace be upon Him; and his people

Allah tells us about Nuh, peace be upon him, whom He sent him to his people to warn them of the severe punishment of Allah and His severe vengeance on those who associated partners with Him, defied His commands and disbelieved His Messengers:

(and he said: "O my people! Worship Allah! You have no other God but Him. Will you not then have Taqwa") Meaning, "Do you not fear Allah when you associate others in worship with Him" The chiefs or leaders of his people said:

(He is no more than a human being like you, he seeks to make himself superior to you.) meaning, `he is putting himself above you and trying to make himself great by claiming to be a Prophet, but he is a human being like you, so how can he receive revelation when you do not'

(Had Allah willed, He surely could have sent down angels.) meaning, `if Allah had wanted to send a Prophet, He would have sent an angel from Him, not a human being. We have never heard of such a thing -- i.e., sending a man to our forefathers' -- their predecessors in times past.

(He is only a man in whom is madness,) means, `he is crazy in his claim that Allah has sent him and chosen him from among you to receive revelation.'

(so wait for him a while.) means, `wait until he dies, put up with him until you are rid of him.'

Surah: 23 Ayah: 26, Ayah: 27, Ayah: 28, Ayah: 29 & Ayah: 30

قَالَ رَبِّ انصُرْنِي بِمَا كَذَّبُونِ ﴿٢٦﴾

26. (Nûh (Noah)) said: "O my Lord! Help me because they deny me."

$$\text{فَأَوْحَيْنَا إِلَيْهِ أَنِ اصْنَعِ الْفُلْكَ بِأَعْيُنِنَا وَوَحْيِنَا فَإِذَا جَاءَ أَمْرُنَا وَفَارَ التَّنُّورُ فَاسْلُكْ فِيهَا مِن كُلٍّ زَوْجَيْنِ اثْنَيْنِ وَأَهْلَكَ إِلَّا مَن سَبَقَ عَلَيْهِ الْقَوْلُ مِنْهُمْ وَلَا تُخَاطِبْنِي فِي الَّذِينَ ظَلَمُوا إِنَّهُم مُّغْرَقُونَ ﴿٢٧﴾}$$

27. So We revealed to him (saying): "Construct the ship under Our Eyes and under Our Revelation (guidance). Then, when Our Command comes, and water gushes forth from the oven, take on board of each kind two (male and female), and your family, except those thereof against whom the Word has already gone forth. And address Me not in favor of those who have done wrong. Verily, they are to be drowned.

$$\text{فَإِذَا اسْتَوَيْتَ أَنتَ وَمَن مَّعَكَ عَلَى الْفُلْكِ فَقُلِ الْحَمْدُ لِلَّهِ الَّذِي نَجَّانَا مِنَ الْقَوْمِ الظَّالِمِينَ ﴿٢٨﴾}$$

28. And when you have embarked on the ship, you and whoever is with you, then say: "All the praises and thanks are to Allâh, Who has saved us from the people who are Zâlimûn (i.e. oppressors, wrong-doers, polytheists, those who join others in worship with Allâh).

$$\text{وَقُل رَّبِّ أَنزِلْنِي مُنزَلًا مُّبَارَكًا وَأَنتَ خَيْرُ الْمُنزِلِينَ ﴿٢٩﴾}$$

29. And say: "My Lord! Cause me to land at a blessed landing-place, for You are the Best of those who bring to land."

$$\text{إِنَّ فِي ذَلِكَ لَآيَاتٍ وَإِن كُنَّا لَمُبْتَلِينَ ﴿٣٠﴾}$$

30. Verily, in this (what We did as regards drowning of the people of Nûh (Noah)) there are indeed Ayât (proofs, evidences, lessons, signs, etc. for men to understand), for sure We are ever putting (men) to the test.

Transliteration

26. Qala rabbi onsurnee bima kaththabooni 27. Faawhayna ilayhi ani isnaAAi alfulka bi-aAAyunina wawahyina fa-itha jaa amruna wafara alttannooru faosluk feeha min kullin zawjayni ithnayni waahlaka illa man sabaqa AAalayhi alqawlu minhum wala tukhatibnee fee allatheena thalamoo innahum mughraqoona 28. Fa-itha istawayta anta waman maAAaka AAala alfulki faquli alhamdu lillahi allathee najjana mina alqawmi alththalimeena 29. Waqul rabbi anzilnee munzalan mubarakan waanta khayru almunzileena 30. Inna fee thalika laayatin wa-in kunna lamubtaleena

Tafsir Ibn Kathir

Allah tells us that Nuh, peace be upon him, invoked his Lord to help him against his people,

as Allah mentions in another Ayah:

(Then he invoked his Lord (saying): "I have been overcome, so help (me)!") (54:10). Here he says:

(O my Lord! Help me because they deny me.) At that point, Allah commanded him to build a boat and to make it strong and firm, and to carry therein of every kind two, i.e., a male and a female of every species of animals, plants and fruits etc. He was also to carry his family,

(except those thereof against whom the Word has already gone forth.) meaning, those whom Allah had already decreed were to be destroyed. These were the members of his family who did not believe in him, such as his son and his wife. And Allah knows best.

(And address Me not in favor of those who have done wrong. Verily, they are to be drowned.) means, `when you witness the heavy rain falling, do not let yourself be overcome with compassion and pity for your people, or hope for more time for them so that they may believe, for I have decreed that they will be drowned and will die in their state of disbelief and wrongdoing.' The story has already been told in detail in Surah Hud, and there is no need to repeat it here.

(And when you have embarked on the ship, you and whoever is with you, then say: `All the praise be to Allah, Who has saved us from the people who are wrongdoers.') This is like the Ayah:

(and has appointed for you ships and cattle on which you ride: In order that you may mount on their backs, and then may remember the favor of your Lord when you mount thereon, and say: "Glory to Him Who has subjected this to us, and we could never have it (by our efforts). And verily, to Our Lord we indeed are to return!") (43:12-14) So, certainly, Nuh adhered to what he was commanded, as Allah says elsewhere:

(And he said: "Embark therein: in the Name of Allah will be its (moving) course and its (resting) anchorage...")(11:41) So Nuh mentioned Allah at the beginning of his journey and at the end, and Allah said:

(And say: `My Lord! Cause me to land at a blessed landing place, for You are the Best of those who bring to land.")

(Verily in this, there are indeed Ayat,) means in this event, which is the saving of the believers and the destruction of the disbelievers there are signs, i.e., clear evidence and proof that the Prophets speak the truth in the Message they bring from Allah, may He be exalted, and that Allah does what He wills, and He is able to do all things and knows all things.

(for sure We are ever putting (men) to the test.) means, `We try Our servants by means of sending the Messengers.'

Surah: 23 Ayah: 31, Ayah: 32, Ayah: 33, Ayah: 34, Ayah: 35, Ayah: 36, Ayah: 37, Ayah: 38, Ayah: 39, Ayah: 40 & Ayah: 41

ثُمَّ أَنشَأْنَا مِن بَعْدِهِمْ قَرْناً ءَاخَرِينَ ۝

31. Then, after them, We created another generation.

فَأَرْسَلْنَا فِيهِمْ رَسُولاً مِّنْهُمْ أَنِ اعْبُدُواْ اللَّهَ مَا لَكُم مِّنْ إِلَـهٍ غَيْرُهُ أَفَلاَ تَتَّقُونَ ۝

32. And We sent to them a Messenger from among themselves (saying): "Worship Allâh! You have no other Ilâh (God) but Him. Will you not then be afraid (of Him i.e. of His Punishment because of worshipping others besides Him)?"

وَقَالَ الْمَلأُ مِن قَوْمِهِ الَّذِينَ كَفَرُواْ وَكَذَّبُواْ بِلِقَاء الآخِرَةِ وَأَتْرَفْنَاهُمْ فِي الْحَيَاةِ الدُّنْيَا مَا هَـذَا إِلاَّ بَشَرٌ مِّثْلُكُمْ يَأْكُلُ مِمَّا تَأْكُلُونَ مِنْهُ وَيَشْرَبُ مِمَّا تَشْرَبُونَ ۝

33. And the chiefs of his people, who disbelieved and denied the Meeting in the Hereafter, and whom We had given the luxuries and comforts of this life, said: "He is no more than a human being like you, he eats of that which you eat, and drinks of what you drink.

وَلَئِنْ أَطَعْتُم بَشَراً مِثْلَكُمْ إِنَّكُمْ إِذاً لَّخَاسِرُونَ ۝

34. "If you were to obey a human being like yourselves, then verily you indeed would be losers.

أَيَعِدُكُمْ أَنَّكُمْ إِذَا مِتَّمْ وَكُنتُمْ تُرَاباً وَعِظَاماً أَنَّكُم مُّخْرَجُونَ ۝

35. "Does he promise you that when you have died and have become dust and bones, you shall come out alive (resurrected)?

۞ هَيْهَاتَ هَيْهَاتَ لِمَا تُوعَدُونَ ۝

36. "Far, very far is that which you are promised!

إِنْ هِيَ إِلاَّ حَيَاتُنَا الدُّنْيَا نَمُوتُ وَنَحْيَا وَمَا نَحْنُ بِمَبْعُوثِينَ ۝

37. "There is nothing but our life of this world! We die and we live! And we are not going to be resurrected!

إِنْ هُوَ إِلاَّ رَجُلٌ افْتَرَى عَلَى اللَّهِ كَذِباً وَمَا نَحْنُ لَهُ بِمُؤْمِنِينَ ۝

38. "He is only a man who has invented a lie against Allâh, and we are not going to believe in him."

Chapter 23: Al-Mu'minun (The Believers), Verses 001-118

قَالَ رَبِّ ٱنصُرْنِى بِمَا كَذَّبُونِ ۝

39. He said: "O my Lord! Help me because they deny me."

قَالَ عَمَّا قَلِيلٍ لَّيُصْبِحُنَّ نَـٰدِمِينَ ۝

40. (Allâh) said: "In a little while, they are sure to be regretful."

فَأَخَذَتْهُمُ ٱلصَّيْحَةُ بِٱلْحَقِّ فَجَعَلْنَـٰهُمْ غُثَآءً فَبُعْدًا لِّلْقَوْمِ ٱلظَّـٰلِمِينَ ۝

41. So As-Saîhah (torment - awful cry) overtook them in truth (with justice), and We made them as rubbish of dead plants. So away with the people who are Zâlimûn (polytheists, wrong-doers, disbelievers in the Oneness of Allâh, disobedient to His Messengers).

Transliteration

31. Thumma ansha/na min baAAdihim qarnan akhareena 32. Faarsalna feehim rasoolan minhum ani oAAbudoo Allaha ma lakum min ilahin ghayruhu afala tattaqoona 33. Waqala almalao min qawmihi allatheena kafaroo wakaththaboo biliqa-i al-akhirati waatrafnahum fee alhayati alddunya ma hatha illa basharun mithlukum ya/kulu mimma ta/kuloona minhu wayashrabu mimma tashraboona 34. Wala-in ataAAtum basharan mithlakum innakum ithan lakhasiroona 35. AyaAAidukum annakum itha mittum wakuntum turaban waAAithaman annakum mukhrajoona 36. Hayhata hayhata lima tooAAadoona 37. In hiya illa hayatuna alddunya namootu wanahya wama nahnu bimabAAootheena 38. In huwa illa rajulun iftara AAala Allahi kathiban wama nahnu lahu bimu/mineena 39. Qala rabbi onsurnee bima kaththabooni 40. Qala AAamma qaleelin layusbihunna nadimeena 41. Faakhathat-humu alssayhatu bialhaqqi fajaAAalnahum ghuthaan fabuAAdan lilqawmi alththalimeena

Tafsir Ibn Kathir

The Story of `Ad or Thamud

Allah tells us that after the people of Nuh, He created another nation. It was said that this was `Ad, because they were the successors of the people of Nuh. Or it was said that they were Thamud, because Allah says:

(So, the Sayhah overtook them in truth.) Allah sent to them a Messenger from among themselves, and he called them to worship Allah Alone with no partner or associate, but they belied him, opposed him and refused to follow him because he was a human being like them, and they refused to follow a human Messenger. They did not believe in the meeting with Allah on the Day of Resurrection and they denied the idea of physical resurrection. They said:

(Does he promise you that when you have died and have become dust and bones, you shall come out alive (resurrected) Far, very far is that which you are promised!) meaning, very unlikely.

(He is only a man who has invented a lie against Allah,) meaning, `in the Message he has brought to you, and his warnings and promise of resurrection.'

(and we are not going to believe in him. He said: "O my Lord! Help me because they deny me.") meaning, the Messenger prayed against his people and asked his Lord to help him against them. His Lord answered his prayer:

((Allah) said: "In a little while, they are sure to be regretful.") meaning, `for their opposition towards you and their stubborn rejection of the Message you brought to them.'

(So, The Sayhah overtook them in truth,) meaning, they deserved that from Allah because of their disbelief and wrongdoing. The apparent meaning is that the Sayhah was combined with the furious cold wind,

(Destroying everything by the command of its Lord! So they became such that nothing could be seen except their dwellings!) (46:25)

(and We made them as rubbish of dead plants.) means, they are dead and destroyed, like the scum and rubbish left by a flood, i.e., something insignificant and useless that is of no benefit to anyone.

(So, away with the people who are wrongdoers.) As Allah's statement:

(We wronged them not, but they were the wrongdoers.) (43:76) means, who are wrongdoers because of their disbelief and stubborn opposition to the Messenger of Allah, so let those who hear this beware of disbelieving in their Messengers.

Surah: 23 Ayah: 42, Ayah: 43 & Ayah: 44

ثُمَّ أَنشَأْنَا مِنْ بَعْدِهِمْ قُرُونًا ءَاخَرِينَ ﴿٤٢﴾

42. Then, after them, We created other generations.

مَا تَسْبِقُ مِنْ أُمَّةٍ أَجَلَهَا وَمَا يَسْتَـْٔخِرُونَ ﴿٤٣﴾

43. No nation can advance their term, nor can they delay it.

ثُمَّ أَرْسَلْنَا رُسُلَنَا تَتْرَا كُلَّ مَا جَاءَ أُمَّةً رَّسُولُهَا كَذَّبُوهُ فَأَتْبَعْنَا بَعْضَهُم بَعْضًا وَجَعَلْنَـٰهُمْ أَحَادِيثَ فَبُعْدًا لِّقَوْمٍ لَّا يُؤْمِنُونَ ﴿٤٤﴾

44. Then We sent Our Messengers in succession. Every time there came to a nation their Messenger, they denied him, so We made them follow one another (to destruction), and We made them as Ahadîth (the true stories for mankind to learn a lesson from them). So away with a people who believe not!

Chapter 23: Al-Mu'minun (The Believers), Verses 001-118

Transliteration

42. Thumma ansha/na min baAAdihim quroonan akhareena 43. Ma tasbiqu min ommatin ajalaha wama yasta/khiroona 44. Thumma arsalna rusulana tatra kulla ma jaa ommatan rasooluha kaththaboohu faatbaAAna baAAdahum baAAdan wajaAAalnahum ahadeetha fabuAAdan liqawmin la yu/minoona

Tafsir Ibn Kathir

Mention of Other Nations Allah says:

(Then, after them, We created other generations.) meaning, nations and peoples.

(No nation can advance their term, nor can they delay it.) means, they are taken at the appropriate time, as decreed by Allah in His Book that is preserved with Him, before they were created, nation after nation, century after century, generation after generation, successors after predecessors.

(Then We sent Our Messengers in succession.) Ibn `Abbas said, "(This means) following one another in succession." This is like the Ayah:

(And verily, We have sent among every Ummah a Messenger (proclaiming): "Worship Allah, and avoid Taghut (all false deities)." Then of them were some whom Allah guided and of them were some upon whom the straying was justified) (16:36).

(Every time there came to a nation their Messenger, they denied him;) meaning the greater majority of them. This is like the Ayah:

(Alas for mankind! There never came a Messenger to them but they used to mock at him.) (36:30)

(so We made them follow one another,) means, `We destroyed them,' as Allah says:

(And how many generations have We destroyed after Nuh!) (17:17)

(and We made them as Ahadith) meaning, stories and lessons for mankind, as Allah says elsewhere:

(so, We made them as tales (in the land), and We dispersed them all totally) (34:19).

Surah: 23 Ayah: 45, Ayah: 46, Ayah: 47, Ayah: 48 & Ayah: 49

ثُمَّ أَرْسَلْنَا مُوسَىٰ وَأَخَاهُ هَـٰرُونَ بِـَٔايَـٰتِنَا وَسُلْطَـٰنٍ مُّبِينٍ ﴿٤٥﴾

45. Then We sent Mûsâ (Moses) and his brother Hârûnýý (Aaron), with Our Ayât (proofs, evidences, verses, lessons, signs, revelations, etc.) and manifest authority,

إِلَىٰ فِرْعَوْنَ وَمَلَإِيْهِ فَٱسْتَكْبَرُوا۟ وَكَانُوا۟ قَوْمًا عَالِينَ ﴿٤٦﴾

46. To Fir'aun (Pharaoh) and his chiefs, but they behaved insolently and they were people self-exalting (by disobeying their Lord, and exalting themselves over and above the Messenger of Allâh).

فَقَالُوٓا۟ أَنُؤْمِنُ لِبَشَرَيْنِ مِثْلِنَا وَقَوْمُهُمَا لَنَا عَٰبِدُونَ ﴿٤٧﴾

47. They said: "Shall we believe in two men like ourselves, and their people are obedient to us with humility (and we use them to serve us as we like)."

فَكَذَّبُوهُمَا فَكَانُوا۟ مِنَ ٱلْمُهْلَكِينَ ﴿٤٨﴾

48. So they denied them both (Mûsâ (Moses) and Hârûn (Aaron)) and became of those who were destroyed.

وَلَقَدْ ءَاتَيْنَا مُوسَى ٱلْكِتَٰبَ لَعَلَّهُمْ يَهْتَدُونَ ﴿٤٩﴾

49. And indeed We gave Mûsâ (Moses) the Scripture, that they may be guided.

Transliteration

45. Thumma arsalna moosa waakhahu haroona bi-ayatina wasultanin mubeenin 46. Ila firAAawna wamala-ihi faistakbaroo wakanoo qawman AAaleena 47. Faqaloo anu/minu libasharayni mithlina waqawmuhuma lana AAabidoona 48. Fakaththaboohuma fakanoo mina almuhlakeena 49. Walaqad atayna moosa alkitaba laAAallahum yahtadoona

Tafsir Ibn Kathir

The Story of Musa, Peace be upon Him; and Fir`awn

Allah tells us that He sent Musa, peace be upon him, and his brother Harun to Fir`awn and his chiefs with decisive evidence and definitive proof, but Fir`awn and his people were too arrogant to follow them and obey their commands because they were human beings, just as previous nations had denied the Message of the human Messengers. They were of a similar mentality, so Allah destroyed Fir`awn and his chiefs, drowning them all in one day. He revealed the Book to Musa, i.e., the Tawrah, in which were rulings, commands and prohibitions, after He had destroyed Fir`awn and the Egyptians and seized them with a punishment of the All-Mighty, All-Capable to carry out what He wills. After Allah revealed the Tawrah, Allah did not destroy any nation with an overwhelming calamity; instead, He commanded the believers to fight the disbelievers, as He says:

(And indeed We gave Musa -- after We had destroyed the generations of old -- the Scripture as an enlightenment for mankind, and a guidance and a mercy, that they might remember.) (28:43)

Surah: 23 Ayah: 50

وَجَعَلْنَا ٱبْنَ مَرْيَمَ وَأُمَّهُۥٓ ءَايَةً وَءَاوَيْنَٰهُمَآ إِلَىٰ رَبْوَةٍ ذَاتِ قَرَارٍ وَمَعِينٍ ﴿٥٠﴾

50. And We made the son of Maryam (Mary) and his mother as a sign, And We gave them refuge on high ground, a place of rest, security and flowing streams.

Transliteration

50. WajaAAalna ibna maryama waommahu ayatan waawaynahuma ila rabwatin thati qararin wamaAAeenin

Tafsir Ibn Kathir

`Isa and Maryam

Allah tells us about His servant and Messenger `Isa bin Maryam, peace be upon them both, and that He made them as a sign for mankind, i.e., definitive proof of His ability to do what He wills. For He created Adam without a father or a mother, He created Hawwa' from a male without a female, and He created `Isa from a female without a male, but He created the rest of mankind from both male and female.

(and We gave them refuge on high ground, a place of rest, security and flowing streams.) Ad-Dahhak reported that Ibn `Abbas said: "Ar-Rabwah is a raised portion of land, which is the best place for vegetation to grow." This was also the view of Mujahid, `Ikrimah, Sa`id bin Jubayr and Qatadah. Ibn `Abbas said,

(Dhat Qarar)"A fertile place.

(and Ma`in) means water running on the surface." This was also the view of Mujahid, `Ikrimah, Sa`id bin Jubayr and Qatadah. Mujahid said: "A level hill." Sa`id bin Jubayr said that

(Dhat Qarar and Ma`in) means that water was flowing gently through it. Mujahid and Qatadah said:

(and Ma`in ) "Running water." Ibn Abi Hatim recorded from Sa`id bin Al-Musayyib:

(and We gave them refuge on a Rabwah, Dhat Qarar and Ma`in.) "It is Damascus." He said; "Something similar was also narrated from `Abdullah bin Salam, Al-Hasan, Zayd bin Aslam and Khalid bin Ma`dan." Ibn Abi Hatim recorded from `Ikrimah from Ibn `Abbas that this Ayah referred to the rivers of Damascus. Layth bin Abi Sulaym narrated from Mujahid that the words;

(and We gave them refuge on a Rabwah,) referred to `Isa bin Maryam and his mother when they sought refuge in Damascus and the flatlands around it. `Abdur-Razzaq recorded that Abu Hurayrah said:

(on a Rabwah, Dhat Qarar and Ma`in.), "It is Ramlah in Palestine." The most correct opinion on this matter is that which was reported by Al-`Awfi from Ibn `Abbas, who said;

(and We gave them refuge on a Rabwah, Dhat Qarar and Ma`in.) "Ma`in refers to running water, and is the river of which Allah mentioned:

(your Lord has provided a water stream under you.)"(19:24) Ad-Dahhak and Qatadah said;

(on a high ground, a place of rest, security and flowing streams.) refers to Jerusalem. This -- and Allah knows best -- is the most apparent meaning, because it is mentioned in the other Ayah, and parts of the Qur'an explain other parts, so it is more appropriate to interpret it by another Ayah, then the Sahih Hadiths, then other reports.

Surah: 23 Ayah: 51, Ayah: 52, Ayah: 53, Ayah: 54, Ayah: 55 & Ayah: 56

يَٰٓأَيُّهَا ٱلرُّسُلُ كُلُوا۟ مِنَ ٱلطَّيِّبَٰتِ وَٱعْمَلُوا۟ صَٰلِحًا ۖ إِنِّى بِمَا تَعْمَلُونَ عَلِيمٌ ۝

51. O (you) Messengers! Eat of the Taiyibât (all kinds of Halâl (lawful) foods (meat of slaughtered eatable animals, milk products, fats, vegetables, fruits, etc.), and do righteous deeds. Verily! I am Well-Acquainted with what you do.

وَإِنَّ هَٰذِهِۦٓ أُمَّتُكُمْ أُمَّةً وَٰحِدَةً وَأَنَا۠ رَبُّكُمْ فَٱتَّقُونِ ۝

52. And verily! This, your religion (of Islâmic Monotheism), is one religion, and I am your Lord, so keep your duty to Me.

فَتَقَطَّعُوٓا۟ أَمْرَهُم بَيْنَهُمْ زُبُرًا ۖ كُلُّ حِزْبٍۭ بِمَا لَدَيْهِمْ فَرِحُونَ ۝

53. But they (men) have broken their religion among them into sects, each group rejoicing in what with it (as its beliefs).

فَذَرْهُمْ فِى غَمْرَتِهِمْ حَتَّىٰ حِينٍ ۝

54. So leave them in their error for a time.

أَيَحْسَبُونَ أَنَّمَا نُمِدُّهُم بِهِۦ مِن مَّالٍ وَبَنِينَ ۝

55. Do they think that in wealth and children with which We enlarge them

نُسَارِعُ لَهُمْ فِى ٱلْخَيْرَٰتِ ۚ بَل لَّا يَشْعُرُونَ ۝

56. We hasten unto them with good things. Nay, (it is a Fitnah (trial) in this worldly life so that they will have no share of good things in the Hereafter) but they perceive not. (Tafsir Al-Qurtubî)

Transliteration

51. Ya ayyuha alrrusulu kuloo mina alttayyibati waiAAmaloo salihan innee bima taAAmaloona Aaaleemun 52. Wa-inna hathihi ommatukum ommatan wahidatan waana rabbukum faittaqooni 53. FataqattaAAoo amrahum baynahum zuburan kullu hizbin bima ladayhim farihoona 54. Fatharhum fee ghamratihim hatta heenin 55.

Ayahsaboona annama numidduhum bihi min malin wabaneena 56. NusariAAu lahum fee alkhayrati bal la yashAAuroona

Tafsir Ibn Kathir

The Command to eat Lawful Food and to do Righteous Deeds

Allah commands His servants and Messengers, peace be upon them all, to eat lawful food and do righteous deeds, which indicates that eating what is lawful helps one to do righteous deeds. The Prophets, peace be upon them, did this in the most perfect manner, and did all kinds of good deeds in words, actions, guidance and advice. May Allah reward them with good on behalf of the people.

(Eat of the Tayyibat) Sa`id bin Jubayr and Ad-Dahhak said, "This means lawful. In the Sahih it says:

《وَمَا مِنْ نَبِيٍّ إِلَّا رَعَى الْغَنَمَ》

(There is no Prophet who was not a shepherd.) They asked, "And you, O Messenger of Allah" He said,

《نَعَمْ، كُنْتُ أَرْعَاهَا عَلَى قَرَارِيطَ لِأَهْلِ مَكَّةَ》

(Yes, I used to tend the sheep of the people of Makkah for a few Qirats.) In the Sahih, it says:

《إِنَّ دَاوُدَ عَلَيْهِ السَّلَامُ كَانَ يَأْكُلُ مِنْ كَسْبِ يَدِهِ》

(Dawud, upon him be peace, used to eat from the earnings of his own hand.) It was recorded in Sahih Muslim, Jami` At-Tirmidhi and Musnad Al-Imam Ahmad -- from whom this version comes -- that Abu Hurayrah, may Allah be pleased with him, said, "The Messenger of Allah said:

《يَا أَيُّهَا النَّاسُ إِنَّ اللهَ طَيِّبٌ لَا يَقْبَلُ إِلَّا طَيِّبًا، وَإِنَّ اللهَ أَمَرَ الْمُؤْمِنِينَ بِمَا أَمَرَ بِهِ الْمُرْسَلِينَ》

(O people, Allah is Tayyib and only accepts that which s Tayyib, and Allah commands the believers as He had commanded the Messengers) by saying:

(O Messengers! Eat of the Tayyibat and do rightecus deeds. Verily, I am Well-Acquainted with what you do.) (23:51) and

(O you who believe! Eat of the Tayyibat that We have provided you with)(2:172).) Then he mentioned how a man may travel on a long journey, dusty and unkempt,

«وَمَطْعَمُهُ حَرَامٌ، وَمَشْرَبُهُ حَرَامٌ، وَمَلْبَسُهُ حَرَامٌ، وَغُذِّيَ بِالْحَرَامِ يَمُدُّ يَدَيْهِ إِلَى السَّمَاءِ: يَا رَبِّ يَا رَبِّ فَأَنَّى يُسْتَجَابُ لِذَلِك»

(and his food, drink and clothing are unlawful, and he has nourished himself with what is unlawful, and he extends his hands towards the sky, saying, `O Lord, O Lord!' -- how can his prayer be answered.) At-Tirmidhi said that it is "Hasan Gharib."

The Religion of all the Prophets is Tawhid; and the Warning against splitting into different Groups

(And verily, this your religion is one religion,) means, `your religion, O Prophets, is one religion and one group, which is the call to worship Allah Alone with no partner or associate.' Allah said:

(and I am your Lord, so have Taqwa.) We have already discussed this in Surat Al-Anbiya'. The phrase

(one nation) is descriptive.

(But they have broken their religion among them into sects,) the nations to whom Prophets were sent.

(each group rejoicing in what is with it.) means, they rejoice in their misguidance because they think that they are rightly-guided. Allah says, threatening and warning:

(So, leave them in their error) meaning their misguidance,

(for a time.) means, until the appointed time of their destruction comes. This is like the Ayah:

(So give a respite to the disbelievers; deal gently with them for a while.) (86:17) And Allah says:

(Leave them to eat and enjoy, and let them be preoccupied with (false) hope. They will come to know!) (15:3)

(Do they think that in wealth and children with which We prolong them, We hasten unto them with good things. Nay, but they perceive not.) means, `do these deceived people think that what We give them of wealth and children is because they are honored and precious in Our sight No, the matter is not as they claim when they say,

(We are more in wealth and in children, and we are not going to be punished.) (34:35) But this thinking is wrong, and their hopes will be dashed. We only give those things to them in order to make them go further (in sin) and to give them more time.' Allah says:

(but they perceive not.) as He says elsewhere:

(So, let not their wealth nor their children amaze you; in reality Allah's plan is to punish them with these things in the life of this world...) (9:55)

(We postpone the punishment only so that they may increase in sinfulness) (3:178).

(Then leave Me Alone with such as belie this Qur'an. We shall punish them gradually from directions they perceive not. And I will grant them a respite.) (68:44-45)

(Leave Me Alone (to deal) with whom I created lonely.) until His saying:

(opposing) (74: 11-16)

(And it is not your wealth, nor your children that bring you nearer to Us, but only he who believes, and does righteous deeds...) (34:37) And there are many other Ayat which say similar things. Imam Ahmad recorded that `Abdullah bin Mas`ud said, "The Messenger of Allah said:

»إِنَّ اللهَ قَسَمَ بَيْنَكُمْ أَخْلَاقَكُمْ كَمَا قَسَمَ بَيْنَكُمْ أَرْزَاقَكُمْ، وَإِنَّ اللهَ يُعْطِي الدُّنْيَا مَنْ يُحِبُّ وَمَنْ لَا يُحِبُّ، وَلَا يُعْطِي الدِّينَ إِلَّا لِمَنْ أَحَبَّ، فَمَنْ أَعْطَاهُ اللهُ الدِّينَ فَقَدْ أَحَبَّهُ، وَالَّذِي نَفْسِي بِيَدِهِ لَا يُسْلِمُ عَبْدٌ حَتَّى يَسْلَمَ قَلْبُهُ وَلِسَانُهُ، وَلَا يُؤْمِنُ حَتَّى يَأْمَنَ جَارُهُ بَوَائِقَهُ«

(Allah has distributed your behavior to you just as He has distritbuted your provision. Allah gives the things of this world to those whom He loves and those whom He does not love, but He only gives religious commitment to those whom He loves. Whoever is given religious commitment by Allah is loved by Him. By the One in Whose Hand is my soul, no servant truly submits until his heart and his tongue submit, and he does not truly believe until his neighbor is safe from his harm.) They said, `What is his harm, O Messenger of Allah' He said,

»غَشْمُهُ وَظُلْمُهُ، وَلَا يَكْسِبُ عَبْدٌ مَالًا مِنْ حَرَامٍ فَيُنْفِقَ مِنْهُ فَيُبَارَكَ لَهُ فِيهِ، وَلَا يَتَصَدَّقَ بِهِ فَيُقْبَلَ مِنْهُ، وَلَا يَتْرُكَهُ خَلْفَ ظَهْرِهِ إِلَّا كَانَ زَادَهُ إِلَى النَّارِ، إِنَّ اللهَ لَا يَمْحُو السَّيِّءَ بِالسَّيِّءِ وَلَكِنْ يَمْحُو السَّيِّءَ بِالْحَسَنِ، إِنَّ الْخَبِيثَ لَا يَمْحُو

«الْخَبِيثُ»

(His wrongdoing and misbehavior. No person who earns unlawful wealth and spends it will be blessed in that; if he gives it in charity, it will not be accepted from him and if he leaves it behind (when he dies), it will be his provision in the Fire. Allah does not wash away an evil deed with another, but he washes away evil deeds with good deeds, for impurity cannot wash away with another impurity.))

Surah: 23 Ayah: 57, Ayah: 58, Ayah: 59, Ayah: 60 & Ayah: 61

إِنَّ ٱلَّذِينَ هُم مِّنْ خَشْيَةِ رَبِّهِم مُّشْفِقُونَ ۝

57. Verily! Those who live in awe for fear of their Lord;

وَٱلَّذِينَ هُم بِـَٔايَـٰتِ رَبِّهِمْ يُؤْمِنُونَ ۝

58. And those who believe in the Ayât (proofs, evidences, verses, lessons, signs, revelations, etc.) of their Lord;

وَٱلَّذِينَ هُم بِرَبِّهِمْ لَا يُشْرِكُونَ ۝

59. And those who join not anyone (in worship) as partners with their Lord;

وَٱلَّذِينَ يُؤْتُونَ مَآ ءَاتَواْ وَّقُلُوبُهُمْ وَجِلَةٌ أَنَّهُمْ إِلَىٰ رَبِّهِمْ رَٰجِعُونَ ۝

60. And those who give that (their charity) which they give (and also do other good deeds) with their hearts full of fear (whether their alms and charities have been accepted or not), because they are sure to return to their Lord (for reckoning).

أُوْلَـٰٓئِكَ يُسَـٰرِعُونَ فِى ٱلْخَيْرَٰتِ وَهُمْ لَهَا سَـٰبِقُونَ ۝

61. It is these who race for the good deeds, and they are foremost in them (e.g. offering the compulsory Salât (prayers) in their (early) stated, fixed times and so on).

Transliteration

57. Inna allatheena hum min khashyati rabbihim mushfiqoona 58. Waallatheena hum bi-ayati rabbihim yu/minoona 59. Waallatheena hum birabbihim la yushrikoona 60. Waallatheena yu/toona ma ataw waquloobuhum wajilatun annahum ila rabbihim rajiAAoona 61. Ola-ika yusariAAoona fee alkhayrati wahum laha sabiqoona

Tafsir Ibn Kathir

Description of the People of Good Deeds

(Verily, those who live in awe for fear of their Lord;) means, even though they have reached the level of Ihsan and have faith and do righteous deeds, they are still in awe

Chapter 23: Al-Mu'minun (The Believers), Verses 001-118

of Allah and fear Him and His hidden plans for them, as Al-Hasan Al-Basri said, "The believer combines Ihsan with awe, while the disbelievers combine evil deeds with a sense of security."

(And those who believe in the Ayat of their Lord;) means, they believe in His universal and legislative signs, as Allah says about Maryam, peace be upon her:

(and she testified to the truth of the Words of her Lord, and His Scriptures) (66:12), meaning that she believed that whatever existed was by the will and decree of Allah, and that whatever Allah decreed, if it was a command, it would be something that He liked and accepted; if it was a prohibition, it would be something that He disliked and rejected; and if it was good, it would be true. This is like the Ayah:

(And those who join not anyone (in worship) as partners with their Lord;) meaning, they do not worship anyone or anything else besides Him, but they worship Him Alone and know that there is no god except Allah Alone, the One, the Self-Sufficient Master, Who does not take a wife or have any offspring, and there is none comparable or equal unto Him.

(And those who give that which they give with their hearts full of fear, because they are sure to return to their Lord.) means, they give in charity, fearing that it may not be accepted from them because of some shortcoming or failure to meet the required conditions of giving. This has to do with fear and taking precautions, as Imam Ahmad recorded from `A'ishah: I said: "O Messenger of Allah,

(وَالَّذِينَ يُؤْتُونَ مَآ ءَاتَوا وَّقُلُوبُهُمْ وَجِلَةٌ)

(And those who give that which they give with their hearts full of fear...) Are these the ones who steal and commit Zina and drink alcohol while fearing Allah" The Messenger of Allah replied:

«لَا، يَا بِنْتَ أَبِي بَكْرٍ يَا بِنْتَ الصِّدِّيقِ، وَلَكِنَّهُ الَّذِي يُصَلِّي وَيَصُومُ وَيَتَصَدَّقُ وَهُوَ يَخَافُ اللهَ عَزَّ وَجَل»

(No, O daughter of Abu Bakr. O daughter of As-Siddic, the one who prays, fast and gives in charity, fearing Allah.) This was recorded by At-Tirmidhi, and Ibn Abi Hatim recorded something similar in which the Prophet said:

«لَا يَا بِنْتَ الصِّدِّيقِ، وَلَكِنَّهُمُ الَّذِينَ يُصَلُّونَ وَيَصُومُونَ وَيَتَصَدَّقُونَ وَهُمْ يَخَافُونَ أَلَّا يُقْبَلَ مِنْهُمْ:»

$$(أُولَٰئِكَ يُسَارِعُونَ فِي الْخَيْرَاتِ)$$

(No, O daughter of As-Siddiq, they are the ones who pray and fast and give in charity while fearing that it will not be accepted from them, (It is these who hasten in the good deeds.)) This is also how Ibn `Abbas, Muhammad bin Ka`b Al-Qurazi and Al-Hasan Al-Basri interpreted this Ayah.

Surah: 23 Ayah: 62, Ayah: 63, Ayah: 64, Ayah: 65, Ayah: 66 & Ayah: 67

$$وَلَا نُكَلِّفُ نَفْسًا إِلَّا وُسْعَهَا ۖ وَلَدَيْنَا كِتَابٌ يَنطِقُ بِالْحَقِّ ۚ وَهُمْ لَا يُظْلَمُونَ ﴿٦٢﴾$$

62. And We tax not any person except according to his capacity, and with Us is a Record which speaks the truth, and they will not be wronged.

$$بَلْ قُلُوبُهُمْ فِي غَمْرَةٍ مِّنْ هَٰذَا وَلَهُمْ أَعْمَالٌ مِّن دُونِ ذَٰلِكَ هُمْ لَهَا عَامِلُونَ ﴿٦٣﴾$$

63. Nay, but their hearts are covered from (understanding) this (the Qur'ân), and they have other (evil) deeds, besides, which they are doing.

$$حَتَّىٰ إِذَا أَخَذْنَا مُتْرَفِيهِم بِالْعَذَابِ إِذَا هُمْ يَجْأَرُونَ ﴿٦٤﴾$$

64. Until, when We seize those of them who lead a luxurious life with punishment: behold they make humble invocation with a loud voice.

$$لَا تَجْأَرُوا الْيَوْمَ ۖ إِنَّكُم مِّنَّا لَا تُنصَرُونَ ﴿٦٥﴾$$

65. Invoke not loudly this day! Certainly you shall not be helped by Us.

$$قَدْ كَانَتْ آيَاتِي تُتْلَىٰ عَلَيْكُمْ فَكُنتُمْ عَلَىٰ أَعْقَابِكُمْ تَنكِصُونَ ﴿٦٦﴾$$

66. Indeed My Verses used to be recited to you, but you used to turn back on your heels (denying them, and refusing with hatred to listen to them).

$$مُسْتَكْبِرِينَ بِهِ سَامِرًا تَهْجُرُونَ ﴿٦٧﴾$$

67. In pride (they - Quraish pagans and polytheists of Makkah used to feel proud that they are the dwellers of Makkah sanctuary - Haram), talking evil about it (the Qur'ân) by night.

Transliteration

62. Wala nukallifu nafsan illa wusAAaha waladayna kitabun yantiqu bialhaqqi wahum la yuthlamoona 63. Bal quloobuhum fee ghamratin min hatha walahum aAAmalun min dooni thalika hum laha Aaamiloona 64. Hatta itha akhathna mutrafeehim bialAAathabi itha hum yaj-aroona 65. La taj-aroo alyawma innakum minna la

tunsaroona 66. Qad kanat ayatee tutla AAalaykum fakuntum AAala aAAqabikum tankisoona 67. Mustakbireena bihi samiran tahjuroona

Tafsir Ibn Kathir

The Justice of Allah and the Frivolity of the Idolators

Allah tells us of His justice towards His servants in this world, in that He does not task any person except according to his capacity, i.e., He does not burden any soul with more than it can bear. On the Day of Resurrection He will call them to account for their deeds, which He has recorded in a written Book from which nothing is omitted. He says:

(and with Us is a Record which speaks the truth,) meaning, the Book of deeds

(and they will not be wronged.) means, nothing will be omitted from their record of good deeds. As for evil deeds, He will forgive and overlook many of them in the case of His believing servants. Then Allah says, denouncing the disbelievers and idolators of the Quraysh:

(Nay, but their hearts are covered), meaning because of negligence and misguidance,

(from this.) means, the Qur'an which Allah revealed to His Messenger .

(and they have other deeds, besides which they are doing.) Al-Hakam bin Aban narrated from `Ikrimah, from Ibn `Abbas that

(and they have other deeds,) means, evil deeds apart from that, i.e., Shirk,

(which they are doing.) means, which they will inevitably do. This was also narrated from Mujahid, Al-Hasan and others. Others said that this phrase means:

(And they have other deeds, besides which they are doing.) It was decreed that they would do evil deeds, and they will inevitably do them before they die, so that the word of punishment may be justified against them. A similar view was narrated from Muqatil bin Hayyan, As-Suddi and `Abdur-Rahman bin Zayd bin Aslam. This is a clear and appropriate meaning. We have already quoted from the Hadith of Ibn Mas`ud:

«فَوَ الَّذِي لَا إِلَهَ غَيْرُهُ إِنَّ الرَّجُلَ لَيَعْمَلُ بِعَمَلِ أَهْلِ الْجَنَّةِ حَتَّى مَا يَكُونُ بَيْنَهُ وَبَيْنَهَا إِلَّا ذِرَاعٌ، فَيَسْبِقُ عَلَيْهِ الْكِتَابُ فَيَعْمَلُ بِعَمَلِ أَهْلِ النَّارِ فَيَدْخُلُهَا»

(By Him besides Whom there is no other God, a man may do the deeds of the people of Paradise until there is no more than a forearm's length between him and it, then the decree will overtake him and he will do the deeds of the people of Hell, then he will enter Hell...)

(Until when We seize those of them who lead a luxurious life with punishment; behold, they make humble invocation with a loud voice.) means, when the punishment and vengeance of Allah comes to those who are living a happy life of luxury in this world and overtakes them,

(behold, they make humble invocation with a loud voice.) means, they scream their calls for help. This is like the Ayat:

(And leave Me Alone (to deal) with the beliers, those who are in possession of good things of life. And give them respite for a little while. Verily, with Us are fetters, and a raging Fire.) (73:11-12)

(How many a generation have We destroyed before them! And they cried out when there was no longer time for escape.) (38:3)

(Invoke not loudly this day! Certainly you shall not be helped by Us.) means, no one is going to save you from what has happened to you, whether you scream aloud or remain silent. There is no escape and no way out. It is inevitable: the punishment will surely come to you. Then Allah mentions the greatest of their sins:

(Indeed My Ayat used to be recited to you, but you used to turn back on your heels.) meaning, when you were called, you refused and resisted.

("This is because, when Allah Alone was invoked, you disbelieved, but when partners were joined to Him, you believed! So the judgment is only with Allah, the Most High, the Most Great!") (40:12)

(In pride, talking evil about it by night.) refers to the arrogant pride which the Quraysh felt because they believed themselves to be the guardians of the Ka`bah, when in fact this was not the case. As An-Nasa'i said in his Tafsir of this Ayah in his Sunan: Ahmad bin Sulayman told us that `Ubaydullah told us from Isra`il, from `Abdul-A`la that he heard Sa`id bin Jubayr narrating that Ibn `Abbas said, "Talking by late night became disapproved of when this Ayah was revealed:

(In pride, talking evil about it by night.) He said, "They boasted about the Ka`bah and said, `We are its people who stay up talking at night.' They used to boast and stay up and talk at night around the Ka`bah. They did not use it for the proper purpose, and so in effect they had abandoned it."

Surah: 23 Ayah: 68, Ayah: 69, Ayah: 70, Ayah: 71, Ayah: 72, Ayah: 73, Ayah: 74 & Ayah: 75

أَفَلَمْ يَدَّبَّرُوا۟ ٱلْقَوْلَ أَمْ جَآءَهُم مَّا لَمْ يَأْتِ ءَابَآءَهُمُ ٱلْأَوَّلِينَ ۝

68. Have they not pondered over the Word (of Allâh, i.e. what is sent down to the Prophet (peace be upon him)) or has there come to them what had not come to their fathers of old?

أَمْ لَمْ يَعْرِفُوا۟ رَسُولَهُمْ فَهُمْ لَهُۥ مُنكِرُونَ ۝

69. Or is it that they did not recognize their Messenger (Muhammad (peace be upon him)) so they deny him?

أَمْ يَقُولُونَ بِهِ جِنَّةٌ ۚ بَلْ جَآءَهُم بِٱلْحَقِّ وَأَكْثَرُهُمْ لِلْحَقِّ كَٰرِهُونَ ۝

70. Or say they: "There is madness in him?" Nay, but he brought them the truth (i.e. Tauhîd: Worshipping Allâh Alone in all aspects, the Qur'ân and the religion of Islâm), but most of them (the disbelievers) are averse to the truth.

وَلَوِ ٱتَّبَعَ ٱلْحَقُّ أَهْوَآءَهُمْ لَفَسَدَتِ ٱلسَّمَٰوَٰتُ وَٱلْأَرْضُ وَمَن فِيهِنَّ ۚ بَلْ أَتَيْنَٰهُم بِذِكْرِهِمْ فَهُمْ عَن ذِكْرِهِم مُّعْرِضُونَ ۝

71. And if the truth had been in accordance with their desires, verily, the heavens and the earth, and whosoever is therein would have been corrupted! Nay, We have brought them their reminder, but they turn away from their reminder.

أَمْ تَسْـَٔلُهُمْ خَرْجًا فَخَرَاجُ رَبِّكَ خَيْرٌ ۖ وَهُوَ خَيْرُ ٱلرَّٰزِقِينَ ۝

72. Or is it that you (O Muhammad (peace be upon him)) ask them for some wages? But the recompense of your Lord is better, and He is the Best of those who give sustenance.

وَإِنَّكَ لَتَدْعُوهُمْ إِلَىٰ صِرَٰطٍ مُّسْتَقِيمٍ ۝

73. And certainly, you (O Muhammad (peace be upon him)) call them to the Straight Path (true religion - Islâmic Monotheism).

وَإِنَّ ٱلَّذِينَ لَا يُؤْمِنُونَ بِٱلْءَاخِرَةِ عَنِ ٱلصِّرَٰطِ لَنَٰكِبُونَ ۝

74. And verily, those who believe not in the Hereafter are indeed deviating far astray from the Path (true religion - Islâmic Monotheism).

۞ وَلَوْ رَحِمْنَٰهُمْ وَكَشَفْنَا مَا بِهِم مِّن ضُرٍّ لَّلَجُّوا۟ فِى طُغْيَٰنِهِمْ يَعْمَهُونَ ۝

75. And though We had mercy on them and removed the distress, which is on them, still they would obstinately persist in their transgression, wandering blindly.

Transliteration

68. Afalam yaddabbaroo alqawla am jaahum ma lam ya/ti abaahumu al-awwaleena   69. Am lam yaAArifoo rasoolahum fahum lahu munkiroona   70. Or say they: "There is madness in him?" Nay, but he brought them the truth [i.e. "(A) Tauhîd: Worshipping Allâh Alone in all aspects (B) The Qur'ân (C) The religion of Islâm,"] but most of them (the disbelievers) are averse to the truth.   71. Walawi ittabaAAa alhaqqu ahwaahum lafasadati alssamawatu waal-ardu waman feehinna bal ataynahum bithikrihim fahum AAan thikrihim muAAridoona   72. Am tas-aluhum kharjan fakharaju rabbika khayrun wahuwa khayru alrraziqeena   73. Wa-innaka latadAAoohum ila siratin mustaqeemin

74. Wa-inna allatheena la yu/minoona bial-akhirati AAani alssirati lanakiboona   75. Walaw rahimnahum wakashafna ma bihim min durrin lalajjoo fee tughyanihim yaAAmahoona

Tafsir Ibn Kathir

Refutation and Condemnation of the Idolators

Allah denounces the idolators for not understanding the Qur'an or contemplating its meaning, and for turning away from it, even though they had been addressed specifically in this Book which Allah did not reveal to any Messenger more perfect and noble, and especially since no Book or warner had come to their forefathers who had died during the Jahiliyyah. What these people, upon whom the blessing had been bestowed, should have done, was to accept it and give thanks for it, and try to understand it and act in accordance with it night and day, as was done by the wise ones among them who became Muslim and followed the Messenger , may Allah be pleased with them.

(Have they not pondered over the Word,) Qatadah said, "Because, by Allah, if the people had pondered the meaning and understood it properly, they would have found in the Qur'an a deterrent to disobeying Allah. But they only paid attention to the Ayat which are not entirely clear, and so they were destroyed because of that." Then Allah says, denouncing the disbelievers of the Quraysh:

(Or is it that they did not recognize their Messenger so they deny him) means, `do they not recognize Muhammad and the honesty, trustworthiness and good character with which he grew up among them Can they deny that or argue against it' Ja`far bin Abi Talib said to An-Najashi, the king of Ethiopia: "O King, Allah has sent to us a Messenger whose lineage, honesty and trustworthiness are known to us." Al-Mughirah bin Shu`bah said something similar to the deputy of Kisra when he wanted to challenge him. When the Byzantine ruler Heraclius asked Abu Sufyan Sakhr bin Harb and his companions -- who were still disbelievers and had not yet become Muslim -- about the characteristics, lineage, honesty and trustworthiness of the Prophet , they could only tell the truth and admit that he was indeed noble and truthful.

(Or they say: There is madness in him) This is a narration of what the Quraysh said about the Prophet . They said that he was making up the Qur'an by himself, or that he was crazy and did not know what he was saying. Allah tells us that their hearts did not believe that, they knew that what they were saying about the Qur'an was falsehood, for it had come to them from the Words of Allah and could not be resisted or rejected. So Allah challenged them and all the people of the world to produce something like it if they could -- but they could not and would never be able to do so. So Allah says:

(Nay, but he brought them Al-Haqq, but most of them are averse to the truth.)

Truth does not follow Whims and Desires

Allah says;

(And if Al-Haqq had followed their desires, verily, the heavens and the earth, and whosoever is therein would have been corrupted!) Mujahid, Abu Salih and As-Suddi said, "Al-Haqq is Allah, may He be glorified." What is meant by the Ayah is that if Allah had responded to the desires in their hearts and prescribed things accordingly, the heavens and the earth and whosoever is therein, would have been corrupted, i.e., because of their corrupt and inconsistent desires. As Allah says of them elsewhere:

("Why is not this Qur'an sent down to some great man of the two towns") (43:31) Then He says:

(Is it they who would portion out the mercy of your Lord) (43:32) And Allah says:

(Say: "If you possessed the treasure of the mercy of my Lord, then you would surely hold back for fear of spending it. ") (17:100),

(Or have they a share in the dominion Then in that case they would not give mankind even a Naqir.) (4:53) All of this goes to show how incapable mankind is and how divergent and inconsistent their ideas and desires are. Only Allah, may He be glorified, is Perfect in all His attributes, words, actions, laws, power and control of His creation, may He be exalted and sanctified. There is no God but He and no Lord besides Him. Then He says:

(Nay, We have brought them their reminder,) meaning the Qur'an,

(but they turn away from their reminder.)

The Prophet does not ask for any payment, and he calls to the straight path.

(Or is it that you ask them for some Kharj) Al-Hasan said, "A reward." Qatadah said, "Some payment."

(But the recompense of your Lord is better,) means, you are not asking for any wages or payment or anything for calling them to right guidance, rather you are hoping for a great reward from Allah, as He says:

(Say: "Whatever wage I might have asked of you is yours. My wage is from Allah only.") (34:47)

(Say: "No wage do I ask of you for this, nor am I one of the pretenders.") (38:86)

(Say: "No reward do I ask of you for this except to be kind to me for my kinship with you.") (42:23)

(And there came a man running from the farthest part of the town. He said: "O my people! Obey the Messengers. Obey those who ask no wages of you, and who are rightly guided.") (35:20-21)

(And certainly, you call them to the straight path. And verily, those who believe not in the Hereafter are indeed deviating far astray from the path.)

The Situation of the Disbelievers

(And verily, those who believe not in the Hereafter are indeed deviating far astray from the path.) meaning, they have gone astray and deviated.

(And though We had mercy on them and removed the distress which is on them, still they would obstinately persist in their transgression, wandering blindly.) Here Allah tells of their stubbornness in their disbelief, in that even if He had removed the calamity from them and made them understand the Qur'an, they still would not follow it; they would still persist in their disbelief and stubborn transgression. This is like the Ayat:

(Had Allah known of any good in them, He would indeed have made them listen; and even if He had made them listen, they would but have turned away with aversion.) (8:23)

(And if (Lauw) you could but see when they will be held over the (Hell) Fire! They will say: "Would that we were but sent back (to the world)! Then we would not deny the Ayat of our Lord, and we would be of the believers!" Nay, it has become manifest to them what they had been concealing before. But if they were returned (to the world), they would certainly revert to that which they were forbidden.) (6:27-29) Until His statement:

(be resurrected) This has to do with the knowledge of Allah. He knows about something that will not happen, but if it were to happen, He knows how it would be. Ad-Dahhak reported from Ibn `Abbas: "Every- thing that is implied in the word:

(If (Lauw)) is something that will never happen."

Surah: 23 Ayah: 76, Ayah: 77, Ayah: 78, Ayah: 79, Ayah: 80, Ayah: 81, Ayah: 82 & Ayah: 83

وَلَقَدْ أَخَذْنَـٰهُم بِٱلْعَذَابِ فَمَا ٱسْتَكَانُوا۟ لِرَبِّهِمْ وَمَا يَتَضَرَّعُونَ ۝

76. And indeed We seized them with punishment, but they humbled not themselves to their Lord, nor did they invoke (Allâh) with submission to Him.

حَتَّىٰٓ إِذَا فَتَحْنَا عَلَيْهِم بَابًا ذَا عَذَابٍ شَدِيدٍ إِذَا هُمْ فِيهِ مُبْلِسُونَ ۝

77. Until, when We open for them the gate of severe punishment, then lo! they will be plunged into destruction with deep regrets, sorrows and in despair.

وَهُوَ ٱلَّذِىٓ أَنشَأَ لَكُمُ ٱلسَّمْعَ وَٱلْأَبْصَـٰرَ وَٱلْأَفْـِٔدَةَ قَلِيلًا مَّا تَشْكُرُونَ ۝

78. It is He, Who has created for you (the sense of) hearing (ears), eyes (sight), and hearts (understanding). Little thanks you give.

وَهُوَ ٱلَّذِى ذَرَأَكُمْ فِى ٱلْأَرْضِ وَإِلَيْهِ تُحْشَرُونَ ۝

Chapter 23: Al-Mu'minun (The Believers), Verses 001-118

79. And it is He Who has created you on the earth, and to Him you shall be gathered back.

وَهُوَ ٱلَّذِى يُحْىِ وَيُمِيتُ وَلَهُ ٱخْتِلَـٰفُ ٱلَّيْلِ وَٱلنَّهَارِ أَفَلَا تَعْقِلُونَ ۝

80. And it is He Who gives life and causes death, and His is the alternation of night and day. Will you not then understand?

بَلْ قَالُوا۟ مِثْلَ مَا قَالَ ٱلْأَوَّلُونَ ۝

81. Nay, but they say the like of what the men of old said.

قَالُوٓا۟ أَءِذَا مِتْنَا وَكُنَّا تُرَابًا وَعِظَـٰمًا أَءِنَّا لَمَبْعُوثُونَ ۝

82. They said: "When we are dead and have become dust and bones, shall we be resurrected indeed?

لَقَدْ وُعِدْنَا نَحْنُ وَءَابَآؤُنَا هَـٰذَا مِن قَبْلُ إِنْ هَـٰذَآ إِلَّآ أَسَـٰطِيرُ ٱلْأَوَّلِينَ ۝

83. "Verily, this we have been promised - we and our fathers before (us)! This is only the tales of the ancients!"

Transliteration

76. Walaqad akhathnahum bialAAathabi fama istakanoo lirabbihim wama yatadarraAAoona 77. Hatta itha fatahna AAalayhim baban tha AAathabin shadeedin itha hum feehi mublisoona 78. Wahuwa allathee anshaa lakumu alssamAAa waal-absara waal-af-idata qaleelan ma tashkuroona 79. Wahuwa allathee tharaakum fee al-ardi wa-ilayhi tuhsharoona 80. Wahuwa allathee yuhyee wayumeetu walahu ikhtilafu allayli waalnnahari afala taAAqiloona 81. Bal qaloo mithla ma qala al-awwaloona 82. Qaloo a-itha mitna wakunna turaban waAAithaman a-inna lamabAAoothoona 83. Laqad wuAAidna nahnu waabaona hatha min qablu in hatha illa asateeru al-awwaleena

Tafsir Ibn Kathir

(And indeed We seized them with punishment,) means, `We tried and tested them with difficulties and calamities.' His saying:

(but they humbled not themselves to their Lord, nor did they invoke with submission to Him.) means, that did not deter them from their disbelief and resistance, rather they persisted in their sin and misguidance,

(but they humbled not themselves)

(nor did they invoke (Allah) with submission to Him.) they did not call on Him. This is like the Ayah:

(When Our torment reached them, why then did they not humble themselves But their hearts became hardened,) (6:43) Ibn Abi Hatim recorded that Ibn `Abbas said,

"Abu Sufyan came to the Messenger of Allah and said, `O Muhammad, I ask you by Allah and by the ties of kinship between us, we have been reduced to eating camel hair and blood.' Then Allah revealed,

(And indeed We seized them with punishment, but they humbled not themselves.) This was also recorded by An-Nasa'i. The basis of this Hadith is in the Two Sahihs, where it says that the Messenger of Allah prayed against the Quraysh when he could not make any headway with them, and he said,

«اللَّهُمَّ أَعِنِّي عَلَيْهِمْ بِسَبْعٍ كَسَبْعِ يُوسُفَ»

(O Allah, help me against them sending on them seven years (of famine) like the seven (years of drought) of Yusuf.)

(Until, when We open for them the gate of severe punishment, then lo! they will be plunged in despair.) When the command of Allah reaches them and the Hour comes to them suddenly, and they are overtaken by the punishment of Allah which they were not expecting, then they will despair of any ease and goodness, and all their hopes will disappear.

A reminder of the Blessings of Allah and His immense Power

Then Allah mentions His blessings to His servants, in that He has given them hearing, sight and understanding through which they come to know things and draw lessons from them, the signs which attest to the Oneness of Allah and indicate that He is the One Who does what He wills and chooses what He wants.

(Little thanks you give.) means, how little you thank Allah for the blessings He has given you. This is like the Ayah:

(And most of mankind will not believe even if you desire it eagerly.) (12:103) Then Allah tells us about His great power and overwhelming authority, for He is the One Who originated creation and put people in all parts of the earth, with their different nations, languages and characteristics, then on the Day of Resurrection He will gather them all together, the first of them and the last, at a fixed time on a day appointed, and none will be left out, young or old, male or female, noble or insignificant, but all will be brought back as they were originally created. Allah said:

(And it is He Who gives life and causes death,) meaning, He will bring the scattered bones back to life and cause the death of the nations,

(and His is the alternation of night and day.) meaning, by His command night and day are subjugated, each of them following the other and never departing from that pattern, as Allah says:

(It is not for the sun to overtake the moon, nor does the night outstrip the day)(36:40).

(Will you not then understand) means, do you not have minds that tell you of the Almighty, All-Knowing to Whom all things are subjugated, Who has power over all things and to Whom all things submit

The Idolators thought that Resurrection after Death was very unlikely

Then Allah tells us about those who denied the resurrection, who were like the disbelievers who came before them:

(Nay, but they say the like of what the men of old said. They said: "When we are dead and have become dust and bones, shall we be resurrected indeed") They thought it very unlikely that this would happen after they had disintegrated into nothing.

("Verily, this we have been promised -- we and our fathers before (us)! This is only the tales of the ancients!") This means, "It is impossible that we could be brought back. This was said by those who learned it from the books and disputes of the ancients." This denial and rejection on their part is like the Ayah where Allah tells us about them:

("Even after we are crumbled bones" They say: "It would in that case, be a return with loss!" But it will be only a single Zajrah, When behold, they find themselves on the surface of the earth alive after their death.) (79:11-14)

(Does not man see that We have created him from Nutfah. Yet behold he (stands forth) as an open opponent. And he puts forth for Us a parable, and forgets his own creation. He says: "Who will give life to these bones after they are rotten and have become dust" Say: "He will give life to them Who created them for the first time! And He is the All-Knower of every creation!") (36:77-79)

Surah: 23 Ayah: 84, Ayah: 85, Ayah: 86, Ayah: 87, Ayah: 88, Ayah: 89 & Ayah: 90

قُل لِّمَنِ ٱلۡأَرۡضُ وَمَن فِيهَآ إِن كُنتُمۡ تَعۡلَمُونَ ۝

84. Say: "Whose is the earth and whosoever is therein? If you know!"

سَيَقُولُونَ لِلَّهِ ۚ قُلۡ أَفَلَا تَذَكَّرُونَ ۝

85. They will say: "It is Allâh's!" Say: "Will you not then remember?"

قُلۡ مَن رَّبُّ ٱلسَّمَٰوَٰتِ ٱلسَّبۡعِ وَرَبُّ ٱلۡعَرۡشِ ٱلۡعَظِيمِ ۝

86. Say: "Who is (the) Lord of the seven heavens, and (the) Lord of the Great Throne?"

سَيَقُولُونَ لِلَّهِ ۚ قُلۡ أَفَلَا تَتَّقُونَ ۝

87. They will say: "Allâh." Say: "Will you not then fear Allâh (believe in His Oneness, obey Him, believe in the Resurrection and Recompense for every good or bad deed)?"

قُلْ مَن بِيَدِهِ مَلَكُوتُ كُلِّ شَىْءٍ وَهُوَ يُجِيرُ وَلَا يُجَارُ عَلَيْهِ إِن كُنتُمْ تَعْلَمُونَ ﴿٨٨﴾

88. Say "In Whose Hand is the sovereignty of everything (i.e. treasures of each and everything)? And He protects (all), while against Whom there is no protector, (i.e. if Allâh saves anyone none can punish or harm him, and if Allâh punishes or harms anyone none can save him), if you know?" (Tafsir Al-Qurtubî)

سَيَقُولُونَ لِلَّهِ قُلْ فَأَنَّىٰ تُسْحَرُونَ ﴿٨٩﴾

89. They will say: "(All that belongs) to Allâh." Say: "How then are you deceived and turn away from the truth?"

بَلْ أَتَيْنَـٰهُم بِٱلْحَقِّ وَإِنَّهُمْ لَكَـٰذِبُونَ ﴿٩٠﴾

90. Nay, but We have brought them the truth (Islâmic Monotheism), and verily, they (disbelievers) are liars.

Transliteration

84. Qul limani al-ardu waman feeha in kuntum taAAlamoona 85. Sayaqooloona lillahi qul afala tathakkaroona 86. Qul man rabbu alssamawati alssabAAi warabbu alAAarshi alAAatheemi 87. Sayaqooloona lillahi qul afala tattaqoona 88. Qul man biyadihi malakootu kulli shay-in wahuwa yujeeru wala yujaru AAalayhi in kuntum taAAlamoona 89. Sayaqooloona lillahi qul faanna tusharoona 90. Bal ataynahum bialhaqqi wa-innahum lakathiboona

Tafsir Ibn Kathir

The Idolators believe in Tawhid Ar-Rububiyyah, which requires them to believe in Tawhid Al-Uluhiyyah

Allah states that the fact that He is One and that He is independent in His creation, control, dominion and guides one to realize that there is no God except Him and that none should be worshipped except Him Alone, with no partner or associate. He tells His Messenger Muhammad to say to the idolators who worship others besides Him, even though they admit His Lordship, that He has no partner in Lordship. But despite this they still attributed partners in divinity to Him, and worshipped others besides Him even though they recognized the fact that those whom they worshipped could not create anything, did not own anything, nor do they have any control over anything. However, they still believed that these creatures could bring them closer to Allah,

(We worship them only that they may bring us near to Allah) (39:3). So Allah says:

(Say: "Whose is the earth and whosoever is therein") meaning, "Who is the Owner Who has created it and whatever is in it of animals, plants, fruits and all other kinds of creation"

("If you know!" They will say: "It is Allah's!") means, they will admit that this belongs to Allah Alone with no partner or associate. If that is the case,

(Say: "Will you not then remember") that none should be worshipped except the Creator and Provider.

(Say: "Who is Lord of the seven heavens, and Lord of the Great Throne") means, "Who is the Creator of the higher realm with its planets, lights and angels who submit to Him in all regions and in all directions Who is the Lord of the Great Throne, which is the highest of all created things" Allah says here:

(and Lord of the Great Throne), meaning the Mighty Throne. At the end of the Surah, Allah says:

(the Lord of the Supreme Throne!) (23:116), meaning splendid and magnificent. The Throne combines the features of height and vastness with splendor and magnificence. This is why it was said that it is made of red rubies. Ibn Mas`ud said, "There is no night or day with your Lord, and the light of the Throne is from the Light of His Face."

(They will say: "Allah." Say: "Will you not then have Taqwa") meaning, since you admit that He is the Lord of the heavens and the Lord of the Mighty Throne, will you not fear His punishment for worshipping others besides Him and associating others with Him

(Say: "In Whose Hand is the sovereignty of everything") i.e., sovereignty is in His Hands.

(There is not a moving creature but He has grasp of its forelock) (11:56). meaning, He has control over it. The Messenger of Allah used to say,

«لَا وَالَّذِي نَفْسِي بِيَدِه»

(By the One in Whose hand is my soul.) When he swore an oath, he would say,

«لَا وَمُقَلِّبِ الْقُلُوب»

(By the One Who turns over (controls) the hearts.) He, may He be glorified, is the Creator, the Sovereign, the Controller,

(And He protects (all), while against Whom there is no protector, if you know) Among the Arabs, if a leader announced his protection to a person, no one could go against him in that, yet no one could offer protection against that leader. Allah says:

(And He protects (all), while against Whom there is no protector,) meaning, He is the greatest Master, and there is none greater than Him. His is the power to create and to command, and none can overturn or oppose His ruling. What He wills happens, and what He does not, will not happen. Allah says:

(He cannot be questioned about what He does, while they will be questioned.) (21:23) He cannot be asked about what He does because of His greatness, Pride, overwhelming power, wisdom and justice, but all of His creation will be asked about what they did, as Allah says:

(So, by your Lord, We shall certainly call all of them to account. For all that they used to do.) (15:92-93)

(They will say: "(All that belongs) to Allah.") means, they will admit that the Almighty Master Who protects all while against Him there is no protector is Allah Alone, with no partner or associate.

(Say: "How then are you deceived and turn away from the truth") means, how can your minds accept the idea of worshipping others besides Him when you recognize and acknowledge that Then Allah says:

(Nay, but We have brought them the truth,) which is the declaration that there is no god worthy of worship besides Allah, and the establishment of clear, definitive and sound proof to that effect,

(and verily, they are liars.) means, in their worship of others alongside Allah when they have no evidence for doing so, as Allah says at the end of this Surah:

(And whoever invokes, besides Allah, any other god, of whom he has no proof; then his reckoning is only with his Lord. Surely, the disbelievers will not be successful.) (23:117) The idolators have no evidence for what they are doing, which has led them into lies and misguidance. Rather they are following their forefathers and predecessors who were confused and ignorant, as Allah describes them:

("We found our fathers following a certain way and religion, and we will indeed follow their footsteps.") (43:23)

Surah: 23 Ayah: 91 & Ayah: 92

مَا ٱتَّخَذَ ٱللَّهُ مِن وَلَدٍ وَمَا كَانَ مَعَهُ مِنْ إِلَٰهٍ إِذًا لَّذَهَبَ كُلُّ إِلَٰهٍ بِمَا خَلَقَ وَلَعَلَا بَعْضُهُمْ عَلَىٰ بَعْضٍ سُبْحَٰنَ ٱللَّهِ عَمَّا يَصِفُونَ ۝

91. No son (or offspring) did Allâh beget, nor is there any ilâh (god) along with Him; (if there had been many gods), then each god would have taken away what he had created, and some would have tried to overcome others! Glorified is Allâh above all that they attribute to Him!

Chapter 23: Al-Mu'minun (The Believers), Verses 001-118

$$\text{عَلِمِ ٱلْغَيْبِ وَٱلشَّهَٰدَةِ فَتَعَٰلَىٰ عَمَّا يُشْرِكُونَ} \quad \text{﴿٩٢﴾}$$

92. All-Knower of the unseen and the seen! Exalted is He over all that they associate as partners to Him!

Transliteration

91. Ma ittakhatha Allahu min waladin wama kana maAAahu min ilahin ithan lathahaba kullu ilahin bima khalaqa walaAAala baAAduhum AAala baAAdin subhana Allahi AAamma yasifoona 92. AAalimi alghaybi waalshshahadati fataAAala AAamma yushrikoona

Tafsir Ibn Kathir

Allah has no Partner or Associate

Allah declares Himself to be above having any child or partner in dominion, control and worship. He says:

(No son did Allah beget, nor is there any god along with Him. (If there had been many gods), then each god would have taken away what he had created, and some would have tried to overcome others.) meaning, if it were decreed that there should be a plurality of deities, each of them would have exclusive control over whatever he had created, so there would never be any order in the universe. But what we see is that the universe is ordered and cohesive, with the upper and lower realms connected to one another in the most perfect fashion.

(you can see no fault in the creation of the Most Gracious) (65:3). Moreover, if there were a number of gods, each of them would try to subdue the other with enmity, and one would prevail over the other. This has been mentioned by the scholars of `Ilm-ul-Kalam, who discussed it using the evidence of mutual resistance or counteraction. This idea states that if there were two or more creators, one would want to make a body move while the other would want to keep it immobile, and if neither of them could achieve what they wanted, then both would be incapable, but the One Whose existence is essential (i.e., Allah) cannot be incapable. It is impossible for the will of both to be fulfilled because of the conflict. This dilemma only arises when a plurality of gods is suggested, so it is impossible for there to be such a plurality, because if the will of one is fulfilled and not the other, the one who prevails will be the one whose existence is essential (i.e., God) and the one who is prevailed over will be merely possible (i.e., he is not divine), because it is not befitting for the one to be defeated whose existence is essential. Allah says:

(and some would have tried to overcome others! Glorified be Allah above all that they attribute to Him!) meaning, high above all that the stubborn wrongdoers say when they claim that He has a son or partner.

(All-Knower of the unseen and the seen!) means, He knows what is hidden from His creatures and what they see.

(Exalted be He over all that they associate as partners to Him!) means, sanctified and glorified and exalted be He above all that the wrongdoers and liars say.

Surah: 23 Ayah: 93, Ayah: 94, Ayah: 95, Ayah: 96, Ayah: 97 & Ayah: 98

$$\text{قُل رَّبِّ إِمَّا تُرِيَنِّي مَا يُوعَدُونَ ۝}$$

93. Say (O Muhammad (peace be upon him)) " My Lord! If You would show me that with which they are threatened (torment),

$$\text{رَبِّ فَلَا تَجْعَلْنِي فِي ٱلْقَوْمِ ٱلظَّـٰلِمِينَ ۝}$$

94. "My Lord! Then (save me from Your Punishment), and put me not amongst the people who are the Zâlimûn (polytheists and wrong-doers)."

$$\text{وَإِنَّا عَلَىٰ أَن نُّرِيَكَ مَا نَعِدُهُمْ لَقَـٰدِرُونَ ۝}$$

95. And indeed We are Able to show you (O Muhammad (peace be upon him)) that with which We have threatened them.

$$\text{ٱدْفَعْ بِٱلَّتِي هِيَ أَحْسَنُ ٱلسَّيِّئَةَ ۚ نَحْنُ أَعْلَمُ بِمَا يَصِفُونَ ۝}$$

96. Repel evil with that which is better. We are Best-Acquainted with the things they utter.

$$\text{وَقُل رَّبِّ أَعُوذُ بِكَ مِنْ هَمَزَٰتِ ٱلشَّيَـٰطِينِ ۝}$$

97. And say: "My Lord! I seek refuge with You from the whisperings (suggestions) of the Shayâtin (devils).

$$\text{وَأَعُوذُ بِكَ رَبِّ أَن يَحْضُرُونِ ۝}$$

98. "And I seek refuge with You, My Lord! lest they should come near me."

Transliteration

93. Qul rabbi imma turiyannee ma yooAAadoona 94. Rabbi fala tajAAalnee fee alqawmi alththalimeena 95. Wa-inna AAala an nuriyaka ma naAAiduhum laqadiroona 96. IdfaAA biallatee hiya ahsanu alssayyi-ata nahnu aAAlamu bima yasifoona 97. Waqul rabbi aAAoothu bika min hamazati alshshayateeni 98. WaaAAoothu bika rabbi an yahdurooni

Tafsir Ibn Kathir

The Command to call on Allah when Calamity strikes, to repel Evil with that which is better, and to seek refuge with Allah

Allah commands His Prophet Muhammad to call on Him with this supplication when calamity strikes:

(My Lord! If You would show me that with which they are threatened.) meaning, `if You punish them while I am witnessing that, then do not cause me to be one of them.' As was said in the Hadith recorded by Imam Ahmad and At-Tirmidhi, who graded it Sahih:

《وَإِذَا أَرَدْتَ بِقَوْمٍ فِتْنَةً فَتَوَفَّنِي إِلَيْكَ غَيْرَ مَفْتُونٍ》

(If You want to test people, then take me to You (cause me to die) without having to undergo the test.)

(And indeed We are able to show you that with which We have threatened them.) means, `if We willed, We could show you the punishment and test that We will send upon them.' Then Allah shows him the best way to behave when mixing with people, which is to treat kindly the one who treats him badly, so as to soften his heart and turn his enmity to friendship, and to turn his hatred to love. Allah says:

(Repel evil with that which is better.) This is like the Ayah:

(Repel (the evil) with one which is better, then verily he, between whom and you there was enmity, (will become) as though he was a close friend. But none is granted it except those who are patient) (41:34-35). meaning, nobody will be helped or inspired to follow this advice or attain this quality,

(except those who are patient) meaning, those who patiently bear people's insults and bad treatment and deal with them in a good manner when they are on the receiving end of bad treatment from them.

(and none is granted it except the owner of the great portion) means, in this world and the Hereafter. And Allah says:

(And say: "My Lord! I seek refuge with You from the whisperings of the Shayatin.") Allah commanded him to seek refuge with Him from the Shayatin, because no trick could help you against them and you cannot protect yourself by being kind to them. We have already stated, when discussing Isti`adhah (seeking refuge), that the Messenger of Allah used to say,

《أَعُوذُ بِاللهِ السَّمِيعِ الْعَلِيمِ مِنَ الشَّيْطَانِ الرَّجِيمِ مِنْ هَمْزِهِ وَنَفْخِهِ وَنَفْثِهِ》

(I seek refuge with Allah, the All-Hearing, All-Seeing, from the accursed Shayatin, from his whisperings, evil suggestions and insinuations.) His saying:

("And I seek refuge with You, My Lord! lest they should come near me.") means, in any issue of my life. So we are commanded to mention Allah at the beginning of any undertaking, in order to ward off the Shayatin at the time of eating, intercourse, slaughtering animals for food, etc. Abu Dawud recorded that the Messenger of Allah used to say:

(O Allah, I seek refuge with You from old age, I seek refuge with You from being crushed or drowned, and I seek refuge with you from being assaulted by the Shayatin at the time of death.)

Surah: 23 Ayah: 99 & Ayah: 100

حَتَّىٰ إِذَا جَآءَ أَحَدَهُمُ ٱلْمَوْتُ قَالَ رَبِّ ٱرْجِعُونِ ۝

99. Until, when death comes to one of them (those who join partners with Allâh), he says: "My Lord! Send me back,

لَعَلِّى أَعْمَلُ صَٰلِحًا فِيمَا تَرَكْتُ ۚ كَلَّآ ۚ إِنَّهَا كَلِمَةٌ هُوَ قَآئِلُهَا ۖ وَمِن وَرَآئِهِم بَرْزَخٌ إِلَىٰ يَوْمِ يُبْعَثُونَ ۝

100. "So that I may do good in that which I have left behind!" No! It is but a word that he speaks; and behind them is Barzakh (a barrier) until the Day when they will be resurrected.

Transliteration

99. Hatta itha jaa ahadahumu almawtu qala rabbi irjiAAooni 100. LaAAallee aAAmalu salihan feema taraktu kalla innaha kalimatun huwa qa-iluha wamin waraihim barzakhun ila yawmi yubAAathoona

Tafsir Ibn Kathir

The Disbelievers' Hope when death approaches

Allah tells us about what happens when death approaches one of the disbelievers or one of those who have been negligent with the commands of Allah. He tells us what he says and how he asks to come back to this world so that he can rectify whatever wrongs he committed during his lifetime. Allah says:

("My Lord! Send me back, so that I may do good in that which I have left behind!" No!) This is like the Ayat:

(And spend of that with which We have provided you before death comes to one of you,) until His saying:

(And Allah is All-Aware of what you do) (63:10-11)

(And warn mankind of the Day when the torment will come unto them)

upto His saying; (that you would not leave (the world for the Hereafter).) (14:44) And His saying:

(On the Day the event is finally fulfilled, those who neglected it before will say: "Verily, the Messengers of our Lord did come with the truth, now are there any intercessors for us that they might intercede on our behalf Or could we be sent back so that we might do deeds other than those deeds which we used to do") (7:53) And:

(And if you only could see when the criminals shall hang their heads before their Lord (saying): "Our Lord! We have now seen and heard, so send us back, that we will do righteous good deeds. Verily, we now believe with certainty.") (32:12) And;

(If you could but see when they will be held over the (Hell) Fire! They will say: "Would that we were but sent back! Then we would not deny the Ayat of our Lord...") until His saying;

(And indeed they are liars.) (6:27-28)

(And you will see the wrongdoers, when they behold the torment, they will say: "Is there any way of return") (42:44)

(They will say: "Our Lord! You have made us to die twice, and You have given us life twice! Now we confess our sins, then is there any way to get out") (40:11) and the Ayah after it:

(Therein they will cry: "Our Lord! Bring us out, we shall do righteous good deeds, not what we used to do." (Allah will reply:) "Did We not give you lives long enough, so that whosoever would receive admonition could receive it And the warner came to you. So taste you (the evil of your deeds). For the wrongdoers there is no helper.") (35:37) Allah says that they will ask to go back, when death approaches, on the Day of Resurrection, when they are gathered for judgment before the Compeller (Allah) and when they are in the agonies of the punishment of Hell, but their prayer will not be answered. Here Allah says:

(No! It is but a word that he speaks;) The word Kalla (No!) is a word that is used to rebuke, and the meaning is: "No, We will not respond to what he asks for and We will not accept it from him."

(It is but a word that he speaks) refers to his asking to go back so that he can do righteous deeds; this is just talk on his part, it would not be accompanied by any action. If he were to go back, he would not do any righteous good deeds, he is merely lying, as Allah says:

(But if they were returned, they would certainly revert to that which they were forbidden. And indeed they are liars) (6:28). Qatadah said: "By Allah, he will not wish to go back to his family and tribe, or to accumulate more of the things of this world or satisfy his desires, but he will wish that he could go back to do acts of obedience to

Allah. May Allah have mercy on a man who does that which the disbeliever will wish he had done when he sees the punishment of Hell."

Barzakh and Punishment therein

(and in front of them is Barzakh until the Day when they will be resurrected.) Abu Salih and others said that:

(and in front of them) means before them. Mujahid said, Al-Barzakh is a barrier between this world and the Hereafter. Muhammad bin Ka`b said, "Al-Barzakh is what is between this world and the Hereafter, neither they are the people of this world, eating and drinking, nor are they with the people of the Hereafter, being rewarded or punished for their deeds." Abu Sakhr said, "Al-Barzakh refers to the graves. They are neither in this world nor the Hereafter, and they will stay there until the Day of Resurrection."

(and in front of them is Barzakh). In these words is a threat to those wrongdoers at the time of death, of the punishment of Barzakh. This is similar to the Ayat:

(In front of them there is Hell) (45:10).

(and in front of him will be a great torment) (14: 17).

(until the Day when they will be resurrected). means, he will be punished continually until the Day of Resurrection, as it says in the Hadith:

《فَلَا يَزَالُ مُعَذَّبًا فِيهَا》

(He will continue to be punished in it.) meaning, in the earth.

Surah: 23 Ayah: 101, Ayah: 102, Ayah: 103 & Ayah: 104

فَإِذَا نُفِخَ فِى ٱلصُّورِ فَلَآ أَنسَابَ بَيْنَهُمْ يَوْمَئِذٍ وَلَا يَتَسَآءَلُونَ

101. Then, when the Trumpet is blown, there will be no kinship among them that Day, nor will they ask of one another.

فَمَن ثَقُلَتْ مَوَٰزِينُهُۥ فَأُوْلَٰٓئِكَ هُمُ ٱلْمُفْلِحُونَ

102. Then, those whose scales (of good deeds) are heavy, they are the successful.

وَمَنْ خَفَّتْ مَوَٰزِينُهُۥ فَأُوْلَٰٓئِكَ ٱلَّذِينَ خَسِرُوٓاْ أَنفُسَهُمْ فِى جَهَنَّمَ خَٰلِدُونَ

103. And those whose scales (of good deeds) are light, they are those who lose their Own selves, in Hell will they abide.

Chapter 23: Al-Mu'minun (The Believers), Verses 001-118

تَلْفَحُ وُجُوهَهُمُ ٱلنَّارُ وَهُمْ فِيهَا كَٰلِحُونَ ۝

104. The Fire will burn their faces, and therein they will grin, with displaced lips (disfigured).

Transliteration

101. Fa-itha nufikha fee alssoori fala ansaba baynahum yawma-ithin wala yatasaaloona 102. Faman thaqulat mawazeenuhu faola-ika humu almuflihoona 103. Waman khaffat mawazeenuhu faola-ika allatheena khasiroo anfusahum fee jahannama khalidoona 104. Talfahu wujoohahumu alnnaru wahum feeha kalihoona

Tafsir Ibn Kathir

The sounding of the Trumpet and the weighing of Deeds in the Scales.

Allah says that when the Trumpet is blown for the Resurrection, and the people rise from their graves,

(there will be no kinship among them that Day, nor will they ask of one another.) meaning that lineage will be of no avail on that Day, and a father will not ask about his son or care about him. Allah says:

(And no friend will ask a friend (about his condition), though they shall be made to see one another) (70:10-11). meaning, no relative will ask about another relative, even if he can see him and even if he is carrying a heavy burden. Even if he was the dearest of people to him in this world, he will not care about him or take even the slightest part of his burden from him. Allah says:

(That Day shall a man flee from his brother. And from his mother and his father. And from his wife and his children.) (80:34-36) Ibn Mas`ud said, "On the Day of Resurrection, Allah will gather the first and the last, then a voice will call out, `Whoever is owed something by another, let him come forth and take it.' And a man will rejoice if he is owed something or had been mistreated by his father or child or wife, even if it is little. '' This is confirmed in the Book of Allah, where Allah says:

(Then, when the Trumpet is blown, there will be no kinship among them that Day, nor will they ask of one another.) This was recorded by Ibn Abi Hatim.

(Then, those whose Scales are heavy, these! they are the successful.) means, the one whose good deeds outweigh his bad deeds, even by one. This was the view of Ibn `Abbas.

(they are the successful.) means, those who have attained victory and been saved from Hell and admitted to Paradise. Ibn `Abbas said, "These are the ones who have attained what they wanted and been saved from an evil from which there is no escape.''

(And those whose Scales are light,) means, their evil deeds outweigh their good deeds.

(they are those who lose themselves,) means, they are doomed and have ended up with the worst deal. Allah says:

(in Hell will they abide.) meaning, they will stay there forever and will never leave.

(The Fire will burn their faces,) This is like the Ayah:

(and fire will cover their faces) (14:50). and:

(If only those who disbelieved knew (the time) when they will not be able to ward off the Fire from their faces, nor from their backs) (21:39).

(and therein they will grin, with displaced lips.) `Ali bin Abi Talhah narrated from Ibn `Abbas, "Frowning."

Surah: 23 Ayah: 105, Ayah: 106 & Ayah: 107

أَلَمْ تَكُنْ ءَايَـٰتِى تُتْلَىٰ عَلَيْكُمْ فَكُنتُم بِهَا تُكَذِّبُونَ ﴿١٠٥﴾

105. "Were not My Verses (this Qur'ân) recited to you, and then you used to deny them?"

قَالُوا۟ رَبَّنَا غَلَبَتْ عَلَيْنَا شِقْوَتُنَا وَكُنَّا قَوْمًا ضَآلِّينَ ﴿١٠٦﴾

106. They will say: "Our Lord! Our wretchedness overcame us, and we were (an) erring people.

رَبَّنَآ أَخْرِجْنَا مِنْهَا فَإِنْ عُدْنَا فَإِنَّا ظَـٰلِمُونَ ﴿١٠٧﴾

107. "Our Lord! Bring us out of this. If ever we return (to evil), then indeed we shall be Zâlimûn: (polytheists, oppressors, unjust, and wrong-doers)."

Transliteration

105. Alam takun ayatee tutla AAalaykum fakuntum biha tukaththiboona 106. Qaloo rabbana ghalabat AAalayna shiqwatuna wakunna qawman dalleena 107. Rabbana akhrijna minha fa-in AAudna fa-inna thalimoona

Tafsir Ibn Kathir

Rebuking the People of Hell, their admission of Their Wretchedness and their Request to be brought out of Hell

This is a rebuke from Allah to the people of Hell for the disbelief, sins, unlawful deeds and evil actions that they committed, because of which they were doomed. Allah says:

Chapter 23: Al-Mu'minun (The Believers), Verses 001-118

("Were not My Ayat recited to you, and then you used to deny them") meaning, `I sent Messengers to you, and revealed Books, and cleared the confusion for you, so you have no excuse.' This is like the Ayat:

(in order that mankind should have no plea against Allah after the Messengers) (4:165)

(And We never punish until We have sent a Messenger) (17:15).

(Every time a group is cast therein, its keeper will ask: "Did no warner come to you") Until His saying;

(So, away with the dwellers of the blazing Fire!) They will say:

(Our Lord! Our wretchedness overcame us, and we were (an) erring people.) meaning, evidence has been established against us, but we were so doomed that we could not follow it, so we went astray and were not guided. Then they will say:

(Our Lord! Bring us out of this. If ever we return (to evil), then indeed we shall be wrongdoers.) meaning, send us back to the world, and if we go back to what we used to do before, then we will indeed be wrongdoers who deserve punishment. This is like the Ayat:

(Now we confess our sins, then is there any way to get out) Until His statement:

(So the judgment is only with Allah, the Most High, the Most Great!") (40:11-12) meaning, there will be no way out, because you used to associate partners in worship with Allah whereas the believers worshipped Him Alone.

Surah: 23 Ayah: 108, Ayah: 109, Ayah: 110 & Ayah: 111

قَالَ ٱخْسَـُٔوا۟ فِيهَا وَلَا تُكَلِّمُونِ ۝

108. He (Allâh) will say: "Remain you in it with ignominy! And speak you not to Me!"

إِنَّهُۥ كَانَ فَرِيقٌ مِّنْ عِبَادِى يَقُولُونَ رَبَّنَآ ءَامَنَّا فَٱغْفِرْ لَنَا وَٱرْحَمْنَا وَأَنتَ خَيْرُ ٱلرَّٰحِمِينَ ۝

109. Verily! There was a party of My slaves, who used to say: "Our Lord! We believe, so forgive us, and have mercy on us, for You are the Best of all who show mercy!"

فَٱتَّخَذْتُمُوهُمْ سِخْرِيًّا حَتَّىٰٓ أَنسَوْكُمْ ذِكْرِى وَكُنتُم مِّنْهُمْ تَضْحَكُونَ ۝

110. But you took them for a laughingstock, so much so that they made you forget My Remembrance while you used to laugh at them!

$$\text{إِنِّى جَزَيْتُهُمُ ٱلْيَوْمَ بِمَا صَبَرُوٓاْ أَنَّهُمْ هُمُ ٱلْفَآئِزُونَ ﴿١١١﴾}$$

111. Verily! I have rewarded them this Day for their patience: they are indeed the ones that are successful.

Transliteration

108. Qala ikhsaoo feeha wala tukallimooni 109. Innahu kana fareequn min AAibadee yaqooloona rabbana amanna faighfir lana wairhamna waanta khayru alrrahimeena 110. Faittakhathtumoohum sikhriyyan hatta ansawkum thikree wakuntum minhum tadhakoona 111. Innee jazaytuhumu alyawma bima sabaroo annahum humu alfaizoona

Tafsir Ibn Kathir

Allah's Response and Rejection of the Disbelievers

This is the response of Allah to the disbelievers when they ask Him to bring them out of the Fire and send them back to this world. He will say:

(Remain you in it with ignominy!) meaning, abide therein, humiliated, despised and scorned.

(And speak you not to Me!) means, `do not ask for this again, for I will not respond to you. Al-`Awfi reported from Ibn `Abbas concerning this Ayah,

(Remain you in it with ignominy! And speak you not to Me!) "These are the words of Ar-Rahman when silencing them." Ibn Abi Hatim recorded that `Abdullah bin `Amr said, "The people of Hell will call on Malik for forty years, and he will not answer them. Then he will respond and tell them that they are to abide therein. By Allah, their cries will mean nothing to Malik or to the Lord of Malik. Then they will call on their Lord and will say,

(Our Lord! Our wretchedness overcame us, and we were (an) erring people. Our Lord! Bring us out of this. If ever we return (to evil), then indeed we shall be wrongdoers.) (23:106-107) Allah will not answer them for a time span equivalent to twice the duration of this world. Then He will reply:

(Remain you in it with ignominy! And speak you not to Me!) By Allah, the people will not utter a single word after that, and they will merely be in the Fire of Hell, sighing in a high and low tone. Their voices are likened to those of donkeys, which start in a high tone and end in a low tone." Then Allah will remind them of their sins in this world and how they used to make fun of His believing servants and close friends:

(Verily, there was a party of My servants who used to say: "Our Lord! We believe, so forgive us and have mercy on us, for You are the Best of all who show mercy!" But you took them for a laughing stock,) meaning, `you made fun of them for calling on Me and praying to Me,' (so much so that they made you forget My remembrance) means, your hatred for them made you forget what I would do to you.

(while you used to laugh at them!) means, at their deeds and worship. This is like the Ayah:

(Verily, those who committed crimes used to laugh at those who believed. And, whenever they passed by them, used to wink one to another.) (83:29-30) meaning, they used to slander them in mockery. Then Allah tells us how He will reward His friends and righteous servants, and says:

(Verily, I have rewarded them this Day for their patience;) meaning, `for the harm and mockery that you inflicted on them,

(they are indeed the ones that are successful.) I have caused them to attain the victory of joy, safety, Paradise and salvation from the Fire.'

Surah: 23 Ayah: 112, Ayah: 113, Ayah: 114, Ayah: 115 & Ayah: 116

قَـٰلَ كَمْ لَبِثْتُمْ فِى ٱلْأَرْضِ عَدَدَ سِنِينَ ۝

112. He (Allâh) will say: "What number of years did you stay on earth?"

قَالُوا۟ لَبِثْنَا يَوْمًا أَوْ بَعْضَ يَوْمٍ فَسْـَٔلِ ٱلْعَآدِّينَ ۝

113. They will say: "We stayed a day or part of a day. Ask of those who keep account."

قَـٰلَ إِن لَّبِثْتُمْ إِلَّا قَلِيلًا ۖ لَّوْ أَنَّكُمْ كُنتُمْ تَعْلَمُونَ ۝

114. He (Allâh) will say: "You stayed not but a little, if you had only known!

أَفَحَسِبْتُمْ أَنَّمَا خَلَقْنَـٰكُمْ عَبَثًا وَأَنَّكُمْ إِلَيْنَا لَا تُرْجَعُونَ ۝

115. "Did you think that We had created you in play (without any purpose), and that you would not be brought back to Us?"

فَتَعَـٰلَى ٱللَّهُ ٱلْمَلِكُ ٱلْحَقُّ ۖ لَآ إِلَـٰهَ إِلَّا هُوَ رَبُّ ٱلْعَرْشِ ٱلْكَرِيمِ ۝

116. So Exalted is Allâh, the True King: Lâ ilâha illa Huwa (none has the right to be worshipped but He), the Lord of the Supreme Throne!

Transliteration

112. Qala kam labithtum fee al-ardi AAadada sineena 113. Qaloo labithna yawman aw baAAda yawmin fais-ali alAAaddeena 114. Qala in labithtum illa qaleelan law annakum kuntum taAAlamoona 115. Afahasibtum annama khalaqnakum AAabathan waannakum ilayna la turjaAAoona 116. FataAAala Allahu almaliku alhaqqu la ilaha illa huwa rabbu alAAarshi alkareemi

Tafsir Ibn Kathir

Allah tells them how much they wasted in their short lives in this world by failing to obey Allah and worship Him Alone.

If they had been patient during their short stay in this world, they would have attained victory just like His pious close friends.

(He will say: "What number of years did you stay on earth") means, how long did you stay in this world

(They will say: "We stayed a day or part of a day. Ask of those who keep account.") meaning, those who keep the records.

(He will say: "You stayed not but a little...") meaning, it was only a short time, no matter how you look at it.

(if you had only known!) means, you would not have preferred the transient to the eternal, and treated yourself in this bad way, and earned the wrath of Allah in this short period. If you had patiently obeyed Allah and worshipped Him as the believers did, you would have attained victory just as they did.

Allah did not create His Servants in vain

(Did you think that We had created you in play,) means, `did you think that you were created in vain, with no purpose, with nothing required of you and no wisdom on Our part' Or it was said that "in play" meant to play and amuse yourselves, like the animals were created, who have no reward or punishment. But you were created to worship Allah and carry out His commands.

(and that you would not be brought back to Us) means, that you would not be brought back to the Hereafter. This is like the Ayah:

(Does man think that he will be left neglected) (75:36)

(So Exalted be Allah, the True King.) means, sanctified be He above the idea that he should create anything in vain, for He is the True King Who is far above doing such a thing.

(None has the right to be worshipped but He, the Lord of Al-`Arsh Al-Karim!) The Throne is mentioned because it is the highest point of all creation, and it is described as Karim, meaning beautiful in appearance and splendid in form, as Allah says elsewhere:

(every good kind We cause to grow therein) (26:7).

Surah: 23 Ayah: 117 & Ayah: 118

$$\text{وَمَن يَدْعُ مَعَ ٱللَّهِ إِلَٰهًا ءَاخَرَ لَا بُرْهَٰنَ لَهُۥ بِهِۦ فَإِنَّمَا حِسَابُهُۥ عِندَ رَبِّهِۦٓ ۚ إِنَّهُۥ لَا يُفْلِحُ ٱلْكَٰفِرُونَ ۝}$$

117. And whoever invokes (or worships), besides Allâh, any other ilâh (god), of whom he has no proof; then his reckoning is only with his Lord. Surely! Al-Kâfirûn (the disbelievers in Allâh and in the Oneness of Allâh, polytheists, pagans, idolaters) will not be successful.

$$\text{وَقُل رَّبِّ ٱغْفِرْ وَٱرْحَمْ وَأَنتَ خَيْرُ ٱلرَّٰحِمِينَ ۝}$$

118. And say (O Muhammad (peace be upon him)) "My Lord! Forgive and have mercy, for You are the Best of those who show mercy!"

Transliteration

117. Waman yadAAu maAAa Allahi ilahan akhara la burhana lahu bihi fa-innama hisabuhu AAinda rabbihi innahu la yuflihu alkafiroona   118. Waqul rabbi ighfir wairham waanta khayru alrrahimeena

Tafsir Ibn Kathir

Shirk is the Worst form of Wrong, its Practitioner shall never succeed.

Allah threatens those who associate anything else with Him and worship anything with Him. He informs that those who associate others with Allah:

(of whom he has no proof), meaning no evidence for what he says. Then Allah says:

(And whoever invokes, besides Allah, any other god, of whom he has no proof;) this is a conditional sentence, whose fulfilling clause is:

(then his reckoning is only with his Lord.) meaning, Allah will call him to account for that. Then Allah tells us:

(Surely, disbelievers will not be successful.) meaning, they will not be successful with Him on the Day of Resurrection; they will not prosper or be saved.

(And say: "My Lord! Forgive and have mercy, for You are the best of those who show mercy!") Here Allah is teaching us to recite this supplication, for forgiveness, in a general sense, means wiping away sins and concealing them from people, and mercy means guiding a person and helping him to say and do good things.

CHAPTER (SURAH) 24: AN-NOOR (THE LIGHT), VERSES 001–064

$$\text{(بِسْمِ اللَّهِ الرَّحْمَٰنِ الرَّحِيمِ)}$$

In the Name of Allah, the Most Gracious, the Most Merciful

Surah: 24 Ayah: 1 & Ayah: 2

سُورَةٌ أَنزَلْنَٰهَا وَفَرَضْنَٰهَا وَأَنزَلْنَا فِيهَآ ءَايَٰتٍۭ بَيِّنَٰتٍ لَّعَلَّكُمْ تَذَكَّرُونَ ۝

1. (This is) a Sûrah (chapter of the Qur'ân) which We have sent down and which We have enjoined, (ordained its laws); and in it We have revealed manifest Ayât (proofs, evidences, verses, lessons, signs, revelations -lawful and unlawful things, and set boundaries of Islâmic Religion), that you may remember.

ٱلزَّانِيَةُ وَٱلزَّانِى فَٱجْلِدُوا۟ كُلَّ وَٰحِدٍ مِّنْهُمَا مِا۟ئَةَ جَلْدَةٍ ۖ وَلَا تَأْخُذْكُم بِهِمَا رَأْفَةٌ فِى دِينِ ٱللَّهِ إِن كُنتُمْ تُؤْمِنُونَ بِٱللَّهِ وَٱلْيَوْمِ ٱلْءَاخِرِ ۖ وَلْيَشْهَدْ عَذَابَهُمَا طَآئِفَةٌ مِّنَ ٱلْمُؤْمِنِينَ ۝

2. The woman and the man guilty of illegal sexual intercourse, flog each of them with a hundred stripes. Let not pity withhold you in their case, in a punishment prescribed by Allâh, if you believe in Allâh and the Last Day. And let a party of the believers witness their punishment. (This punishment is for unmarried persons guilty of the above crime, but if married persons commit it, the punishment is to stone them to death, according to Allâh's Law).

Transliteration

1. Sooratun anzalnaha wafaradnaha waanzalna feeha ayatin bayyinatin laAAallakum tathakkaroona 2. Alzzaniyatu waalzzanee faijlidoo kulla wahidin minhuma mi-ata jaldatin wala ta/khuthkum bihima ra/fatun fee deeni Allahi in kuntum tu/minoona biAllahi waalyawmi al-akhiri walyashhad AAathabahuma ta-ifatun mina almu/mineena

Tafsir Ibn Kathir

The Importance of Surat An-Nur

(A Surah which We have sent down) Here Allah is pointing out the high esteem in which He holds this Surah, which is not to say that other Surahs are not important.

(and which We have enjoined,) Mujahid and Qatadah said, "This means: We have explained what is lawful and unlawful, commands and prohibitions, and the prescribed punishments." Al-Bukhari said, "Those who read it: Faradnaha, say that it means: "We have enjoined them upon you and those who come after you."

(and in it We have revealed manifest Ayat,) means, clearly explained,

(that you may remember.)

Chapter 24: An-Noor (The Light), Verses 001-064

The Explanation of the Prescribed Punishment for Zina (Illicit Sex)

Then Allah says:

(The Zaniyah and the Zani, flog each of them with a hundred stripes.) This honorable Ayah contains the ruling on the law of retaliation for the person who commits illegal sex, and details of the punishment. Such a person will either be unmarried, meaning that he has never been married, or he will be married, meaning that he has had intercourse within the bounds of a lawful marriage, and he is free, adult and of sound mind. As for the virgin who is unwedded, the prescribed punishment is one hundred stripes, as stated in this Ayah. In addition to this he is to be banished from his homeland for one year, as was recorded in the Two Sahihs from Abu Hurayrah and Zayd bin Khalid Al-Juhani in the Hadith about the two bedouins who came to the Messenger of Allah . One of them said, "O Messenger of Allah, this son of mine was employed by this man, and committed Zina with his wife. I paid a ransom with him on behalf of my son one hundred sheep and a slave-girl, but when I asked the people of knowledge, they said that my son should be given one hundred stripes and banished for a year, and that this man's wife should be stoned to death." The Messenger of Allah said:

«وَالَّذِي نَفْسِي بِيَدِهِ لَأَقْضِيَنَّ بَيْنَكُمَا بِكِتَابِ اللهِ تَعَالَى، الْوَلِيدَةُ وَالْغَنَمُ رَدٌّ عَلَيْكَ، وَعَلَى ابْنِكَ جَلْدُ مِائَةٍ وَتَغْرِيبُ عَامٍ، وَاغْدُ يَا أُنَيْسُ لِرَجُلٍ مِنْ أَسْلَمَ إِلَى امْرَأَةِ هذَا، فَإِنِ اعْتَرَفَتْ فَارْجُمْهَا»

(By the One in Whose Hand is my soul, I will judge between you both according to the Book of Allah. Take back the slave-girl and sheep, and your son is to be given one hundred stripes and banished for one year. O Unays -- he said to a man from the tribe of Aslam -- go to this man's wife, and if she confesses, then stone her to death.) Unays went to her and she confessed, so he stoned her to death. This indicates that if the person who is guilty of illegal sex is a virgin and unmarried, he should be banished in addition to being given one hundred stripes. But if married, meaning he has had intercourse within the bounds of lawful marriage, and he is free, adult and of sound mind, then he should be stoned to death. Imam Malik recorded that `Umar, may Allah be pleased with him, stood up and praised and glorified Allah, then he said; "O people! Allah sent Muhammad with the truth, and revealed to him the Book. One of the things that was revealed to him was the Ayah of stoning to death, which we have recited and understood. The Messenger of Allah carried out the punishment of stoning and after him we did so, but I am afraid that as time goes by, some will say that they did not find the Ayah of stoning in the Book of Allah, and they will go astray because they abandoned one of the obligations revealed by Allah. Stoning is something that is prescribed in the Book of Allah for the person -- man or woman -- who commits illegal sex, if he or she is married, if decisive evidence is produced, or if pregnancy results from that, or if they confess to it." It was also recorded in the Two Sahihs in the lengthy Hadith of Malik, from which we have quoted briefly only the portion that is relevant to the current discussion.

Do not feel pity for Them when carrying out the Prescribed Punishment

(Let not pity withhold you in their case, in a punishment prescribed by Allah,) Meaning, with a ruling prescribed by Allah. So the meaning of the Ayah is: "Do not feel too sorry for them where the laws of Allah are established." This does not mean that we should not naturally feel pity when carrying out the punishment. What is prohibited here is the kind of pity that may make the judge ignore the punishment altogether. This is what is not permitted for the judge. Mujahid said,

(Let not pity withhold you in their case, in a punishment prescribed by Allah,) "If the matter is taken to the ruling authority, the punishment has to be carried out and cannot be stopped." This was also narrated from Sa`id bin Jubayr and `Ata' bin Abi Rabah. It was recorded in a Hadith:

«تَعَافَوُا الْحُدُودَ فِيمَا بَيْنَكُمْ، فَمَا بَلَغَنِي مِنْ حَدَ فَقَدْ وَجَبَ»

(Compromise with the matter of prescribed punishment mutually sorting it out among yourselves, for once a matter where the prescribed punishment is required reaches me, I am obliged to carry it out.) Allah's saying:

(if you believe in Allah and the Last Day.) means, then do that, carry out the punishments on those who commit illegal sex, and strike them hard without causing any wound, so that he and others like him will be deterred by the terror of that. In Al-Musnad, it was recorded that one of the Companions said, "O Messenger of Allah, when I slaughter a sheep I feel pity for it." He said,

«وَلَكَ فِي ذَلِكَ أَجْرٌ»

(You be rewarded for that.)

Carry out the Prescribed Punishment in Public

(And let a party of the believers witness their punishment.) This is more humiliating for the people who are guilty of illegal sex, if they are flogged in front of the people. This is because it is more effective as a deterrent and it conveys the sense of scandal and rebuke. Al-Hasan Al-Basri said,

(And let a party of the believers witness their punishment.) "Publicly."

Chapter 24: An-Noor (The Light), Verses 001-064

Surah: 24 Ayah: 3

ٱلزَّانِى لَا يَنكِحُ إِلَّا زَانِيَةً أَوۡ مُشۡرِكَةً وَٱلزَّانِيَةُ لَا يَنكِحُهَآ إِلَّا زَانٍ أَوۡ مُشۡرِكٌ ۚ وَحُرِّمَ ذَٰلِكَ عَلَى ٱلۡمُؤۡمِنِينَ ۝

3. The adulterer marries not but an adulteress or a Mushrikah and the adulteress none marries her except an adulterer or a Muskrik (and that means that the man who agrees to marry (have a sexual relation with) a Mushrikah (female polytheist, pagan or idolatress) or a prostitute, then surely he is either an adulterer, or a Mushrik (polytheist, pagan or idolater). And the woman who agrees to marry (have a sexual relation with) a Mushrik (polytheist, pagan or idolater) or an adulterer, then she is either a prostitute or a Mushrikah (female polytheist, pagan, or idolatress)) Such a thing is forbidden to the believers (of Islâmic Monotheism).

Transliteration

3. Alzzanee la yankihu illa zaniyatan aw mushrikatan waalzzaniyatu la yankihuha illa zanin aw mushrikun wahurrima thalika AAala almu/mineena

Tafsir Ibn Kathir

Here Allah tells us that the Zani (male who is guilty of illegal sex) does not have intercourse except with a Zaniyah (female who is guilty of illegal sex) or a Mushrikah (female idolator), meaning that no one would go along with him in this action except a sinful woman who is also guilty of Zina, or a Mushrikah who does not think it is unlawful. By the same token,

(and the Zaniyah, none marries her except a Zani) a sinful man who is guilty of fornication,

(or a Mushrik) (a man) who does not think it is unlawful.

(Such a thing is forbidden to the believers.) meaning, indulging in this, or marrying prostitutes, or marrying chaste women to immoral men. Qatadah and Muqatil bin Hayyan said: "Allah forbade the believers from marrying prostitutes." This Ayah is like the Ayah (about marrying slave-girls):

(they should be chaste, not committing illegal sex, nor taking boyfriends.) (4:25) And His saying:

(desiring chastity not committing illegal sexual intercourse, nor taking them as girlfriends) (5:5). Imam Ahmad recorded that `Abdullah bin `Amr, may Allah be pleased with him, said that a man among the believers asked the Messenger of Allah for permission (to marry) a woman known as Umm Mahzul, who used to commit adultery, and who had stated the condition that she should spend on him. So he asked the Messenger of Allah for permission, or he mentioned the matter to him. The Messenger of Allah recited to him:

(The Zani marries not but a Zaniyah or a Mushrikah; and the Zaniyah, none marries her except Zani or a Mushrik. Such a thing is forbidden to the believers.) (24:3) Ibn Abi Hatim recorded that Abu Hurayrah said,

«لَا يَنْكِحُ الزَّانِي الْمَجْلُودُ إِلَّا مِثْلَهُ»

(A Zani who has been flogged should not marry anyone except someone who is like him.) A similar report was recorded by Abu Dawud in his Sunan.

Surah: 24 Ayah: 4 & Ayah: 5

وَٱلَّذِينَ يَرْمُونَ ٱلْمُحْصَنَٰتِ ثُمَّ لَمْ يَأْتُوا بِأَرْبَعَةِ شُهَدَآءَ فَٱجْلِدُوهُمْ ثَمَٰنِينَ جَلْدَةً وَلَا تَقْبَلُوا لَهُمْ شَهَٰدَةً أَبَدًا ۚ وَأُوْلَٰٓئِكَ هُمُ ٱلْفَٰسِقُونَ ۝

4. And those who accuse chaste women, and produce not four witnesses, flog them with eighty stripes, and reject their testimony forever. They indeed are the Fâsiqûn (liars, rebellious, disobedient to Allâh).

إِلَّا ٱلَّذِينَ تَابُوا مِنۢ بَعْدِ ذَٰلِكَ وَأَصْلَحُوا فَإِنَّ ٱللَّهَ غَفُورٌ رَّحِيمٌ ۝

5. Except those who repent thereafter and do righteous deeds, (for such) verily, Allâh is Oft-Forgiving, Most Merciful.

Transliteration

4. Waallatheena yarmoona almuhsanati thumma lam ya/too bi-arbaAAati shuhadaa faijlidoohum thamaneena jaldatan wala taqbaloo lahum shahadatan abadan waola-ika humu alfasiqoona   5. Illa allatheena taboo min baAAdi thalika waaslahoo fa-inna Allaha ghafoorun raheemun

Tafsir Ibn Kathir

The Prescribed Punishment for slandering Chaste Women

This Ayah states the prescribed punishment for making false accusations against chaste women, i.e., those who are free, adult and chaste. If the person who is falsely accused is a man, the same punishment of flogging also applies. If the accuser produces evidence that what he is saying is true, then the punishment does not apply. Allah said:

(and produce not four witnesses, flog them with eighty stripes, and reject their testimony forever. They indeed are the rebellious.) If the accuser cannot prove that what he is saying is true, then three rulings apply to him: (firstly) that he should be flogged with eighty stripes, (secondly) that his testimony should be rejected forever, and (thirdly) that he should be labelled as a rebellious who is not of good character, whether in the sight of Allah or of mankind.

Explaining the Repentance of the One Who makes a False Accusation

Then Allah says:

(Except those who repent thereafter and do righteous deeds; (for such) verily, Allah is Oft-Forgiving, Most Merciful.) This exception refers to the second and third rulings mentioned above. The flogging has been carried out regardless of whether he repents or persists, and after that there is no further punishment, as is agreed among the scholars. If he repents, then his testimony may be accepted, and he is no longer to be regarded as a rebellious. This was the view of Sa`id bin Al-Musayyib -- the leader of the Tabi`in -- and also a group among the Salaf. Ash-Sha`bi and Ad-Dahhak said, "His testimony cannot be accepted even if he does repent, unless he himself admits that he said something false, in which case his testimony may be accepted." And Allah knows best.

Surah: 24 Ayah: 6, Ayah: 7, Ayah: 9, Ayah: 9 & Ayah: 10

وَٱلَّذِينَ يَرْمُونَ أَزْوَٰجَهُمْ وَلَمْ يَكُن لَّهُمْ شُهَدَآءُ إِلَّآ أَنفُسُهُمْ فَشَهَٰدَةُ أَحَدِهِمْ أَرْبَعُ شَهَٰدَٰتٍۭ بِٱللَّهِ ۙ إِنَّهُۥ لَمِنَ ٱلصَّٰدِقِينَ ۝

6. And for those who accuse their wives, but have no witnesses except themselves, let the testimony of one of them be four testimonies (i.e. testifies four times) by Allâh that he is one of those who speak the truth.

وَٱلْخَٰمِسَةُ أَنَّ لَعْنَتَ ٱللَّهِ عَلَيْهِ إِن كَانَ مِنَ ٱلْكَٰذِبِينَ ۝

7. And the fifth (testimony) (should be) the invoking of the Curse of Allâh on him if he be of those who tell a lie (against her).

وَيَدْرَؤُاْ عَنْهَا ٱلْعَذَابَ أَن تَشْهَدَ أَرْبَعَ شَهَٰدَٰتٍۭ بِٱللَّهِ ۙ إِنَّهُۥ لَمِنَ ٱلْكَٰذِبِينَ ۝

8. But it shall avert the punishment (of stoning to death) from her, if she bears witness four times by Allâh, that he (her husband) is telling a lie.

وَٱلْخَٰمِسَةَ أَنَّ غَضَبَ ٱللَّهِ عَلَيْهَآ إِن كَانَ مِنَ ٱلصَّٰدِقِينَ ۝

9. And the fifth (testimony) should be that the Wrath of Allâh be upon her if he (her husband) speaks the truth.

وَلَوْلَا فَضْلُ ٱللَّهِ عَلَيْكُمْ وَرَحْمَتُهُۥ وَأَنَّ ٱللَّهَ تَوَّابٌ حَكِيمٌ ۝

10. And had it not been for the Grace of Allâh and His Mercy on you (He would have hastened the punishment upon you)! And that Allâh is the One Who forgives and accepts repentance, the All-Wise.

Transliteration

6. Waallatheena yarmoona azwajahum walam yakun lahum shuhadao illa anfusuhum fashahadatu ahadihim arbaAAu shahadatin biAllahi innahu lamina alssadiqeena 7. Waalkhamisatu anna laAAnata Allahi AAalayhi in kana mina alkathibeena 8. Wayadrao AAanha alAAathaba an tashhada arbaAAa shahadatin biAllahi innahu lamina alkathibeena 9. Waalkhamisata anna ghadaba Allahi AAalayha in kana mina alssadiqeena 10. Walawla fadlu Allahi AAalaykum warahmatuhu waanna Allaha tawwabun hakeemun

Tafsir Ibn Kathir

Details of Al-Li`an

This Ayah offers a way out for husbands. If a husband has accused his wife but cannot come up with proof, he can swear the Li`an (the oath of condemnation) as Allah commanded. This means that he brings her before the Imam and states what he is accusing her of. The ruler then asks him to swear four times by Allah in front of four witnesses

(that he is one of those who speak the truth) in his accusation of her adultery.

(And the fifth; the invoking of the curse of Allah on him if he be of those who tell a lie.) If he says that, then she is divorced from him by the very act of this Li`an; she is forever forbidden for him and he must give her Mahr to her. The punishment for Zina should be carried out on her, and nothing can prevent the punishment except if she also swears the oath of condemnation (Li`an) and swears by Allah four times that he is one of those who lied, i.e., in what he is accusing her of;

(And the fifth; should be that the crath of Allah be upon her if he speaks the truth.) Allah says:

(But she shall avert the punishment) meaning, the prescribed punishment.

(if she bears witness four times by Allah, that he is telling a lie. And the fifth; should be that the wrath of Allah be upon her if he speaks the truth.) The wrath of Allah is mentioned specially in the case of the woman, because usually a man would not go to the extent of exposing his wife and accusing her of Zina unless he is telling the truth and has good reason to do this, and she knows that what he is accusing her of is true. So in her case the fifth testimony calls for the wrath of Allah to be upon her, for the one upon whom is the wrath of Allah, is the one who knows the truth yet deviates from it. Then Allah mentions His grace and kindness to His creation in that He has prescribed for them a way out of their difficulties. Allah says:

(And had it not been for the grace of Allah and His mercy on you!) meaning, many of your affairs would have been too difficult for you,

(And that Allah is the One Who forgives and accepts repentance,) means, from His servants, even if that comes after they have sworn a confirmed oath.

(the All-Wise.) in what He prescribes and commands and forbids. There are Hadiths which explain how we are to put this Ayah into effect, why it was revealed and concerning whom among the Companions it was revealed.

The Reason why the Ayah of Li`an was revealed

Imam Ahmad recorded that Ibn `Abbas said: "When the Ayah

(And those who accuse chaste women, and produce not four witnesses, flog them with eighty stripes, and reject their testimony forever) (24:4) was revealed, Sa`d bin `Ubadah, may Allah be pleased with him, -- the leader of the Ansar -- said, `Is this how it was revealed, O Messenger of Allah' The Messenger of Allah said:

«يَا مَعْشَرَ الْأَنْصَارِ أَلَا تَسْمَعُونَ مَا يَقُولُ سَيِّدُكُمْ؟»

(O Ansar, did you hear what your leader said) They said, `O Messenger of Allah, do not blame him, for he is a jealous man. By Allah, he never married a woman who was not a virgin, and he never divorced a woman but none of us would dare to marry her because he is so jealous.' Sa`d said, `By Allah, O Messenger of Allah, I know that it (the Ayah) is true and is from Allah, but I am surprised. If I found some wicked man lying down with my wife, should I not disturb him until I have brought four witnesses By Allah, he would have finished what he was doing before I could bring them!' A little while later, Hilal bin Umayyah -- one of the three whose repentance had been accepted -- came back from his lands at night and found a man with his wife. He saw with his own eyes and heard with his own ears, but he did not disturb him until the morning. In the morning he went to the Messenger of Allah and said, `O Messenger of Allah, I came to my wife at night and found a man with her, and I saw with my own eyes and heard with my own ears.' The Messenger of Allah did not like what he had said and got very upset. The Ansar gathered around him and said, `We were being tested by what Sa`d bin Ubadah said, and now the Messenger of Allah will punish Hilal bin Umayyah and declare his testimony before people to be unacceptable.' Hilal said: `By Allah, I hope that Allah will make for me a way out from this problem.' Hilal said, `O Messenger of Allah, I see how upset you are by what I have said, but Allah knows that I am telling the truth.' By Allah, the Messenger of Allah wanted to have him flogged, but then Allah sent revelation to His Messenger . When the revelation came upon him, they knew about it from the change in his face, so they would leave him alone until the revelation was finished. Allah revealed the Ayah:

(And for those who accuse their wives, but have no witnesses except themselves, let the testimony of one of them be four testimonies by Allah...,) Then the revelation was finished and the Messenger of Allah said,

«أَبْشِرْ يَا هِلَالُ فَقَدْ جَعَلَ اللهُ لَكَ فَرَجًا وَمَخْرَجًا»

(Rejoice, O Hilal, for Allah has made a way out for you.) Hilal said, `I had been hoping for this from my Lord, may He be glorified.' The Messenger of Allah said:

«أَرْسِلُوا إِلَيْهَا»

(Send for her.) So they sent for her and she came. The Messenger of Allah recited this Ayah to them both, and reminded them that the punishment of the Hereafter is more severe than the punishment in this world. Hilal said, `By Allah, O Messenger of Allah, I have spoken the truth about her.' She said, `He is lying.' The Messenger of Allah said,

«لَاعِنُوا بَيْنَهُمَا»

(Make them both swear the Li`an.) So Hilal was told, `Testify.' So he testified four times by Allah that he was one of those who speak the truth. When he came to the fifth testimony, he was told, `O Hilal, have Taqwa of Allah, for the punishment of this world is easier than the punishment of the Hereafter, and this will mean that the punishment will be inevitable for you.' He said, `By Allah, Allah will not punish me for it, just as He has not caused me to be flogged for it.' So he testified for the fifth time that the curse of Allah would be upon him if he was telling a lie. Then it was said to his wife, `Testify four times by Allah that he is telling a lie.' And when his wife reached the fifth testimony, she was told, `Have Taqwa of Allah, for the punishment of this world is easier than the punishment of the Hereafter, and this will mean that the punishment will be inevitable for you.' She hesitated for a while, and was about to admit her guilt, then she said: `By Allah, I will not expose my people to shame, and she swore the fifth oath that the wrath of Allah would be upon her if he was telling the truth.' Then the Messenger of Allah separated them, and decreed that her child should not be attributed to any father, nor should the child be accused, and whoever accused her or her child, they would be subject to punishment. He also decreed that (Hilal) was not obliged to house her or feed her, because they had not been separated by divorce, nor had he died and left her a widow. He said,

«إِنْ جَاءَتْ بِهِ أُصَيْهِبَ (أُرَيْسِحَ) حَمْشَ السَّاقَيْنِ، فَهُوَ لِهِلَالٍ، وَإِنْ جَاءَتْ بِهِ أَوْرَقَ جَعْدًا جُمَالِيًّا خَدَلَّجَ السَّاقَيْنِ سَابِغَ الْأَلْيَتَيْنِ، فَهُوَ لِلَّذِي رُمِيَتْبِهِ»

(If she gives birth to a red-haired child (with skinny thighs) and thin legs, then he is Hilal's child, but if she gives birth to a curly-haired child with thick legs and plump buttocks, then this is what she is accused of.) She subsequently gave birth to a child who was curly-haired with thick legs and plump buttocks, and the Messenger of Allah said,

«لَوْلَا الْأَيْمَانُ لَكَانَ لِي وَلَهَا شَأْنٌ»

(Were it not for the oath that she swore, I would deal with her.)" `Ikrimah said, "The child grew up to become the governor of Egypt, and he was given his mother's name

Chapter 24: An-Noor (The Light), Verses 001-064

and was not attributed to any father." Abu Dawud recorded a similar but briefer report. This Hadith has corroborating reports in the books of Sahih and elsewhere, with many chains of narration, including the report narrated by Al-Bukhari from Ibn `Abbas, that Hilal bin Umayyah accused his wife before the Prophet with Sharik bin Sahma'. The Prophet said,

«الْبَيِّنَةَ أَوْ حَدٌّ فِي ظَهْرِكَ»

(Evidence or the punishment on your back.) He said, "O Messenger of Allah, if any one of us saw a man with his wife, how could he go and get evidence" The Prophet again said,

«الْبَيِّنَةَ وَإِلَّا حَدٌّ فِي ظَهْرِكَ»

(Evidence otherwise the punishment on your back.) Hilal said, "By the One Who sent you with the truth! I am telling the truth and Allah will reveal something that will protect my back from the punishment. " Then Jibril came down and brought the revelation,

(And for those who accuse their wives,) Then he recited until he reached:

(that he is one of those who speak the truth) (24:5). When the revelation had finished, the Prophet sent for them both. Hilal came and gave his testimony, and the Prophet said,

«إِنَّ اللهَ يَعْلَمُ أَنَّ أَحَدَكُمَا كَاذِبٌ، فَهَلْ مِنْكُمَا تَائِبٌ؟»

(Allah knows that one of you is lying. Will one of you repent) Then she stood up and gave her testimony, and when she reached the fifth oath, they stopped her and said, "If you swear the fifth oath and you are lying, the curse of Allah will be inevitable." Ibn `Abbas said, "She hesitated and kept quiet until we thought that she had changed her mind, then she said, `I will not dishonor my people today', and she went ahead. Then the Messenger of Allah said,

«أَبْصِرُوهَا، فَإِنْ جَاءَتْ بِهِ أَكْحَلَ الْعَيْنَيْنِ سَابِغَ الْأَلْيَتَيْنِ خَدَلَّجَ السَّاقَيْنِ، فَهُوَ لِشَرِيكِ ابْنِ سَحْمَاءَ»

(Wait until she gives birth, and if she gives birth to a child whose eyes look as if they are ringed with kohl and who has plump buttocks and thick legs, then he is the child of Sharik bin Sahma'.) She gave birth to a child who matched this description, and the Prophet said,

$$\text{«لَوْلَا مَا مَضَى مِنْ كِتَابِ اللَّهِ لَكَانَ لِي وَ لَهَا شَأْنٌ»}$$

(Were it not for the Book of Allah, I would deal with her.) This version was recorded only by Al-Bukhari, but the event has been narrated with additional chains of narration from Ibn `Abbas and others. Imam Ahmad recorded that Sa`id bin Jubayr said: During the governorship of Ibn Az-Zubayr I was asked about the couple who engage in Li`an, and whether they should be separated, and I did not know the answer. I got up and went to the house of Ibn `Umar, and said, "O Abu `Abdur-Rahman, should the couple who engage in Li`an be separated" He said, "Subhan Allah, the first one to ask about this was so-and-so the son of so-and-so. He said, `O Messenger of Allah, what do you think of a man who sees his wife committing an immoral sin If he speaks he will be speaking about something very serious, and if he keeps quiet he will be keeping quiet about something very serious.' (The Prophet) kept quiet and did not answer him. Later on, he came to him and said, `What I asked you about is something with which I myself being tested with.' Then Allah revealed the Ayat,

(And for those who accuse their wives,) until he reached:

(That the wrath of Allah be upon her if he speaks the truth.) He started to advise the man and remind him about Allah, and told him that the punishment of this world is easier than the punishment of the Hereafter. The man said: `By the One Who sent you with the truth, I was not telling you a lie.' Then the Prophet turned to the woman and advised the woman and reminded her about Allah, and told her that the punishment of this world is easier than the punishment of the Hereafter. The woman said, `By the One Who sent you with the truth, he is lying.' So (the Prophet) started with the man, who swore four times by Allah that he was one of those who speak the truth, and swore the fifth oath that the curse of Allah would be upon him if he were lying. Then he turned to the woman, who swore four times by Allah that he was lying, and swore the fifth oath that the wrath of Allah would be upon her if he was telling the truth. Then he separated them." It was also recorded by An-Nasa'i in his Tafsir, and by Al-Bukhari and Muslim in the Two Sahihs.

Surah: 24 Ayah: 11

$$\text{إِنَّ ٱلَّذِينَ جَآءُو بِٱلْإِفْكِ عُصْبَةٌ مِّنكُمْ ۚ لَا تَحْسَبُوهُ شَرًّا لَّكُم ۖ بَلْ هُوَ خَيْرٌ لَّكُمْ ۚ لِكُلِّ ٱمْرِئٍ مِّنْهُم مَّا ٱكْتَسَبَ مِنَ ٱلْإِثْمِ ۚ وَٱلَّذِى تَوَلَّىٰ كِبْرَهُۥ مِنْهُمْ لَهُۥ عَذَابٌ عَظِيمٌ}$$

11. Verily! Those who brought forth the slander (against 'Aishah (may Allah be pleased with her) the wife of the Prophet (peace be upon him)) are a group among you. Consider it not a bad thing for you. Nay, it is good for you. Unto every man among them will be paid that which he had earned of the sin, and as for him among them who had the greater share therein, his will be a great torment.

Transliteration

11. Inna allatheena jaoo bial-ifki AAusbatun minkum la tahsaboohu sharran lakum bal huwa khayrun lakum likulli imri-in minhum ma iktasaba mina al-ithmi waallathee tawalla kibrahu minhum lahu AAathabun AAatheemun

Tafsir Ibn Kathir

Al-Ifk (the Slander)

The next ten Ayat were all revealed concerning `A'ishah, the mother of the believers, may Allah be pleased with her, when the people of slander and falsehood among the hypocrites made their accusations against her and spread lies about her. Allah became jealous on her behalf and on behalf of His Prophet , and revealed her innocence to protect the honor of the Messenger of Allah . He said:

(Verily, those who brought forth the slander are a group among you.) meaning they were not one or two, but a group. Foremost among this group was `Abdullah bin Ubayy bin Salul, the leader of the hypocrites, who fabricated the lie and whispered it to others, until some of the Muslims started to believe it, and others thought it might be possible and began to talk about it. This is how matters remained for almost a month, until Qur'an was revealed. This is reported in Sahih Hadiths. Imam Ahmad recorded that Az-Zuhri said: Sa`id bin Al-Musayyib, `Urwah bin Az-Zubayr, `Alqamah bin Waqqas and `Ubaydullah bin `Abdullah bin `Utbah bin Mas`ud told me about the story of `A'ishah, the wife of the Prophet , when the people of the slander said what they said about her, and Allah declared her innocence. Each of them told something about the story, and some of them knew more details than others or had memorized more than others. I learned the story from each of them, who had heard it from `A'ishah herself, and what one told me confirmed what the others said. They mentioned that `A'ishah, may Allah be pleased with her, the wife of the Prophet , said: "When the Messenger of Allah wanted to go on a journey, he would cast lots among his wives, and the one whose lot was drawn would go with him." `A'ishah, may Allah be pleased with her, said, "So he drew lots among us with regard to a campaign he was going out on, and mine was drawn, so I went out with the Messenger of Allah . This was after the commandment of Hijab had been revealed, so I traveled in my howdah and stayed in it when we camped. We traveled until the Messenger of Allah completed his campaign, then we returned. As we were approaching Al-Madinah, we paused for a while, then they announced that the journey was to be resumed. When I heard this, I walked quickly away from the army to answer the call of nature, then I came back to my howdah. Then I put my hand to my chest and noticed that a necklace of mine that was made of onyx and cornelian had broken, so I went back and looked for it, and was delayed because of that. In the meantime, the people who used to lift my howdah onto my camel came along and put it on the camel, thinking that I was inside. In those times women were more slender and not so heavy, they only ate mouthfuls of food. So the people did not think anything of the howdah being so light when they lifted it up, as I was a young woman. They set off, and I found my necklace after the army had moved on. Then I came back to the place where we had stopped, and I saw no one to call or answer. So I went to the place where I had been, thinking that the people would miss me and come back for me. While I was sitting there, I fell asleep. tSafwan bin Al-Mu`attal As-Sulami Adh-Dhakwani had rested during the night behind the army. Then he set out just before daybreak and reached the place where I was in the morning, where he saw the outline of a person sleeping. He came to me and recognized me when he saw me, as he had seen me before Hijab was made obligatory for me. When he saw me and said `Truly, to Allah we belong, and truly, to Him we shall return,' I woke up, and covered my face with my Jilbab (outer garment). By Allah, he did not speak a word to me and I did not hear him say anything except `Truly, to Allah we belong, and truly, to Him we shall return,' until he brought his camel and made it kneel so that I could ride upon it, then he set out leading the camel until we caught up with the army at Zuhr time.

There are people who are doomed because of what happened to me, and the one who had the greater share therein was `Abdullah bin Ubayy bin Salul. When we came back to Al-Madinah, I was ill for a month, and the people were talking about what the people of the slander were saying, and I knew nothing about it. What upset me when I was ill was that I did not see the kindness I used to see on the part of the Messenger of Allah . When I was ill; he would just come in and say,

《كَيْفَ تِيكُمْ؟》

(How is that (lady)) That is what upset me. I did not feel that there was anything wrong until I went out after I felt better, and Umm Mistah went out with me, walking towards Al-Manasi`, which is where we used to go to relieve ourselves, and we would not go out for that purpose except at night. This was before we had lavatories close to our houses; our habit was similar to that of the early Arabs in that we went out into the deserts to relieve ourselves, because we considered it troublesome and harmful to have lavatories in our houses. So I went out with Umm Mistah, who was the daughter of Abu Ruhm bin Al-Muttalib bin `Abd Manaf, and her mother was the daughter of Sakhr bin `Amir, the paternal aunt of Abu Bakr As-Siddiq. Her son was Mistah bin Uthathah bin `Abbad bin Al-Muttalib. When we finished what we had to do, the daughter of Abu Ruhm Umm Mistah and I came back towards my house. Umm Mistah stumbled over her apron and said, `May Mistah be ruined!' I said to her, `What a bad thing you have said! Are you abusing a man who was present at Badr' She said, `Good grief, have you not heard what he said' I said, `What did he say' So she told me what the people of the slander were saying, which made me even more ill. When I returned home, the Messenger of Allah came in to me and greeted me, then he said,

《كَيْفَ تِيكُمْ؟》

(How is that (lady)) I said to him, `Will you give me permission to go to my parents' At that time I wanted to confirm the news by hearing it from them. The Messenger of Allah gave me permission, so I went to my parents and asked my mother, `O my mother, what are the people talking about' My mother said, `Calm down, for by Allah, there is no beautiful woman who is loved by her husband and has co-wives but those co-wives would find fault with her.' I said, `Subhan Allah! Are the people really talking

Chapter 24: An-Noor (The Light), Verses 001-064

about that' I wept throughout the whole night until morning. My tears never ceased and I did not sleep at all, and morning came while I was still weeping. Because the revelation had ceased, the Messenger of Allah called `Ali bin Abi Talib and Usamah bin Zayd, and consulted with them about divorcing his wife. As for Usamah bin Zayd, he told the Messenger of Allah about what he knew of his wife's innocence and his fondness for her. He said, `O Messenger of Allah, she is your wife, and we do not know anything about her but good.' But `Ali bin Abi Talib said, `O Messenger of Allah, Allah has not imposed restrictions on you, and there are plenty of other women besides her. If you ask her servant girl, she will tell you the truth.' So the Messenger of Allah called Barirah and said,

«أَيْ بَرِيرَةُ هَلْ رَأَيْتِ مِنْ شَيْءٍ يَرِيبُكِ مِنْ عَائِشَةَ؟»

(O Barirah, have you ever seen anything that might make you suspicious about `A'ishah) Barirah said to him, `By the One Who sent you with the truth, I have never seen anything for which I could blame her, apart from the fact that she is a young girl who sometimes falls asleep and leaves her family's dough unprotected so that the domestic goats come and eat it.' So then the Messenger of Allah got up and (addressed the people) and asked who could sort out `Abdullah bin Ubayy bin Salul for him. While he was standing on the Minbar, the Messenger of Allah said,

«يَامَعْشَرَ الْمُسْلِمِينَ مَنْ يَعْذِرُنِي مِنْ رَجُلٍ قَدْ بَلَغَنِي أَذَاهُ فِي أَهْلِ بَيْتِي، فَوَاللهِ مَا عَلِمْتُ عَلَى أَهْلِي إِلَّا خَيْرًا، وَلَقَدْ ذَكَرُوا رَجُلًا مَا عَلِمْتُ عَلَيْهِ إِلَّا خَيْرًا، وَمَا كَانَ يَدْخُلُ عَلَى أَهْلِي إِلَّا مَعِي»

(O Muslims, who will help me against a man who has hurt me by slandering my family By Allah, I know nothing about my family but good, and the people are blaming a man of whom I know nothing except good, and he has never entered upon my family except with me.) Sa`d bin Mu`adh Al-Ansari stood up and said, `O Messenger of Allah, by Allah I will deal with him for you. If he is from (the tribe of) Al-Aws, then I will cut off his head, and if he is from our brothers of (the tribe of) Al-Khazraj, tell us what to do and we will do it.' Then Sa`d bin `Ubadah stood up. He was the leader of Al-Khazraj, and he was a righteous man, but he was overwhelmed with tribal chauvinism. He said to Sa`d bin Mu`adh, `By Allah, you will not kill him and you will never be able to kill him.' Then Usayd bin Hudayr, who was the cousin of Sa`d bin Mu`adh, stood up and said to Sa`d bin `Ubadah, `You are lying! By Allah, we will kill him, and you are a hypocrite arguing on behalf of the hypocrites!' Then the two groups, Al-Aws and Al-Khazraj, started to get angry and were about to come to blows, with the Messenger of Allah standing there on the Minbar, trying to calm them down until they became quiet, then the Messenger of Allah also fell silent. On that day I kept on weeping so much, my tears never ceased and I did not sleep at all. My parents thought that my liver would burst from all that weeping. While they were sitting with me and I was weeping, a woman of the Ansar asked for permission to see me. I let her in, and she sat and wept with me. While we were in that state, the Messenger of Allah came in, greeted us and sat down. He had never sat with me since the rumors began, and a month had passed by without any revelation coming to him concerning my case. The Messenger of Allah recited the Tashahhud when he sat down, then he said,

«أَمَّا بَعْدُ، يَا عَائِشَةُ فَإِنَّهُ قَدْ بَلَغَنِي عَنْكِ كَذَا وَكَذَا، فَإِنْ كُنْتِ بَرِيئَةً فَسَيُبَرِّئُكِ اللهُ، وَإِنْ كُنْتِ أَلْمَمْتِ بِذَنْبٍ فَاسْتَغْفِرِي اللهَ ثُمَّ تُوبِي إِلَيْهِ، فَإِنَّ الْعَبْدَ إِذَا اعْتَرَفَ بِذَنْبِهِ ثُمَّ تَابَ، تَابَ اللهُ عَلَيْهِ»

(Thereafter, O `A'ishah, I have been told such and such a thing about you, and if you are innocent, then Allah will reveal your innocence, but if you have committed a sin, then seek Allah's forgiveness and turn in repentance to Him, for when a servant confesses his sin and repents to Allah, He accepts his repentance.) When the Messenger of Allah finished what he had to say, my tears stopped completely and I not longer felt even one drop. Then I said to my father, `Answer the Messenger of Allah on my behalf.' He said, `I do not know what I should say to the Messenger of Allah.' So I said to my mother, `Answer the Messenger of Allah on my behalf.' She said, `I do not know what I should say to the Messenger of Allah.' So even though I was just a young girl who had not memorized much of the Qur'an, I said: `By Allah, I know that you have heard so much of this story that it has become planted in your minds and you believe it. So now if I tell you that I am innocent -- and Allah knows that I am innocent -- you will not believe me; but if I admit something to you -- and Allah knows that I am innocent -- you will believe me. By Allah, I cannot find any example to give you except for that which the Prophet Yusuf's father said,

(So (for me) patience is most fitting. And it is Allah Whose help can be sought against that (lie) which you describe) (12:18). Then I turned my face away and lay down on my bed. By Allah, at that point I knew I was innocent and that Allah would prove my innocence because I was innocent, but by Allah, I did not think that Allah would reveal Qur'an that would be forever recited concerning my situation, because I thought of myself as too insignificant for Allah to reveal anything concerning me. But I hoped that the Messenger of Allah would see a dream in which Allah would prove my innocence. By Allah, the Messenger of Allah did not move from where he was sitting and no one left the house before Allah sent down revelation to His Prophet , and he was overtaken by the state that always overtook him when the revelation came upon him, until drops of sweat like pearls would run down him, even on a winter's day; this was because of the heaviness of the words which were being revealed to him. When that state passed -- and the Messenger of Allah was smiling -- the first thing he said was,

«أَبْشِرِي يَا عَائِشَةُ، أَمَّا اللهُ عَزَّ وَجَلَّ فَقَدْ بَرَّأَكِ»

Chapter 24: An-Noor (The Light), Verses 001-064

(Be glad O `A'ishah, Allah has declared your innocence.) My mother said to me, `Get up and go to him.' I said, `By Allah, I will not go to him and I will not give praise to anyone except Allah, may He be glorified, for He is the One Who has proven my innocence.' So Allah revealed:

(Verily, those who brought forth the slander are a group among you.), until the ten Ayat. Allah revealed these Ayat concerning my innocence. Abu Bakr, may Allah be pleased with him, who used to spend on Mistah bin Uthathah because he was a close relative and because he was poor, said, `By Allah, I will never spend anything on him again after what he has said about `A'ishah.' Then Allah revealed,

(And let not those among you who are blessed with graces and wealth swear not to give to their kinsmen.) until His saying:

(Do you not love that Allah should forgive you And Allah is Oft-Forgiving, Most Merciful) (24:22). So Abu Bakr said, `By Allah, certainly I love that Allah should forgive me.' So he resumed spending on Mistah as he had spent on him before, and he said, `By Allah, I shall never stop spending on him.' The Messenger of Allah asked Zaynab bint Jahsh about my situation, and said,

«يَا زَيْنَبُ مَاذَا عَلِمْتِ أَوْ رَأَيْتِ؟»

(O Zaynab, what do you know and what have you seen) She said, `O Messenger of Allah, may Allah protect my hearing and my sight. By Allah, I know nothing but good.' She is the one who used to compete with me among the wives of the Prophet , but Allah protected her (from telling lies) because of her piety. But her sister Hamnah bint Jahsh kept on fighting on her behalf, so she was doomed along with those who were doomed." Ibn Shihab said, "This is as much as we know about this group of people." It was also by Al-Bukhari and Muslim in their Sahihs from the Hadith of Az-Zuhri, and by Ibn Ishaq also from Az-Zuhri. He also said: "Yahya bin `Abbad bin `Abdullah bin Az-Zubayr told me from his father, from `A'ishah, may Allah be pleased with her, and `Abdullah bin Abi Bakr bin Muhammad bin `Amr bin Hazm Al-Ansari told me from `Amrah, from `A'ishah, (a report) similar to that quoted above. And Allah knows best. Allah's saying:

(Verily, those who brought forth the slander) means, the lies, falsehood and fabrications.

(are a group) means, a gang among you.

(Consider it not a bad thing for you.) O family of Abu Bakr,

(Nay, it is good for you.) means, in this world and the Hereafter, honorable mention in this world and raised status in the Hereafter. Allah demonstrated the esteem with which He regarded the family of Abu Bakr when He defended `A'ishah the Mother of the believers, may Allah be pleased with her, by revealing her innocence in the Qur'an,

(Falsehood cannot come to it from before it or behind it. ..) (41:42). Ibn `Abbas, may Allah be pleased with him, entered upon her when she was dying, he said to her, "Rejoice, for you are the wife of the Messenger of Allah and he used to love you; he did not marry any virgin other than you, and your innocence was revealed from heaven."

(Unto every man among them will be paid that which he had earned of the sin,) means, each of those who spoke about this matter and accused the Mother of the believers `A'ishah, may Allah be pleased with her, of any immoral action, will have a great share of punishment.

(and as for him among them who had the greater share therein,) It was said that this referred to the one who initiated the rumors, or that it was the one who collected rumors and spread them among the people.

(his will be a great torment.) means, for that. He was `Abdullah bin Ubayy bin Salul, may Allah disfigure him and curse him.

Surah: 24 Ayah: 12 & Ayah: 13

لَوْلَا إِذْ سَمِعْتُمُوهُ ظَنَّ ٱلْمُؤْمِنُونَ وَٱلْمُؤْمِنَـٰتُ بِأَنفُسِهِمْ خَيْرًا وَقَالُوا۟ هَـٰذَآ إِفْكٌ مُّبِينٌ ﴿١٢﴾

12. Why then, did not the believers, men and women, when you heard it (the slander) think good of their own people and say: "This (charge) is an obvious lie?"

لَّوْلَا جَآءُو عَلَيْهِ بِأَرْبَعَةِ شُهَدَآءَ ۚ فَإِذْ لَمْ يَأْتُوا۟ بِٱلشُّهَدَآءِ فَأُو۟لَـٰٓئِكَ عِندَ ٱللَّهِ هُمُ ٱلْكَـٰذِبُونَ ﴿١٣﴾

13. Why did they not produce four witnesses? Since they (the slanderers) have not produced witnesses! Then with Allâh they are the liars.

Transliteration

12. Lawla ith samiAAtumoohu thanna almu/minoona waalmu/minatu bi-anfusihim khayran waqaloo hatha ifkun mubeenun   13. Lawla jaoo AAalayhi bi-arbaAAati shuhadaa fa-ith lam ya/too bialshshuhada-i faola-ika AAinda Allahi humu alkathiboona

Tafsir Ibn Kathir

Disciplining the Believers for spreading the Slander

Here Allah disciplines the believers with regard to the matter of `A'ishah, because some of them spread this evil talk and the slander that had been mentioned. So Allah says:

Chapter 24: An-Noor (The Light), Verses 001-064

(Why then, when you heard it,) meaning, the talk which accused the Mother of the believers, may Allah be pleased with her,

(the believers, men and women, think good of their own people) means, why did they not compare what was said to themselves -- if it was not befitting for them then it was even less appropriate for the Mother of the believers, and she was more likely to be innocent. Or it was said that this was revealed about Abu Ayyub Khalid bin Zayd Al-Ansari and his wife, may Allah be pleased with them. Imam Muhammad bin Ishaq bin Yasar narrated, "The wife of Abu Ayyub Khalid bin Zayd Al-Ansari, Umm Ayyub, said to him, `O Abu Ayyub, have you heard what the people are saying about `A'ishah' He said, `Yes, and it is all lies. Would you do that, O Umm Ayyub' She said, `No, by Allah, I would not do that.' He said, `And by Allah, `A'ishah is better than you.' When the Qur'an was revealed, Allah mentioned those who spoke about the evil deed among the people of the slander,

(Verily, those who brought forth the slander are a group among you.) (24:1) This refers to Hassan and his companions who said what they said. Then Allah said,

(Why then, did not the believers, men, when you heard it, think...) means, as Abu Ayyub and his wife did." Allah's saying:

(the believers, men think...) meaning, `why did they not think good, because the Mother of the believers is his wife and is closer to him.' This is concerned with innermost feelings;

(and say:) means, with their tongues, verbally,

("This (charge) is an obvious lie") means, a clear untruth told about the Mother of the believers, may Allah be pleased with her. What happened should not have been the cause of suspicion. The fact that the Mother of the believers came openly, riding on the camel of Safwan bin Al-Mu`attal at midday, with the entire army watching and the Messenger of Allah among them, should have made it clear that there was no cause for suspicion. If there had been anything suspicious about the matter, they would not have come openly in this manner in front of so many witnesses; they would have come secretly. On this basis, what the people of the slander said accusing the Mother of the believers was an utter lie, false speech and evil foolish talk, by which people who indulged in it lost out. Allah said:

(Why did they not produce four witnesses against him) meaning, to prove that what they were saying was true.

(Since they have not produced witnesses! Then with Allah they are the liars.)Allah has ruled that they are indeed wicked liars.

Surah: 24 Ayah: 14 & Ayah: 15

وَلَوْلَا فَضْلُ ٱللَّهِ عَلَيْكُمْ وَرَحْمَتُهُۥ فِى ٱلدُّنْيَا وَٱلْءَاخِرَةِ لَمَسَّكُمْ فِى مَآ أَفَضْتُمْ فِيهِ عَذَابٌ عَظِيمٌ ۝

14. Had it not been for the Grace of Allâh and His Mercy unto you in this world and in the Hereafter, a great torment would have touched you for that whereof you had spoken.

إِذْ تَلَقَّوْنَهُۥ بِأَلْسِنَتِكُمْ وَتَقُولُونَ بِأَفْوَاهِكُم مَّا لَيْسَ لَكُم بِهِۦ عِلْمٌ وَتَحْسَبُونَهُۥ هَيِّنًا وَهُوَ عِندَ ٱللَّهِ عَظِيمٌ ۝

15. When you were propagating it with your tongues, and uttering with your mouths that whereof you had no knowledge, you counted it a little thing, while with Allâh it was very great.

Transliteration

14. Walawla fadlu Allahi AAalaykum warahmatuhu fee alddunya waal-akhirati lamassakum fee ma afadtum feehi AAathabun AAatheemun 15. Ith talaqqawnahu bi-alsinatikum wataqooloona bi-afwahikum ma laysa lakum bihi AAilmun watahsaboonahu hayyinan wahuwa AAinda Allahi AAatheemun

Tafsir Ibn Kathir

The Grace of Allah towards the People of the Slander by giving Them the Opportunity to repent

Allah says,

(Had it not been for the grace of Allah and His mercy unto you in this world and in the Hereafter,) This is addressed to those who were indulging in discussing the matter of `A'ishah, informing them that Allah has accepted their repentance in this world, and forgiven them because of their faith in the Hereafter.

(would have touched you for that whereof you had spoken.) with regard to the slander.

(a great torment) This refers to those who had faith in Allah because of their repentance, such as Mistah, Hassan and Hamnah bint Jahsh the sister of Zaynab bint Jahsh. As for the hypocrites who indulged in the slander, such as `Abdullah bin Ubayy bin Salul and his like, they are not the ones who are referred to in this Ayah, because they did not have sufficient faith and righteous deeds to balance or cancel out what they had done. By the same token, the threats that were narrated for a specific deed are bound to be carried out, if there is no repentance or sufficient righteous deeds to balance or outweigh it. Then Allah says:

Chapter 24: An-Noor (The Light), Verses 001-064

(When you were propagating it with your tongues,) Mujahid and Sa`id bin Jubayr said, "Some of you were relating it to others," where one says, `I heard this from so-and-so, and so-and-so said such and such, and some of them mentioned such and such.' Others recited the Ayah: (بِأَلْسِنَتِكُمْ تَلِقُونَهُ إِذْ) ("When you were inventing a lie with your tongues...") In Sahih Al-Bukhari, it is recorded that `A'ishah recited it like that. According to her, the meaning refers to lies which a person persists in telling. The first recitation is preferred and more popular, and the majority recite it that way, but the second is reported from `A'ishah, the Mother of the believers.

(and uttering with your mouths that whereof you had no knowledge,) means, you were speaking about something which you knew nothing about. Then Allah says:

(you counted it a little thing, while with Allah it was very great.) means, `you said what you said about the Mother of the believers and you thought that it was a trifling and insignificant matter, but even if she was not the wife of the Prophet, it still would not be an insignificant matter -- so how about when she is the wife of the Unlettered Prophet, the Seal of the Prophets and Leader of the Messengers ' It is a very serious matter with Allah that such a thing should be said about the wife of His Messenger! For Allah, may He be glorified and exalted, feels great fury and anger over such matters, and He would never decree such a thing for the wife of any of His Prophets. If that is the case, then how about the best of the wives of any Prophet, the wife of the best of the sons of Adam in this world and the next Allah says:

(you counted it a little thing, while with Allah it was very great.) In the Two Sahihs it is reported that:

«إِنَّ الرَّجُلَ لَيَتَكَلَّمُ بِالْكَلِمَةِ مِنْ سَخَطِ اللهِ، لَا يَدْرِي مَا تَبْلُغُ، يَهْوِي بِهَا فِي النَّارِ أَبْعَدَ مَا بَيْنَ السَّمَاءِ وَالْأَرْضِ»

(A man may say a word that angers Allah without realizing how far it will go, and because of that he will be thrown into Hell a distance greater than that between heaven and earth.) According to another report:

«لَا يُلْقِي لَهَا بَالًا»

(And he may not pay any attention to it.)

Surah: 24 Ayah: 16, Ayah: 17 & Ayah: 18

وَلَوْلَا إِذْ سَمِعْتُمُوهُ قُلْتُم مَّا يَكُونُ لَنَا أَن نَّتَكَلَّمَ بِهَـذَا سُبْحَـنَكَ هَـذَا بُهْتَـنٌ عَظِيمٌ ۝

16. And why did you not, when you heard it, say? "It is not right for us to speak of this. Glory is to You (O Allâh)! This is a great lie."

$$\text{يَعِظُكُمُ ٱللَّهُ أَن تَعُودُواْ لِمِثْلِهِۦٓ أَبَدًا إِن كُنتُم مُّؤْمِنِينَ ﴿١٧﴾}$$

17. Allâh forbids you from it and warns you not to repeat the like of it forever, if you are believers.

$$\text{وَيُبَيِّنُ ٱللَّهُ لَكُمُ ٱلْءَايَـٰتِ وَٱللَّهُ عَلِيمٌ حَكِيمٌ ﴿١٨﴾}$$

18. And Allâh makes the Ayât (proofs, evidences, verses, lessons, signs, revelations, etc.) plain to you, and Allâh is All-Knowing, All-Wise.

Transliteration

16. Walawla ith samiAAtumoohu qultum ma yakoonu lana an natakallama bihatha subhanaka hatha buhtanun Aaatheemun 17. YaAAithukumu Allahu an taAAoodoo limithlihi abadan in kuntum mu/mineena 18. Wayubayyinu Allahu lakumu al-ayati waAllahu AAaleemun hakeemun

Tafsir Ibn Kathir

Further Discipline

This is further discipline, in addition to the command to think well of people, i.e., if something unbefitting is mentioned about good people, then one should think well of them, and not feel towards them anything but good. Then if a person has any unsuitable thoughts about them, insinuated into his mind and imagination by Shaytan, he should not speak about that, for the Prophet said:

$$\text{«إِنَّ اللهَ تَعَالَى تَجَاوَزَ لِأُمَّتِي عَمَّا حَدَّثَتْ بِهِ أَنْفُسُهَا مَا لَمْ تَقُلْ أَوْ تَعْمَلْ»}$$

(Allah will excuse my Ummah for anything that occurs to their minds, so long as they do not speak about it or act upon it.) This was reported in the Two Sahihs. Allah's saying:

(And why did you not, when you heard it, say: "It is not right for us to speak of this".) meaning, we should not talk about it or mention it to anyone.

(Glory be to You (O Allah)! This is a great lie.) means, glory be to Allah that such a thing should be said about the wife of His Prophet and close Friend . Then Allah says,

(Allah forbids you from it and warns you not to repeat the like of it forever,) meaning, Allah is forbidding you and warning you from doing anything like this again in the future. Allah says,

(if you are believers.) meaning, if you believe in Allah and His Laws, and you respect His Messenger . As for those who are described as disbelievers, a different ruling applies in their case. Then Allah says,

(And Allah makes the Ayat plain to you,) meaning, He makes clear to you the rulings of Shari`ah and His divine decrees.

Chapter 24: An-Noor (The Light), Verses 001-064

(and Allah is All-Knowing, All-Wise.) means, He knows what is right for His servants and He is Wise in His Laws and decrees.

Surah: 24 Ayah: 19

إِنَّ ٱلَّذِينَ يُحِبُّونَ أَن تَشِيعَ ٱلْفَـٰحِشَةُ فِى ٱلَّذِينَ ءَامَنُوا۟ لَهُمْ عَذَابٌ أَلِيمٌ فِى ٱلدُّنْيَا وَٱلْـَٔاخِرَةِ ۚ وَٱللَّهُ يَعْلَمُ وَأَنتُمْ لَا تَعْلَمُونَ ۝

19. Verily, those who like that (the crime of) illegal sexual intercourse should be propagated among those who believe, they will have a painful torment in this world and in the Hereafter. And Allâh knows and you know not.

Transliteration

19. Inna allatheena yuhibboona an tasheeAAa alfahishatu fee allatheena amanoo lahum AAathabun aleemun fee alddunya waal-akhirati waAllahu yaAAlamu waantum la taAAlamoona

Tafsir Ibn Kathir

Disciplining Those Who like that Illegal Sexual Intercourse should be circulated among the Believers

This is a third instance of discipline directed at those who hear evil talk, believe it to some extent, and start to spread it; they should not spread such talk or pass it on to others. Allah says:

(Verily, those who like that Fahshah should be circulated among those who believe, they will have a painful torment) meaning, those who like to see evil talk about them (the believers) appear,

(they will have a painful torment in this world) means, because of the prescribed punishment, and in the Hereafter because of the torment in Hell.

(And Allah knows and you know not.) means, return the matter to Him and you will be guided. Imam Ahmad recorded from Thawban that the Prophet said:

«لَا تُؤْذُوا عِبَادَ اللهِ وَلَا تُعَيِّرُوهُمْ، وَلَا تَطْلُبُوا عَوْرَاتِهِمْ، فَإِنَّهُ مَنْ طَلَبَ عَوْرَةَ أَخِيهِ الْمُسْلِمِ طَلَبَ اللهُ عَوْرَتَهُ، حَتَّى يَفْضَحَهُ فِي بَيْتِهِ»

(Do not annoy the servants of Allah, nor abuse them, nor seek their hidden shortcomings. Whoever seeks out the faults of his Muslim brother, Allah will expose his faults and degrade him, even if he is hiding in his house.)

Surah: 24 Ayah: 20 & Ayah: 21

$$\text{وَلَوْلَا فَضْلُ اللَّهِ عَلَيْكُمْ وَرَحْمَتُهُ وَأَنَّ اللَّهَ رَءُوفٌ رَحِيمٌ ۝}$$

20. And had it not been for the Grace of Allâh and His Mercy on you, (Allâh would have hastened the punishment upon you). And that Allâh is full of kindness, Most Merciful.

$$\text{۞ يَا أَيُّهَا الَّذِينَ آمَنُوا لَا تَتَّبِعُوا خُطُوَاتِ الشَّيْطَانِ وَمَن يَتَّبِعْ خُطُوَاتِ الشَّيْطَانِ فَإِنَّهُ يَأْمُرُ بِالْفَحْشَاءِ وَالْمُنكَرِ وَلَوْلَا فَضْلُ اللَّهِ عَلَيْكُمْ وَرَحْمَتُهُ مَا زَكَىٰ مِنكُم مِّنْ أَحَدٍ أَبَدًا وَلَٰكِنَّ اللَّهَ يُزَكِّي مَن يَشَاءُ وَاللَّهُ سَمِيعٌ عَلِيمٌ ۝}$$

21. O you who believe! Follow not the footsteps of Shaitân (Satan). And whosoever follows the footsteps of Shaitân (Satan), then, verily he commands Al-Fahshâ' (i.e. to commit indecency (illegal sexual intercourse)) and Al-Munkar (disbelief and polytheism (i.e. to do evil and wicked deeds; and to speak or to do what is forbidden in Islâm)) And had it not been for the Grace of Allâh and His Mercy on you, not one of you would ever have been pure from sins. But Allâh purifies (guides to Islâm) whom He wills, and Allâh is All-Hearer, All-Knower.

Transliteration

20. Walawla fadlu Allahi AAalaykum warahmatuhu waanna Allaha raoofun raheemun
21. Ya ayyuha allatheena amanoo la tattabiAAoo khutuwati alshshaytani waman yattabiAA khutuwati alshshaytani fa-innahu ya/muru bialfahsha-i waalmunkari walawla fadlu Allahi AAalaykum warahmatuhu ma zaka minkum min ahadin abadan walakinna Allaha yuzakkee man yashao waAllahu sameeAAun AAaleemun

Tafsir Ibn Kathir

A Reminder of the Grace of Allah and a Warning against following the Footsteps of Shaytan

Allah says:

(And had it not been for the grace of Allah and His mercy on you, and that Allah is full of kindness, Most Merciful.) meaning, if it were not for this, it would have been another matter altogether, but He, may He be exalted, is full of kindness towards His servants and Merciful towards them. He accepts the repentance of those who repent to Him from this sin, and purifies those among them who are purified by the prescribed punishment carried out on them. Then Allah says:

(O you who believe! Follow not the Khutuwat of Shaytan.) hmeaning, his ways and paths and what he commands,

Chapter 24: An-Noor (The Light), Verses 001-064

(And whosoever follows the footsteps of Shaytan, then, verily, he commands immorality and the evil deeds.) This is a warning given in the most concise and eloquent manner. `Ali bin Abi Talhah recorded from Ibn `Abbas that

(the Khutuwat of Shaytan) means his deeds. `Ikrimah said that it means his evil whispers. Qatadah said: "Every sin is one of the footsteps of Shaytan." Abu Mijlaz said: "Vowing to commit sin is one of the footsteps of Shaytan." Then Allah says:

(And had it not been for the grace of Allah and His mercy on you, not one of you would ever have been pure from sins.) meaning, if He did not help whomever He wills to repent and come back to Him and be purified from Shirk, evil and sin, and whatever bad characteristics each person has according to his nature, no one would ever attain purity and goodness.

(But Allah purifies whom He wills) means, among His creation, and He sends astray whomever He wills, leaving him to be doomed in his misguidance and sin.

(and Allah is All-Hearer,) means, He hears what His servants say,

(All-Knower.) of who deserves to be guided and who deserves to be misguided.

وَلَا يَأْتَلِ أُولُوا۟ ٱلْفَضْلِ مِنكُمْ وَٱلسَّعَةِ أَن يُؤْتُوٓا۟ أُو۟لِى ٱلْقُرْبَىٰ وَٱلْمَسَٰكِينَ وَٱلْمُهَٰجِرِينَ فِى سَبِيلِ ٱللَّهِ ۖ وَلْيَعْفُوا۟ وَلْيَصْفَحُوٓا۟ ۗ أَلَا تُحِبُّونَ أَن يَغْفِرَ ٱللَّهُ لَكُمْ ۗ وَٱللَّهُ غَفُورٌ رَّحِيمٌ ﴿٢٢﴾

22. And let not those among you who are blessed with graces and wealth swear not to give (any sort of help) to their kinsmen, Al-Masâkîn (the poor), and those who left their homes for Allâh's Cause. Let them pardon and forgive. Do you not love that Allâh should forgive you? And Allâh is Oft-Forgiving, Most Merciful.

Transliteration

22. Wala ya/tali oloo alfadli minkum waalssaAAati an yu/too olee alqurba waalmasakeena waalmuhajireena fee sabeeli Allahi walyaAAfoo walyasfahoo ala tuhibboona an yaghfira Allahu lakum waAllahu ghafoorun raheemun

Tafsir Ibn Kathir

Urging Those Who have been blessed with Wealth to give and to be tolerant

Allah says,

(And let not swear) meaning, make an oath,

(those among you who are blessed with graces) means, those who have the means to give charity and do good,

(and wealth) means, good fortune,

(to give to their kinsmen, the poor, and those who left their homes for Allah's cause.) means, do not swear that you will not uphold the ties of kinship with your relatives who are needy or who migrated for the sake of Allah, which is the ultimate act of kindness in the area of upholding kinship ties. Allah says,

(Let them pardon and forgive.) past insults and bad treatment. This is part of the patience, generosity and kindness of Allah towards His creation, despite the fact that they wrong themselves. This Ayah was revealed concerning As-Siddiq, may Allah be pleased with him, when he swore that he would not help Mistah bin Uthathah after he said what he said about `A'ishah, as we have already seen in the Hadith. When Allah revealed the innocence of the Mother of the believers, `A'ishah, and the believers were happy and content with the outcome of this incident, and those believers who had talked about the matter repented, and the prescribed punishment had been carried out upon those on whom it was carried out, then Allah started to soften the heart of As-Siddiq towards his relative Mistah bin Uthathah. Mistah was the cousin of As-Siddiq, the son of his maternal aunt, and he was a poor man with no wealth except whatever Abu Bakr spent on him. He was one of those who had migrated for the sake of Allah. He had invented the lies and the slander, but then Allah accepted his repentance from that and the prescribed punishment was carried out on him. As-Siddiq was known for his generosity and he did favors to his relatives and strangers alike. When this Ayah was revealed:

(Do you not love that Allah should forgive you), which shows that the reward fits the action, and that `if you forgive others, you will be forgiven,' then As-Siddiq said, "Of course, by Allah, we love -- O our Lord -- that You should forgive us." Then he resumed his spending on Mistah and said, "By Allah I will never stop spending on him." This was to counteract what he had said previously, "By Allah I will never spend on him." This proves that he deserved to be called As-Siddiq, may Allah be pleased with him and his daughter.

Surah: 24 Ayah: 23, Ayah: 24 & Ayah: 25

اَلَّذِينَ يَرْمُونَ ٱلْمُحْصَنَـٰتِ ٱلْغَـٰفِلَـٰتِ ٱلْمُؤْمِنَـٰتِ لُعِنُواْ فِى ٱلدُّنْيَا وَٱلْأَخِرَةِ وَلَهُمْ عَذَابٌ عَظِيمٌ ﴿٢٣﴾

23. Verily, those who accuse chaste women, who never even think of anything touching their chastity and are good believers - are cursed in this life and in the Hereafter, and for them will be a great torment -

يَوْمَ تَشْهَدُ عَلَيْهِمْ أَلْسِنَتُهُمْ وَأَيْدِيهِمْ وَأَرْجُلُهُم بِمَا كَانُواْ يَعْمَلُونَ ﴿٢٤﴾

24. On the Day when their tongues, their hands, and their legs (or feet) will bear witness against them as to what they used to do.

يَوْمَئِذٍ يُوَفِّيهِمُ ٱللَّهُ دِينَهُمُ ٱلْحَقَّ وَيَعْلَمُونَ أَنَّ ٱللَّهَ هُوَ ٱلْحَقُّ ٱلْمُبِينُ ﴿٢٥﴾

25. On that Day Allâh will pay them the recompense of their deeds in full, and they will know that Allâh, He is the Manifest Truth.

Transliteration

23. Inna allatheena yarmoona almuhsanati alghafilati almu/minati luAAinoo fee alddunya waal-akhirati walahum AAathabun Aaatheemun 24. Yawma tashhadu AAalayhim alsinatuhum waaydeehim waarjuluhum bima kanoo yaAAmaloona 25. Yawma-ithin yuwaffeehimu Allahu deenahumu alhaqqa wayaAAlamoona anna Allaha huwa alhaqqu almubeenu

Tafsir Ibn Kathir

A Threat to Those who accuse Chaste Women, Who never even think of anything touching their Chastity and are Good Believers

This is a warning and threat from Allah to those who accuse chaste women, who never even think of anything effecting their chastity since they are good believers. The Mothers of the believers are more entitled to be included in this category than any other chaste woman, especially the one who was the reason for this Ayah being revealed: `A'ishah bint As-Siddiq, may Allah be pleased with them both. All of the scholars agree that whoever slanders her or makes accusations against after what has been said in this Ayah, is a disbeliever, because of his being obstinate with the Qur'an. The same ruling applies to all of the Mothers of the believers.

(are cursed in this life and in the Hereafter,) This is like the Ayah:

(Verily, those who annoy Allah and His Messenger,) (33:57) `Abdur-Rahman bin Zayd bin Aslam said, "This is about `A'ishah, and whoever does anything similar nowadays to Muslim women, the same applies to him, but `A'ishah is the one who is primarily referred to here." Ibn Abi Hatim recorded that Abu Hurayrah said that the Messenger of Allah said:

«اجْتَنِبُوا السَّبْعَ الْمُوبِقَاتِ»

(Shun the seven destructive sins.) He was asked, "What are they, O Messenger of Allah" He said:

«الشِّرْكُ بِاللهِ، وَالسِّحْرُ، وَقَتْلُ النَّفْسِ الَّتِي حَرَّمَ اللهُ إِلَّا بِالْحَقِّ، وَأَكْلُ الرِّبَا، وَأَكْلُ مَالِ الْيَتِيمِ، وَالتَّوَلِّي يَوْمَ الزَّحْفِ، وَقَذْفُ الْمُحْصَنَاتِ الْغَافِلَاتِ الْمُؤْمِنَاتِ»

(Associating partners with Allah; magic; killing a soul whom Allah has forbidden to be killed, except with just cause; consuming Riba; consuming the property of orphans;

desertion at the time of war; and accusing chaste women, who never even think of anything touching their chastity and are good believers.) This was recorded by Al-Bukhari and Muslim in the Two Sahihs.

(On the Day when their tongues, their hands, and their legs will bear witness against them as to what they used to do.) Ibn Abi Hatim recorded that Ibn `Abbas said, "This refers to the idolators when they realize that no one will enter Paradise except the people who used to perform Salah. They will say, `Come, let us deny (everything).' So they will deny (everything), then their mouths will be sealed and their hands and feet will testify against them, and they will not be able to hide anything from Allah." Ibn Abi Hatim also recorded that Anas bin Malik said, "We were with the Prophet and he smiled so broadly that his back teeth could be seen, then he said:

«أَتَدْرُونَ مِمَّ أَضْحَكُ؟»

(Do you know why I am smiling) We said, `Allah and His Messenger know best.' He said,

«مِنْ مُجَادَلَةِ الْعَبْدِ لِرَبِّهِ يَقُولُ: يَا رَبِّ أَلَمْ تُجِرْنِي مِنَ الظُّلْمِ؟ فَيَقُولُ: بَلَى، فَيَقُولُ: لَا أُجِيزُ عَلَيَّ شَاهِدًا إِلَّا مِنْ نَفْسِي، فَيَقُولُ: كَفَى بِنَفْسِكَ الْيَوْمَ عَلَيْكَ شَهِيدًا وَبِالْكِرَامِ عَلَيْكَ شُهُودًا، فَيُخْتَمُ عَلَى فِيهِ وَيُقَالُ لِأَرْكَانِهِ: انْطِقِي فَتَنْطِقَ بِعَمَلِهِ، ثُمَّ يُخَلَّى بَيْنَهُ وَبَيْنَ الْكَلَامِ فَيَقُولُ: بُعْدًا لَكُنَّ وَسُحْقًا فَعَنْكُنَّ كُنْتُ أُنَاضِلُ»

(Because of the way a person will dispute with his Lord. He will say, "O Lord, did you not protect me from doing wrong" Allah will say, "Of course," The person will say, "I will not accept for anyone to give testimony concerning me except myself." Allah will say, "You are sufficient as a witness against yourself." Then a seal will be put upon his mouth and it will be said to his faculties, "Speak." So they will speak about his deeds. Then he will be permitted to speak, and he will say, "Away with you! I was only speaking in your defence!") This was recorded by Muslim and An-Nasa'i.

(On that Day Allah will pay Dinahum,) Ibn `Abbas said,

(Dinahum) "Meaning `their account.' Every time Dinahum appears in the Qur'an it means `their account.'" This was also the view of other scholars.

(and they will know that Allah, He is the Manifest Truth.) means, His promise, His threat and His reckoning are all just and there is no unfairness in them.

Surah: 24 Ayah: 26

ٱلۡخَبِيثَٰتُ لِلۡخَبِيثِينَ وَٱلۡخَبِيثُونَ لِلۡخَبِيثَٰتِ ۖ وَٱلطَّيِّبَٰتُ لِلطَّيِّبِينَ وَٱلطَّيِّبُونَ لِلطَّيِّبَٰتِ ۚ أُوْلَٰٓئِكَ مُبَرَّءُونَ مِمَّا يَقُولُونَ ۖ لَهُم مَّغۡفِرَةٌ وَرِزۡقٌ كَرِيمٌ ۝

26. Bad statements are for bad people (or bad women for bad men) and bad people for bad statements (or bad men for bad women). Good statements are for good people (or good women for good men) and good people for good statements (or good men for good women); such (good people) are innocent of (every) bad statement which they say; for them is Forgiveness, and Rizqun Karîm (generous provision i.e. Paradise).

Transliteration

26. Alkhabeethatu lilkhabeetheena waalkhabeethoona lilkhabeethati waalttayyibatu lilttayyibeena waalttayyiboona lilttayyibati ola-ika mubarraoona mimma yaqooloona lahum maghfiratun warizqun kareemun

Tafsir Ibn Kathir

The Goodness of `A'ishah because She is married to the best of Mankind

Ibn `Abbas said, "Evil words are for evil men, and evil men are for evil words; good words are for good men and good men are for good words. This was revealed concerning `A'ishah and the people of the slander." This was also narrated from Mujahid, `Ata', Sa`id bin Jubayr, Ash-Sha`bi, Al-Hasan bin Abu Al-Hasan Al-Basri, Habib bin Abi Thabit and Ad-Dahhak, and it was also the view favored by Ibn Jarir. He interpreted it to mean that evil speech is more suited to evil people, and good speech is more suited to good people. What the hypocrites attributed to `A'ishah was more suited to them, and she was most suited to innocence and having nothing to do with them. Allah said:

(such (good people) are innocent of (every) bad statement which they say;) `Abdur-Rahman bin Zayd bin Aslam said, "Evil women are for evil men and evil men are for evil women, and good women are for good men and good men are for good women." This also necessarily refers back to what they said, i.e.. Allah would not have made `A'ishah the wife of His Messenger unless she had been good, because he is the best of the best of mankind. If she had been evil, she would not have been a suitable partner either according to His Laws or His decree. Allah said:

(such are innocent of (every) bad statement which they say;) meaning, they are remote from what the people of slander and enmity say.

(for them is forgiveness,) means, because of the lies that were told about them,

(and honored provision.) meaning, with Allah in the Gardens of Delight. This implies a promise that she will be the wife of the Messenger of Allah in Paradise.

Surah: 24 Ayah: 27, Ayah: 28 & Ayah: 29

يَـٰٓأَيُّهَا ٱلَّذِينَ ءَامَنُوا۟ لَا تَدْخُلُوا۟ بُيُوتًا غَيْرَ بُيُوتِكُمْ حَتَّىٰ تَسْتَأْنِسُوا۟ وَتُسَلِّمُوا۟ عَلَىٰٓ أَهْلِهَا ۚ ذَٰلِكُمْ خَيْرٌ لَّكُمْ لَعَلَّكُمْ تَذَكَّرُونَ ۝

27. O you who believe! Enter not houses other than your own, until you have asked permission and greeted those in them; that is better for you, in order that you may remember.

فَإِن لَّمْ تَجِدُوا۟ فِيهَآ أَحَدًا فَلَا تَدْخُلُوهَا حَتَّىٰ يُؤْذَنَ لَكُمْ ۖ وَإِن قِيلَ لَكُمُ ٱرْجِعُوا۟ فَٱرْجِعُوا۟ ۖ هُوَ أَزْكَىٰ لَكُمْ ۚ وَٱللَّهُ بِمَا تَعْمَلُونَ عَلِيمٌ ۝

28. And if you find no one therein, still, enter not until permission has been given. And if you are asked to go back, go back, for it is purer for you. And Allâh is All-Knower of what you do.

لَّيْسَ عَلَيْكُمْ جُنَاحٌ أَن تَدْخُلُوا۟ بُيُوتًا غَيْرَ مَسْكُونَةٍ فِيهَا مَتَـٰعٌ لَّكُمْ ۚ وَٱللَّهُ يَعْلَمُ مَا تُبْدُونَ وَمَا تَكْتُمُونَ ۝

29. There is no sin on you that you enter (without taking permission) houses uninhabited (i.e. not possessed by anybody), (when) you have any interest in them. And Allâh has knowledge of what you reveal and what you conceal.

Transliteration

27. Ya ayyuha allatheena amanoo la tadkhuloo buyootan ghayra buyootikum hatta tasta/nisoo watusallimoo AAala ahliha thalikum khayrun lakum laAAallakum tathakkaroona 28. Fa-in lam tajidoo feeha ahadan fala tadkhulooha hatta yu/thana lakum wa-in qeela lakumu irjiAAoo fairjiAAoo huwa azka lakum waAllahu bima taAAmaloona AAaleemun 29. Laysa AAalaykum junahun an tadkhuloo buyootan ghayra maskoonatin feeha mataAAun lakum waAllahu yaAAlamu ma tubdoona wama taktumoona

Tafsir Ibn Kathir

Seeking Permission and the Etiquette of entering Houses

This is the Islamic etiquette. Allah taught these manners (of seeking permission) to His believing servants and commanded them not to enter houses other than their own until they had asked permission, i.e., to ask for permission before entering and to give the greeting of Salam after asking. One should seek permission three times, and if permission is given, (he may enter), otherwise he should go away. It was reported in the Sahih that when Abu Musa asked `Umar three times for permission to enter and he did not give him permission, he went away. Then `Umar said, "Did I not hear the voice of `Abdullah bin Qays asking for permission to enter Let him come in." So they looked for him, but found that he had gone. When he came later on, `Umar said,

"Why did you go away" He said, "I asked for permission to enter three times, but permission was not given to me, and I heard the Prophet say,

»إِذَا اسْتَأْذَنَ أَحَدُكُمْ ثَلَاثًا فَلَمْ يُؤْذَنْ لَهُ فَلْيَنْصَرِفْ«

(If any one of you asks for permission three times and it is not given, then let him go away.)" `Umar said, "You should certainly bring me evidence for this or I shall beat you!" So he went to a group of the Ansar and told them what `Umar said. They said, "No one will give testimony for you but the youngest of us." So Abu Sa`id Al-Khudri went with him and told `Umar about that. `Umar said, "What kept me from learning that was my being busy in the marketplace." Imam Ahmad recorded a narration stating that Anas or someone else said that the Messenger of Allah asked for permission to enter upon Sa`d bin `Ubadah. He said:

»السَّلَامُ عَلَيْكَ وَرَحْمَةُ اللهِ«

(As-Salamu `Alayka wa Rahmatullah) Sa`d said, "Wa `Alaykas-Salam Wa Rahmatullah," but the Prophet did not hear the returned greeting until he had given the greeting three times and Sa`d had returned the greeting three times, but he did not let him hear him (i.e., Sa`d responded in a low voice). So the Prophet went back, and Sa`d followed him and said,"O Messenger of Allah, may my father and mother be ransomed for you! You did not give any greeting but I responded to you, but I did not let you hear me. I wanted to get more of your Salams and blessings." Then he admitted him to his house and offered him some raisins. The Prophet ate, and when he finished, he said,

»أَكَلَ طَعَامَكُمُ الْأَبْرَارُ، وَصَلَّتْ عَلَيْكُمُ الْمَلَائِكَةُ، وَأَفْطَرَ عِنْدَكُمُ الصَّائِمُونَ«

(May the righteous eat your food, may the angels send blessings upon you and may those who are fasting break their fast with you.) It should also be known that the one who is seeking permission to enter should not stand directly in front of the door; he should have the door on his right or left, because of the Hadith recorded by Abu Dawud from `Abdullah bin Busr, who said, "When the Messenger of Allah came to someone's door, he would never stand directly in front of it, but to the right or left, and he would say,

»السَّلَامُ عَلَيْكُمْ، السَّلَامُ عَلَيْكُمْ«

(As-Salamu `Alaykum, As-Salamu `Alaykum.) That was because at that time the houses had no covers or curtains over their doorways." This report was recorded by Abu Dawud only. In the Two Sahihs, it is recorded that the Messenger of Allah said:

«لَوْ أَنَّ امْرَءًا اطَّلَعَ عَلَيْكَ بِغَيْرِ إِذْنٍ فَخَذَفْتَهُ بِحَصَاةٍ فَفَقَأْتَ عَيْنَهُ، مَا كَانَ عَلَيْكَ مِنْ جُنَاحٍ»

(If a person looks into your house without your permission, and you throw a stone at him and it puts his eye out, there will be no blame on you.) The Group recorded that Jabir said, "I came to the Prophet with something that was owed by my father and knocked at the door. He said,

«مَنْ ذَا؟»

(Who is that) I said, "I am!" He said,

«أَنَا أَنَا»

(I I) as if he disliked it." He did not like it because this word tells you nothing about who is saying it, unless he clearly states his name or the name by which he is known, (nickname) otherwise everyone could call himself "Me", and it does not fulfill the purpose of asking permission to enter, which is to put people at their ease, as commanded in the Ayah. Al-`Awfi narrated from Ibn `Abbas, "Putting people at ease means seeking permission to enter." This was also the view of others. Imam Ahmad recorded from Kaladah bin Al-Hanbal that at the time of the Conquest (of Makkah), Safwan bin Umayyah sent him with milk, a small gazelle, and small cucumbers when the Prophet was at the top of the valley. He said, "I entered upon the Prophet and I did not give the greeting of Salam nor ask for permission to enter. The Prophet said,

«ارْجِعْ فَقُلْ: السَّلَامُ عَلَيْكُمْ أَأَدْخُلُ؟»

(Go back and say: "As-Salamu `Alaykum, may I enter") This was after Safwan had become Muslim." This was also recorded by Abu Dawud, At-Tirmidhi and An-Nasa'i. At-Tirmidhi said, "Hasan Gharib." Ibn Jurayj said that he heard `Ata' bin Abi Rabah narrating that Ibn `Abbas, may Alah be pleased with him, said, "There are three Ayat whose rulings people neglect. Allah says,

(Verily, the most honorable of you with Allah is the one who has the most Taqwa) (49:13), But (now) they say that the most honorable of them with Allah is the one who has the biggest house. As for seeking permission, the people have forgotten all about it." I said, "Should I seek permission to enter upon my orphan sisters who are living with me in one house" He said, "Yes." I asked him to make allowances for me but he refused and said, "Do you want to see them naked" I said, "No." He said, "Then ask for permission to enter." I asked him again and he said, "Do you want to obey Allah" I said, "Yes." He said, "Then ask for permission." Ibn Jurayj said, "Ibn Tawus told me that his father said, `There are no women whom I hate to see naked

Chapter 24: An-Noor (The Light), Verses 001-064

more than those who are my Mahrams.' He was very strict on this point." Ibn Jurayj narrated that Az-Zuhri said, "I heard Huzayl bin Shurahbil Al-Awdi Al-A`ma (say that) he heard Ibn Mas`ud say, `You have to seek permission to enter upon your mothers.'" Ibn Jurayj said, "I said to `Ata': `Does a man have to seek permission to enter upon his wife' He said, `No, it can be understood that this is not obligatory, but it is better for him to let her know that he is coming in so as not to startle her, because she may be in a state where she does not want him to see her. '" Abu Ja`far bin Jarir narrated from the nephew of Zaynab -- the wife of `Abdullah bin Mas`ud -- that Zaynab, may Allah be pleased with her, said, "When `Abdullah came back from some errand and reached the door, he would clear his throat and spit, because he did not want to come suddenly and find us in a state he disliked." Its chain of narration is Sahih.

(O you who believe! Enter not houses other than your own, until you have asked permission and greeted those in them;) Muqatil bin Hayyan said: "During the Jahiliyyah, when a man met his friend, he would not greet him with Salam; rather he would say "Huyyita Sabahan" or "Huyyita Masa'an" (equivalent to "Good morning" or "Good evening"). This was the greeting among the people at that time. They did not seek permission to enter one another's houses; a man might walk straight in and say, "I have come in," and so on. This was difficult for a man to bear, as he might be with his wife. So Allah changed all that by enjoining covering and chastity, making it pure and free of any sin or impropriety. So Allah said:

(O you who believe! Enter not houses other than your own, until you have asked permission and greeted those in them...) What Muqatil said is good. Allah said:

(that is better for you,) meaning, seeking permission to enter in is better for you because it is better for both parties, the one who is seeking permission to enter and the people inside the house.

(in order that you may remember.)

(And if you find no one therein, still enter not until permission has been given.) This has to do with the way in which one deals with other people's property without their permission. If he wants to, he can give permission, and if he wants to he can refrain from giving permission.

(And if you are asked to go back, go back, for it is purer for you.) means, if you are turned away at the door, before or after permission has been given,

(go back, for it is purer for you.) means, going back is purer and better for you.

(And Allah is All-Knower of what you do.) Qatadah said that one of the emigrants said: "All my life I tried to follow this Ayah, but if I asked for permission to enter upon one of my brothers and he asked me to go back, I could not do so happily, although Allah says,

(And if you are asked to go back, go back, for it is purer for you. And Allah is All-Knower of what you do.)"

(And if you are asked to go back, go back....) Sa`id bin Jubayr said, "This means, do not stand at people's doors."

(There is no sin on you that you enter houses uninhabited,) This Ayah is more specific than the one that comes before it, because it states that it is permissible to enter houses where there is nobody, if one has a reason for doing so, such as houses that are prepared for guests -- if he has been given permission once, then this is sufficient. Ibn Jurayj said, "Ibn `Abbas said:

(Enter not houses other than your own,) then this was abrogated and an exception was made, and Allah said:

(There is no sin on you that you enter houses uninhabited, (when) you have any interest in them.) This was also narrated from `Ikrimah and Al-Hasan Al-Basri.

Surah: 24 Ayah: 30

قُل لِّلْمُؤْمِنِينَ يَغُضُّوا۟ مِنْ أَبْصَـٰرِهِمْ وَيَحْفَظُوا۟ فُرُوجَهُمْ ۚ ذَٰلِكَ أَزْكَىٰ لَهُمْ ۗ إِنَّ ٱللَّهَ خَبِيرٌۢ بِمَا يَصْنَعُونَ ۝

30. Tell the believing men to lower their gaze (from looking at forbidden things), and protect their private parts (from illegal sexual acts). That is purer for them. Verily, Allâh is All-Aware of what they do.

Transliteration

30. Qul lilmu/mineena yaghuddoo min absarihum wayahfathoo foroojahum thalika azka lahum inna Allaha khabeerun bima yasnaAAoona

Tafsir Ibn Kathir

The Command to lower the Gaze

This is a command from Allah to His believing servants, to lower their gaze from looking at things that have been prohibited for them. They should look only at what is permissible for them to look at, and lower their gaze from forbidden things. If it so happens that a person's gaze unintentionally falls upon something forbidden, he should quickly look away. Muslim recorded in his Sahih that Jarir bin `Abdullah Al-Bajali, may Allah be pleased with him, said, "I asked the Prophet about the sudden glance, and he commanded me to turn my gaze away. In the Sahih it is narrated that Abu Sa`id said that the Messenger of Allah said:

«إِيَّاكُمْ وَالْجُلُوسَ عَلَى الطُّرُقَاتِ»

(Beware of sitting in the streets.) They said, "O Messenger of Allah, we have no alternative but to sit in the streets to converse with one another." The Messenger of Allah said:

Chapter 24: An-Noor (The Light), Verses 001-064

«إِنْ أَبَيْتُمْ فَأَعْطُوا الطَّرِيقَ حَقَّهُ»

(If you insist, then give the street its rights.) They asked, "What are the rights of the street, O Messenger of Allah" He said,

«غَضُّ الْبَصَرِ، وَكَفُّ الْأَذَى، وَرَدُّ السَّلَامِ، وَالْأَمْرُ بِالْمَعْرُوفِ، وَالنَّهْيُ عَنِ الْمُنْكَرِ»

(Lower your gaze, return the greeting of Salam, enjoin what is good and forbid what is evil.) Abu Al-Qasim Al-Baghawi recorded that Abu Umamah said, "I heard the Messenger of Allah say:

«اكْفُلُوا لِي سِتًّا أَكْفُلْ لَكُمْ بِالْجَنَّةِ: إِذَا حَدَّثَ أَحَدُكُمْ فَلَا يَكْذِبْ، وَإِذَا اثْتُمِنَ فَلَا يَخُنْ، وَإِذَا وَعَدَ فَلَا يُخْلِفْ، وَغُضُّوا أَبْصَارَكُمْ، وَكُفُّوا أَيْدِيَكُمْ، وَاحْفَظُوا فُرُوجَكُمْ»

(Guarantee me six things and I will guarantee you Paradise: when any one of you speaks, he should not lie; if he is entrusted with something, he should not betray that trust; if he makes a promise, he should not break it; lower your gaze; restrain your hands; and protect your private parts.) Since looking provokes the heart to evil, Allah commanded (the believers) to protect their private parts just as he commanded them to protect their gaze which can lead to that. So he said:

(Tell the believing men to lower their gaze, and protect their private parts.) Sometimes protecting the private parts may involve keeping them from committing Zina, as Allah says:

(And those who guard their chastity) (23:5). Sometimes it may involve not looking at certain things, as in the Hadith in Musnad Ahmad and the Sunan:

«احْفَظْ عَوْرَتَكَ إِلَّا مِنْ زَوْجَتِكَ أَوْ مَا مَلَكَتْ يَمِينُكَ»

(Guard your private parts except from your wife and those whom your right hands possess.)

(That is purer for them.) means, it is purer for their hearts and better for their commitment to religion, as it was said: Whoever protects his gaze, Allah will illuminate his understanding, or his heart.

(Verily, Allah is All-Aware of what they do.) This is like the Ayah :

(Allah knows the fraud of the eyes and all that the breasts conceal.) (40:19) In the Sahih it is recorded that Abu Hurayrah, may Allah be pleased with him, said that the Messenger of Allah said:

«كُتِبَ عَلَى ابْنِ آدَمَ حَظُّهُ مِنَ الزِّنَا أَدْرَكَ ذَلِكَ لَا مَحَالَةَ، فَزِنَا الْعَيْنَيْنِ النَّظَرُ، وَزِنَا اللِّسَانِ النُّطْقُ، وَزِنَا الْأُذُنَيْنِ الْاسْتِمَاعُ، وَزِنَا الْيَدَيْنِ الْبَطْشُ، وَزِنَا الرِّجْلَيْنِ الْخُطَى، وَالنَّفْسُ تَمَنَّى وَتَشْتَهِي، وَالْفَرْجُ يُصَدِّقُ ذَلِكَ أَوْ يُكَذِّبُهُ»

(The son of Adam has his share of Zina decreed for him, and he will commit that which has been decreed. The Zina of the eyes is looking; the Zina of the tongue is speaking; the Zina of the ears is listening; the Zina of the hands is striking; and the Zina of the feet is walking. The soul wishes and desires, and the private parts confirm or deny that.) It was recorded by Al-Bukhari without a complete chain. Muslim recorded a similar report with a different chain of narration. Many of the Salaf said, "They used to forbid men from staring at beardless handsome boys."

Surah: 24 Ayah: 31

وَقُل لِّلْمُؤْمِنَاتِ يَغْضُضْنَ مِنْ أَبْصَارِهِنَّ وَيَحْفَظْنَ فُرُوجَهُنَّ وَلَا يُبْدِينَ زِينَتَهُنَّ إِلَّا مَا ظَهَرَ مِنْهَا وَلْيَضْرِبْنَ بِخُمُرِهِنَّ عَلَى جُيُوبِهِنَّ وَلَا يُبْدِينَ زِينَتَهُنَّ إِلَّا لِبُعُولَتِهِنَّ أَوْ آبَائِهِنَّ أَوْ آبَاءِ بُعُولَتِهِنَّ أَوْ أَبْنَائِهِنَّ أَوْ أَبْنَاءِ بُعُولَتِهِنَّ أَوْ إِخْوَانِهِنَّ أَوْ بَنِي إِخْوَانِهِنَّ أَوْ بَنِي أَخَوَاتِهِنَّ أَوْ نِسَائِهِنَّ أَوْ مَا مَلَكَتْ أَيْمَانُهُنَّ أَوِ التَّابِعِينَ غَيْرِ أُولِي الْإِرْبَةِ مِنَ الرِّجَالِ أَوِ الطِّفْلِ الَّذِينَ لَمْ يَظْهَرُوا عَلَى عَوْرَاتِ النِّسَاءِ وَلَا يَضْرِبْنَ بِأَرْجُلِهِنَّ لِيُعْلَمَ مَا يُخْفِينَ مِن زِينَتِهِنَّ وَتُوبُوا إِلَى اللَّهِ جَمِيعًا أَيُّهَ الْمُؤْمِنُونَ لَعَلَّكُمْ تُفْلِحُونَ ۞

31. And tell the believing women to lower their gaze (from looking at forbidden things) And protect their private parts (from illegal sexual acts) and not to show off their adornment except only that which is apparent (both eyes for necessity to see the way, or outer palms of hands or one eye or dress like veil, gloves, head-cover, apron, etc.), and to draw their veils all over Juyubihinna (i.e. their bodies, faces, necks and bosoms) and not to reveal their adornment except to their husbands, or their fathers, or their husband's fathers, or their sons, or their husband's sons, or their brothers or their brother's sons, or their sister's sons, or their (Muslim) women (i.e. their sisters in Islâm), or the (female) slaves whom

their right hands possess, or old male servants who lack vigor, or small children who have no sense of feminine sex. And let them not stamp their feet so as to reveal what they hide of their adornment. And all of you beg Allâh to forgive you all, O believers, that you may be successful.

Transliteration

31. Waqul lilmu/minati yaghdudna min absarihinna wayahfathna furoojahunna wala yubdeena zeenatahunna illa ma thahara minha walyadribna bikhumurihinna AAala juyoobihinna wala yubdeena zeenatahunna illa libuAAoolatihinna aw aba-ihinna aw aba-i buAAoolatihinna aw abna-ihinna aw abna-i buAAoolatihinna aw ikhwanihinna aw banee ikhwanihinna aw banee akhawatihinna aw nisaihinna aw ma malakat aymanuhunna awi alttabiAAeena ghayri olee al-irbati mina alrrijali awi alttifli allatheena lam yathharoo AAala AAawrati alnnisa-i wala yadribna bi-arjulihinna liyuAAlama ma yukhfeena min zeenatihinna watooboo ila Allahi jameeAAan ayyuha almu/minoona laAAallakum tuflihoona

Tafsir Ibn Kathir

The Rulings of Hijab

This is a command from Allah to the believing women, and jealousy on His part over the wives of His believing servants. It is also to distinguish the believing women from the women of the Jahiliyyah and the deeds of the pagan women. The reason for the revelation of this Ayah was mentioned by Muqatil bin Hayyan, when he said: "We heard -- and Allah knows best -- that Jabir bin `Abdullah Al-Ansari narrated that Asma' bint Murshidah was in a house of hers in Bani Harithah, and the women started coming in to her without lower garments so that the anklets on their feet could be seen, along with their chests and forelocks. Asma' said: `How ugly this is!' Then Allah revealed:

(And tell the believing women to lower their gaze...)" And Allah says:

(And tell the believing women to lower their gaze) meaning, from that which Allah has forbidden them to look at, apart from their husbands. (Some) scholars said that it is permissible for women to look at non-Mahram men without desire, as it was recorded in the Sahih that the Messenger of Allah was watching the Ethiopians playing with spears in the Masjid on the day of `Id, and `A'ishah the Mother of the believers was watching them from behind him and he was concealing her from them, until she got bored and went away.

(and protect their private parts). Sa`id bin Jubayr said: "From immoral actions." Abu Al-`Aliyah said: "Every Ayah of the Qur'an in which protecting the private parts is mentioned means protecting them from Zina, except for this Ayah --

(and protect their private parts), which means protecting them from being seen by anybody."

(and not to show off their adornment except that which is apparent,) means, they should not show anything of their adornment to non-Mahram men except for whatever it is impossible to hide. Ibn Mas`ud said: "Such as clothes and outer garments," Meaning what the Arab women used to wear of the veil which covered their clothes and whatever showed from underneath the outer garment. There is no blame on her for this, because this is something that she cannot conceal. Similar to that is what appears of her lower garment and what she cannot conceal. Al-Hasan, Ibn Sirin, Abu Al-Jawza', Ibrahim An-Nakha`i and others also had the same view as Ibn Mas`ud.

(and to draw their veils all over their Juyub) means that they should wear the outer garment in such a way as to cover their chests and ribs, so that they will be different from the women of the Jahiliyyah, who did not do that but would pass in front of men with their chests completely uncovered, and with their necks, forelocks, hair and earrings uncovered. So Allah commanded the believing women to cover themselves, as He says:

(O Prophet! Tell your wives and your daughters and the women of the believers to draw their cloaks all over their bodies. That will be better, that they should be known, so as not to be annoyed) (33:59) And in this noble Ayah He said:

(and to draw their (Khumur) veils all over their Juyub) Khumur (veils) is the plural of Khimar, which means something that covers, and is what is used to cover the head. This is what is known among the people as a veil. Sa`id bin Jubayr said:

(and to draw) means to pull it around and tie it securely.

(their veils all over their Juyub) means, over their necks and chests so that nothing can be seen of them. Al-Bukhari recorded that `A'ishah, may Allah be pleased with her, said: "May Allah have mercy on the women of the early emigrants. When Allah revealed the Ayah:

(and to draw their veils all over their Juyub), they tore their aprons and Akhtamar themselves with them." He also narrated from Safiyyah bint Shaybah that `A'ishah, may Allah be pleased with her, used to say: "When this Ayah:

(and to draw their veils all over their Juyub) was revealed, they took their Izars (waistsheets) and tore them at the edges, and Akhtamar themselves with them."

(and not to reveal their adornment except to their husbands, or their fathers, or their husband's fathers, or their sons, or their husband's sons, or their brothers or their brother's sons, or their sister's sons,) All of these are a woman's close relatives whom she can never marry (Mahram) and it is permissible for her to show her adornments to them, but without making a wanton display of herself. Ibn Al-Mundhir recorded that `Ikrimah commented on this Ayah,

(and not to reveal their adornment except to their husbands, or their fathers, or their husband's fathers...), "The paternal uncle and maternal uncle are not mentioned here, because they may describe a woman to their sons, so a woman should not remove her Khimar in front of her paternal or maternal uncle." With regard to the husband, all of this is for his sake, so she should try her best when adorning herself for him, unlike the way she should appear in front of others.

(or their women,) this means that she may also wear her adornment in front of other Muslim women, but not in front of the women of Ahl Adh-Dhimmah (Jewish and Christian women), lest they describe her to their husbands. This is prohibited for all women, but more so in the case of the women of Ahl Adh-Dhimmah, because there is nothing to prevent them from doing that, but Muslim women know that it is unlawful and so, would be deterred from doing it. The Messenger of Allah said:

«لَا تُبَاشِرِ الْمَرْأَةُ الْمَرْأَةَ فَتَنْعَتَهَا لِزَوْجِهَا كَأَنَّهُ يَنْظُرُ إِلَيْهَا»

(No woman should describe another woman to her husband so that it is as if he is looking at her.) It was recorded in the Two Sahihs from Ibn Mas`ud.

(or their right hand possessions.) Ibn Jarir said, "This means from among the women of the idolators. It is permissible for a Muslim woman to reveal her adornment before such a woman, even if she is an idolatress, because she is her slave-girl." This was also the view of Sa`id bin Al-Musayyib. Allah says;

(Tabi`in among men who do not have desire,) such as hired servants and followers who are not at the same level as the woman and are feeble-minded and have no interest in or desire for women. Ibn `Abbas said, "This is the kind of person who has no desire." `Ikrimah said, "This is the hermaphrodite, who does not experience erections." This was also the view of others among the Salaf. It was narrated in the Sahih from `A'ishah that a hermaphrodite, used to enter upon the family of the Messenger of Allah and they used to consider him as one of those who do not have desire, but then the Messenger of Allah came in when he was describing a woman with four rolls of fat in front and eight behind. The Messenger of Allah said,

«أَلَا أَرَى هَذَا يَعْلَمُ مَا هَهُنَا لَا يَدْخُلَنَّ عَلَيْكُمْ»

(Lo! I think this person knows what is they are; he should never enter upon you.) He expelled him, and he stayed in Al-Bayda' and only came on Fridays to get food.

(or children who are not aware of the nakedness of women.) Because they are so young they do not understand anything about women or their `Awrah or their soft speech or their enticing ways of walking and moving. If a child is small and does not understand that, there is nothing wrong with him entering upon women, but if he is an adolescent or approaching adolescence, so that he knows and understands these things, and can make a distinction between who is beautiful and who is not, then he should not enter upon women. It was recorded in the Two Sahihs that the Messenger of Allah said:

«إِيَّاكُمْ وَالدُّخُولَ عَلَى النِّسَاءِ»

(Avoid entering upon women.) It was said, "O Messenger of Allah, what do you think about the male in-laws" He said:

«الْحَمْوُ: الْمَوْتُ»

(The male in-law is death.)

The Etiquette of Women walking in the Street

Allah's saying:

(And let them not stamp their feet...) During Jahiliyyah, when women walked in the street wearing anklets and no one could hear them, they would stamp their feet so that men could hear their anklets ringing. Allah forbade the believing women to do this. By the same token, if there is any other kind of adornment that is hidden, women are forbidden to make any movements that would reveal what is hidden, because Allah says:

(And let them not stamp their feet...) to the end of it. From that, women are also prohibited from wearing scent and perfume when they are going outside the home, lest men should smell their perfume. Abu `Isa At-Tirmidhi recorded that Abu Musa, may Allah be pleased with him, said that the Prophet said:

«كُلُّ عَيْنٍ زَانِيَةٌ، وَالْمَرْأَةُ إِذَا اسْتَعْطَرَتْ فَمَرَّتْ بِالْمَجْلِسِ فَهِيَ كَذَا وَكَذَا»

(Every eye commits fornication and adultery, and when a woman puts on perfume and passes through a gathering, she is such and such) -- meaning an adulteress. He said, "And there is a similar report from Abu Hurayrah, and this is Hasan Sahih." It was also recorded by Abu Dawud and An-Nasa'i. By the same token, women are also forbidden to walk in the middle of the street, because of what this involves of wanton display. Abu Dawud recorded that Abu Usayd Al-Ansari said that he heard the Messenger of Allah , as he was coming out of the Masjid and men and women were mixing in the street, telling the women:

«اسْتَأْخِرْنَ فَإِنَّهُ لَيْسَ لَكُنَّ أَنْ تَحْقُقْنَ الطَّرِيقَ، عَلَيْكُنَّ بِحَافَّاتِ الطَّرِيقِ»

(Keep back, for you have no right to walk in the middle of the street. You should keep to the sides of the road.) The women used to cling to the walls so much that their clothes would catch on the walls.

(And all of you beg Allah to forgive you all, O believers, that you may be successful.) means, practice what you are commanded in these beautiful manners and praiseworthy characteristics, and give up the evil ways of the people of Jahiliyyah, for the greatest success is to be found in doing what Allah and His Messenger command and avoiding what He forbids. And Allah is the source of strength.

Surah: 24 Ayah: 32, Ayah: 33 & Ayah: 34

وَأَنكِحُوا۟ ٱلْأَيَـٰمَىٰ مِنكُمْ وَٱلصَّـٰلِحِينَ مِنْ عِبَادِكُمْ وَإِمَآئِكُمْ ۚ إِن يَكُونُوا۟ فُقَرَآءَ يُغْنِهِمُ ٱللَّهُ مِن فَضْلِهِۦ ۗ وَٱللَّهُ وَٰسِعٌ عَلِيمٌ ﴿٣٢﴾

32. And marry those among you who are single (i.e. a man who has no wife and the woman who has no husband) and (also marry) the Sâlihûn (pious, fit and capable ones) of your (male) slaves and maid-servants (female slaves). If they be poor, Allâh will enrich them out of His Bounty. And Allâh is All-Sufficient for His creatures' needs, All-Knowing (about the state of the people).

وَلْيَسْتَعْفِفِ ٱلَّذِينَ لَا يَجِدُونَ نِكَاحًا حَتَّىٰ يُغْنِيَهُمُ ٱللَّهُ مِن فَضْلِهِۦ ۗ وَٱلَّذِينَ يَبْتَغُونَ ٱلْكِتَـٰبَ مِمَّا مَلَكَتْ أَيْمَـٰنُكُمْ فَكَاتِبُوهُمْ إِنْ عَلِمْتُمْ فِيهِمْ خَيْرًا ۖ وَءَاتُوهُم مِّن مَّالِ ٱللَّهِ ٱلَّذِىٓ ءَاتَىٰكُمْ ۚ وَلَا تُكْرِهُوا۟ فَتَيَـٰتِكُمْ عَلَى ٱلْبِغَآءِ إِنْ أَرَدْنَ تَحَصُّنًا لِّتَبْتَغُوا۟ عَرَضَ ٱلْحَيَوٰةِ ٱلدُّنْيَا ۚ وَمَن يُكْرِههُّنَّ فَإِنَّ ٱللَّهَ مِنۢ بَعْدِ إِكْرَٰهِهِنَّ غَفُورٌ رَّحِيمٌ ﴿٣٣﴾

33. And let those who find not the financial means for marriage keep themselves chaste, until Allâh enriches them of His Bounty. And such of your slaves as seek a writing (of emancipation), give them such writing, if you find that there is good and honesty in them. And give them something yourselves out of the wealth of Allâh which He has bestowed upon you. And force not your maids to prostitution, if they desire chastity, in order that you may make a gain in the (perishable) goods of this worldly life. But if anyone compels them (to prostitution), then after such compulsion, Allâh is Oft-Forgiving, Most Merciful (to those women, i.e. He will forgive them because they have been forced to do this evil action unwillingly).

وَلَقَدْ أَنزَلْنَآ إِلَيْكُمْ ءَايَـٰتٍ مُّبَيِّنَـٰتٍ وَمَثَلًا مِّنَ ٱلَّذِينَ خَلَوْا۟ مِن قَبْلِكُمْ وَمَوْعِظَةً لِّلْمُتَّقِينَ ﴿٣٤﴾

34. And indeed We have sent down for you Ayât (proofs, evidences, verses, lessons, signs, revelations, etc.) that make things plain, and the example of those who passed away before you, and an admonition for those who are Al-Muttaqûn (the pious and righteous persons - See V.2:2).

Transliteration

32. Waankihoo al-ayama minkum waalssaliheena min AAibadikum wa-ima-ikum in yakoonoo fuqaraa yughnihimu Allahu min fadlihi waAllahu wasiAAun AAaleemun 33. WalyastaAAfifi allatheena la yajidoona nikahan hatta yughniyahumu Allahu min fadlihi waallatheena yabtaghoona alkitaba mimma malakat aymanukum fakatiboohum in AAalimtum feehim khayran waatoohum min mali Allahi allathee atakum wala tukrihoo

fatayatikum AAala albigha-i in aradna tahassunan litabtaghoo AAarada alhayati alddunya waman yukrihhunna fa-inna Allaha min baAAdi ikrahihinna ghafoorun raheemun 34. Walaqad anzalna ilaykum ayatin mubayyinatin wamathalan mina allatheena khalaw min qablikum wamawAAithatan lilmuttaqeena

Tafsir Ibn Kathir

The Command to marry

These clear Ayat include a group of unambiguous rulings and firm commands.

(And marry those among you who are single (Al-Ayama)....) This is a command to marry. The Prophet said:

«يَا مَعْشَرَ الشَّبَابِ، مَنِ اسْتَطَاعَ مِنْكُمُ الْبَاءَةَ فَلْيَتَزَوَّجْ، فَإِنَّهُ أَغَضُّ لِلْبَصَرِ وَأَحْصَنُ لِلْفَرْجِ، وَمَنْ لَمْ يَسْتَطِعْ فَعَلَيْهِ بِالصَّوْمِ فَإِنَّهُ لَهُ وِجَاءٌ»

(O young men, whoever among you can afford to get married, let him marry, for it is more effective in lowering the gaze and protecting the private parts. Whoever cannot do that, then let him fast, for it is a protection for him.) This was recorded in the Two Sahihs from the Hadith of Ibn Mas`ud. In the Sunan, it was recorded from more than one person that the Messenger of Allah said:

«تَزَوَّجُوا تَوَالَدُوا تَنَاسَلُوا فَإِنِّي مُبَاهٍ بِكُمُ الْأُمَمَ يَوْمَ الْقِيَامَةِ»

(Marry and have children, for I will be proud of you before the nations on the Day of Resurrection.) The word Al-Ayama, the plural form of Ayyim, is used to describe a woman who has no husband and a man who has no wife, regardless of whether they have been married and then separated, or have never been married at all. Al-Jawhari reported this from the scholars of the (Arabic) language, and the word is applied to men and women alike.

(If they be poor, Allah will enrich them out of His bounty.) `Ali bin Abi Talhah reported from Ibn `Abbas: "Allah encouraged them to get married, commanded both free men and servants to get married, and He promised to enrich them."

(If they be poor, Allah will enrich them out of His bounty.) It was recorded that Ibn Mas`ud said: "Seek the richness through marriage, for Allah says:

(If they be poor, Allah will enrich them out of His bounty.)" This was recorded by Ibn Jarir. Al-Baghawi also recorded something similar from `Umar. It was reported from Al-Layth from Muhammad bin `Ajlan from Sa`id Al-Maqburi from Abu Hurayrah that the Messenger of Allah said:

«ثَلَاثَةٌ حَقٌّ عَلَى اللهِ عَوْنُهُمْ: النَّاكِحُ يُرِيدُ الْعَفَافَ، وَالْمُكَاتَبُ يُرِيدُ الْأَدَاءَ،

«وَالْغَازِي فِي سَبِيلِ اللَّهِ»

(There are three whom it is a right upon Allah to help: one who gets married seeking chastity; a slave who makes a contract with his master with the aim of buying his freedom; and one who fights for the sake of Allah.) This was recorded by Imam Ahmad, At-Tirmidhi, An-Nasa'i and Ibn Majah. The Prophet performed the marriage of a man who owned nothing but his waist wrap, and could not even buy a ring made of iron, but he still married him to that woman, making the Mahr his promise to teach her whatever he knew of the Qur'an. And it is known from the generosity and kindness of Allah that He provided him with whatever was sufficient for her and for him.

The Command to keep Oneself Chaste if One is not able to get married

Allah's saying:

(And let those who find not the financial means for marriage keep themselves chaste, until Allah enriches them of His bounty.) This is a command from Allah to those who do not have the means to get married: they are to keep themselves chaste and avoid unlawful things, as the Prophet said:

«يَا مَعْشَرَ الشَّبَابِ مَنِ اسْتَطَاعَ مِنْكُمُ الْبَاءَةَ فَلْيَتَزَوَّجْ فَإِنَّهُ أَغَضُّ لِلْبَصَرِ وَأَحْصَنُ لِلْفَرْجِ، وَمَنْ لَمْ يَسْتَطِعْ فَعَلَيْهِ بِالصَّوْمِ فَإِنَّهُ لَهُ وِجَاءٌ»

(O young men, whoever among you can afford to get married, let him marry, for it is more effective in lowering the gaze and protecting the private parts. Whoever cannot do that, then let him fast, for it is a protection for him.) This Ayah is general in meaning, and the Ayah in Surat An-Nisa' is more specific, where Allah says:

(And whoever of you have not the means wherewith to wed free believing women)until His statement;

(but it is better for you that you practise self-restraint) (4:25) meaning, it is better for you to be patient and refrain from marrying slave-girl, because any child that is born will also be a slave.

(and Allah is Oft-Forgiving, Most Merciful) (4:25).

(And let those who find not the financial means for marriage keep themselves chaste,) `Ikrimah said, "This refers to a man who sees a woman and it is as if he feels desire; if he has a wife then let him go to her and fulfill his desire with her, and if he does not have a wife, then let him ponder the kingdom of heaven and earth until Allah grants him means of livelihood."

The Command to grant Slaves a Contract of Emancipation

(And such of your servants as seek a writing (of emancipation), give them such writing, if you find that there is good and honesty in them.) This is a command from Allah to slave-owners: if their servants ask them for a contract of emancipation, they should write it for them, provided that the servant has some skill and means of earning so that he can pay his master the money that is stipulated in the contract. Al-Bukhari said: "Rawh narrated from Ibn Jurayj: `I said to `Ata', "If I know that my servant has money, is it obligatory for me to write him a contract of emancipation" He said, "I do not think it can be anything but obligatory." `Amr bin Dinar said: "I said to `Ata', `Are you narrating this from anybody' He said, `No,' then he told me that Musa bin Anas told him that Sirin, who had a lot of money, asked Anas for a contract of emancipation and he refused. So he went to `Umar (bin Al-Khattab), may Allah be pleased with him, and he said, `Write it for him.' He refused, so `Umar hit him with his whip and recited,

(give them such writing, if you find that there is good and honesty in them.)Then he wrote the contract." This was mentioned by Al-Bukhari with a disconnected chain of narration. It was also narrated by `Abdur-Razzaq who said Ibn Jurayj told them: I said to `Ata', "If I know that my servant has some money, is it obligatory for me to write him a contract of emancipation" He said, `I do not think it can be anything but obligatory.'" (It was also said by `Amr bin Dinar who said, "I said to `Ata', `Are you narrating this from anybody' He said, `No.'") Ibn Jarir recorded that Sirin wanted Anas bin Malik to write a contract of emancipation and he delayed, then `Umar said to him, "You should certainly write him a contract of emancipation." Its chain of narrators is Sahih. Allah's saying:

(if you find that there is good and honesty in them.) Some of them said (this means) trustworthiness. Some said: "Honesty," and others said: "A skill and ability to earn."

(And give them something out of the wealth of Allah which He has bestowed upon you.) This is the share of the wealth of Zakah that Allah stated to be their right. This is the opinion of Al-Hasan, `Abdur-Rahman bin Zayd bin Aslam and his father and Muqatil bin Hayyan. It was also the opinion favored by Ibn Jarir.

(And give them something out of the wealth of Allah which He has bestowed upon you.) Ibrahim An-Nakha`i said, "This is urging the people, their masters and others." This was also the view of Buraydah bin Al-Husayb Al-Aslami and Qatadah. Ibn `Abbas said: "Allah commanded the believers to help in freeing slaves."

The Prohibition of forcing One's Slave-Girls to commit Zina

Allah's saying:

(And force not your slave-girls to prostitution...) Among the people of the Jahiliyyah, there were some who, if he had a slave-girl, he would send her out to commit Zina and would charge money for that, which he would take from her every time. When Islam came, Allah forbade the believers to do that. The reason why this Ayah was revealed, according to the reports of a number of earlier and later scholars of Tafsir, had to do with `Abdullah bin Ubayy bin Salul. He had slave-girls whom he used to force into prostitution so that he could take their earnings and because he wanted them to have children which would enhance his status, or so he claimed.

Reports narrated on this Topic

In his Musnad, Al-Hafiz Abu Bakr Ahmad bin `Amr bin `Abd Al-Khaliq Al-Bazzar, may Allah have mercy on him, recorded that Az-Zuhri said, "`Abdullah bin Ubayy bin Salul had a slave-girl whose name was Mu`adhah, whom he forced into prostitution. When Islam came, the Ayah

(And force not your slave-girls to prostitution...) was revealed." Al-A`mash narrated from Abu Sufyan that Jabir said concerning this Ayah, "This was revealed about a slave-girl belonging to `Abdullah bin Ubayy bin Salul whose name was Musaykah. He used to force her to commit immoral actions, but there was nothing wrong with her and she refused. Then Allah revealed this Ayah:

(And force not your slave-girls to prostitution,) until His saying;

(But if anyone compels them, then after such compulsion, Allah is Oft-Forgiving, Most Merciful.)" An-Nasa'i also recorded something similar. Muqatil bin Hayyan said, "I heard -- and Allah knows best -- that this Ayah was revealed about two men who used to force two slave-girls of theirs (into prostitution). One of them was called Musaykah who belonged to (the Ansari), and Umaymah the mother of Musaykah belonged to `Abdullah bin Ubayy. Mu`adhah and Arwa were in the same situation. Then Musaykah and her mother came to the Prophet and told him about that. Then Allah revealed:

(And force not your slave-girls to prostitution), meaning Zina.

(if they desire chastity,) means, if they want to be chaste, which is the case with the majority of slave-girls.

(in order that you may make a gain in the goods of this worldly life.) meaning, from the money they earn and their children. The Messenger of Allah forbade the money earned by the cupper, the prostitute and the fortune-teller. According to another report:

«مَهْرُ الْبَغِيِّ خَبِيثٌ وَكَسْبُ الْحَجَّامِ خَبِيثٌ، وَثَمَنُ الْكَلْبِ خَبِيثٌ»

(The earnings of a prostitute are evil, the earnings of a cupper are evil, and the price of a dog is evil.)

(But if anyone compels them, then after such compulsion, Allah is Oft-Forgiving, Most Merciful.) meaning, towards them, as has already been stated in the Hadith narrated from Jabir. Ibn Abi Talhah narrated that Ibn `Abbas said, "If you do that, then Allah is Oft-Forgiving, Most Merciful, and their sin will be on the one who forced them to do that." This was also the view of Mujahid, `Ata' Al-Khurasani, Al-A`mash and Qatadah. After explaining these rulings in detail, Allah says:

(And indeed We have sent down for you Ayat that make things plain,) meaning, in the Qur'an there are Ayat which are clear and explain matters in detail.

(and the example of those who passed away before you,) means, reports about the nations of the past and what happened to them when they went against the commandments of Allah, as Allah says:

(And We made them a precedent, and an example to later generations.) (43:56); We made them a lesson, i.e., a rebuke for committing sin and forbidden deeds.

(for those who have Taqwa.) meaning, for those who remember and fear Allah.

Surah: 24 Ayah: 35

اللَّهُ نُورُ ٱلسَّمَـٰوَٰتِ وَٱلۡأَرۡضِۚ مَثَلُ نُورِهِۦ كَمِشۡكَوٰةٍ فِيهَا مِصۡبَاحٌ ٱلۡمِصۡبَاحُ فِى زُجَاجَةٍ ٱلزُّجَاجَةُ كَأَنَّهَا كَوۡكَبٌ دُرِّىٌّ يُوقَدُ مِن شَجَرَةٍ مُّبَـٰرَكَةٍ زَيۡتُونَةٍ لَّا شَرۡقِيَّةٍ وَلَا غَرۡبِيَّةٍ يَكَادُ زَيۡتُهَا يُضِىٓءُ وَلَوۡ لَمۡ تَمۡسَسۡهُ نَارٌۚ نُّورٌ عَلَىٰ نُورٍۚ يَهۡدِى ٱللَّهُ لِنُورِهِۦ مَن يَشَآءُۚ وَيَضۡرِبُ ٱللَّهُ ٱلۡأَمۡثَـٰلَ لِلنَّاسِۗ وَٱللَّهُ بِكُلِّ شَىۡءٍ عَلِيمٌ ۝

35. Allâh is the Light of the heavens and the earth. The parable of His Light is as (if there were) a niche and within it a lamp: the lamp is in glass, the glass as it were a brilliant star, lit from a blessed tree, an olive, neither of the east (i.e. neither it gets sun-rays only in the morning) nor of the west (i.e. nor it gets sun-rays only in the afternoon, but it is exposed to the sun all day long), whose oil would almost glow forth (of itself), though no fire touched it. Light upon Light! Allâh guides to His Light whom He wills. And Allâh sets forth parables for mankind, and Allâh is All-Knower of everything.

Transliteration

35. Allahu nooru alssamawati waal-ardi mathalu noorihi kamishkatin feeha misbahun almisbahu fee zujajatin alzzujajatu kaannaha kawkabun durriyyun yooqadu min shajaratin mubarakatin zaytoonatin la sharqiyyatin wala gharbiyyatin yakadu zaytuha yudee-o walaw lam tamsas-hu narun noorun AAala noorin yahdee Allahu linoorihi man yashao wayadribu Allahu al-amthala lilnnasi waAllahu bikulli shay-in AAaleemun

Tafsir Ibn Kathir

The Parable of the Light of Allah

`Ali bin Abi Talhah reported that Ibn `Abbas said:

(Allah is the Light of the heavens and the earth.) means, the Guide of the inhabitants of the heavens and the earth. Ibn Jurayj said: "Mujahid and Ibn `Abbas said concerning the Ayah:

Chapter 24: An-Noor (The Light), Verses 001-064

(Allah is the Light of the heavens and the earth.) He is controlling their affairs and their stars and sun and moon." As-Suddi said concerning the Ayah:

(Allah is the Light of the heavens and the earth.) by His Light the heavens and earth are illuminated. In the Two Sahihs, it is recorded that Ibn `Abbas, may Allah be pleased with him, said: "When the Messenger of Allah got up to pray at night, he would say:

«اللَّهُمَّ لَكَ الْحَمْدُ، أَنْتَ قَيِّمُ السَّمَوَاتِ وَالْأَرْضِ وَمَنْ فِيهِنَّ، وَلَكَ الْحَمْدُ أَنْتَ نُورُ السَّمَوَاتِ وَالْأَرْضِ وَمَنْ فِيهِنَّ»

(O Allah, to You be praise, You are the Sustainer of heaven and earth and whoever is in them. To You be praise, You are the Light of the heavens and the earth and whoever is in them.) It was narrated that Ibn Mas`ud said, "There is no night or day with your Lord; the Light of the Throne comes from the Light of His Face."

(The parable of His Light) There are two views concerning the meaning of the pronoun (His). The first is that it refers to Allah, may He be glorified and exalted, meaning that the parable of His guidance in the heart of the believer is

(as a niche) This was the view of Ibn `Abbas. The second view is that the pronoun refers to the believer, which is indicated by the context of the words and implies that the parable of the light in the heart of the believer is as a niche. So the heart of the believer and what he is naturally inclined to of guidance and what he learns of the Qur'an which is in accordance with his natural inclinations are, as Allah says:

(Can they who rely on a clear proof from their Lord, and whom a witness from Him recites it (can they be equal with the disbelievers)) (11:17). The heart of the believer in its purity and clarity is likened to a lamp in transparent and jewel-like glass, and the Qur'an and Shari`ah by which it is guided are likened to good, pure, shining oil in which there is no impurity or deviation.

(as (if there were) a niche) Ibn `Abbas, Mujahid, Muhammad bin Ka`b and others said, "This refers to the position of the wick in the lamp." This is well-known, and hence Allah then says:

(and within it a lamp.) This is the flame that burns brightly. Or it was said that the niche is a niche in the house. This is the parable given by Allah of obedience towards Him. Allah calls obedience to Him as light, then He calls it by other numerous names as well. Ubayy bin Ka`b said, "The lamp is the light, and this refers to the Qur'an and the faith that is in his heart." As-Suddi said, "It is the lamp."

(the lamp is in a glass,) means, this light is shining in a clear glass. Ubayy bin Ka`b and others said, "This is the likeness of the heart of the believer."

(the glass as it were a star Durriyyun,) Some authorities recite the word Durriyyun with a Dammah on the Dal and without a Hamzah, which means pearls, i.e., as if it were a star made of pearls (Durr). Others recite it as Dirri'un or Durri'un, with a Kasrah on the Dal, or Dammah on the Dal, and with a Hamzah at the end, which means reflection (Dir'), because if something is shone on the star it becomes brighter than at any other time. The Arabs call the stars they do not know Darari. Ubayy bin Ka`b said: a shining star. Qatadah said: "Huge, bright and clear."

(lit from a blessed tree,) means, it is derived from olive oil, from a blessed tree.

(an olive,) This refers to the blessed tree mentioned previously.

(neither of the east nor of the west,) means, it is not in the eastern part of the land so that it does not get any sun in the first part of the day, nor is it in the western part of the land so that it is shaded from the sun before sunset, but it is in a central position where it gets sun from the beginning of the day until the end, so its oil is good and pure and shining. Ibn Abi Hatim recorded that Ibn `Abbas commented on:

(an olive, neither of the east nor of the west,) "This is a tree in the desert which is not shaded by any other tree or mountain or cave, nothing covers it, and this is best for its oil." Mujahid commented on:

(neither of the east nor of the west,) saying; "It is not in the east where it will get no sun when the sun sets, nor is it in the west where it will get no sun when the sun rises, but it is in a position where it will get sun both at sunrise and sunset." Sa`id bin Jubayr commented:

(an olive, neither of the east nor of the west, whose oil would almost glow forth (of itself)) "This is the best kind of oil. When the sun rises it reaches the tree from the east and when it sets it reaches it from the west, so the sun reaches it morning and evening, so it is not counted as being in the east or in the west."

(whose oil would almost glow forth (of itself), though no fire touched it.) `Abdur-Rahman bin Zayd bin Aslam said (this means) because the oil itself is shining.

(Light upon Light!) Al-`Awfi narrated from Ibn `Abbas that this meant the faith and deeds of a person. As-Suddi said:

(Light upon Light!) "Light of the fire and the light of the oil: when they are combined they give light, and neither of them can give light without the other. Similarly the light of the Qur'an and the light of faith give light when they are combined, and neither can do so without the other."

(Allah guides to His Light whom He wills.) means, Allah shows the way to the ones whom He chooses, as it says in the Hadith recorded by Imam Ahmad from `Abdullah bin `Amr, who said, "I heard the Messenger of Allah say:

«إِنَّ اللهَ تَعَالَى خَلَقَ خَلْقَهُ فِي ظُلْمَةٍ ثُمَّ أَلْقَى عَلَيْهِمْ مِنْ نُورِهِ يَوْمَئِذٍ، فَمَنْ أَصَابَ مِنْ نُورِهِ يَوْمَئِذٍ اهْتَدَى وَمَنْ أَخْطَأَ ضَلَّ فَلِذَلِكَ أَقُولُ: جَفَّ الْقَلَمُ

Chapter 24: An-Noor (The Light), Verses 001-064

»عَلَى عِلْمِ اللهِ عَزَّ وَجَلَّ«

(Allah created His creation in darkness, then on the same day He sent His Light upon them. Whoever was touched by His Light on that day will be guided and whoever was missed will be led astray. Hence I say: the pens have dried in accordance with the knowledge of Allah, may He be glorified.)''

(And Allah sets forth parables for mankind, and Allah is All-Knower of everything.) Having mentioned this parable of the Light of His guidance in the heart of the believer, Allah ends this Ayah with the words:

(And Allah sets forth parables for mankind, and Allah is All-Knower of everything.) meaning, He knows best who deserves to be guided and who deserves to be led astray. Imam Ahmad recorded that Abu Sa`id Al-Khudri said, "The Messenger of Allah said:

»الْقُلُوبُ أَرْبَعَةٌ: قَلْبٌ أَجْرَدُ فِيهِ مِثْلُ السِّرَاجِ يُزْهِرُ، وَقَلْبٌ أَغْلَفُ مَرْبُوطٌ عَلَى غِلَافِهِ، وَقَلْبٌ مَنْكُوسٌ، وَقَلْبٌ مُصْفَحٌ. فَأَمَّا الْقَلْبُ الْأَجْرَدُ: فَقَلْبُ الْمُؤْمِنِ سِرَاجُهُ فِيهِ نُورُهُ، وَأَمَّا الْقَلْبُ الْأَغْلَفُ فَقَلْبُ الْكَافِرِ، وَأَمَّا الْقَلْبُ الْمَنْكُوسُ فَقَلْبُ الْمُنَافِقِ، عَرَفَ ثُمَّ أَنْكَرَ، وَأَمَّا الْقَلْبُ الْمُصْفَحُ فَقَلْبٌ فِيهِ إِيمَانٌ وَنِفَاقٌ، وَمَثَلُ الْإِيمَانِ فِيهِ كَمَثَلِ الْبَقْلَةِ يَمُدُّهَا الْمَاءُ الطَّيِّبُ، وَمَثَلُ النِّفَاقِ فِيهِ كَمَثَلِ الْقَرْحَةِ يَمُدُّهَا الدَّمُ وَالْقَيْحُ، فَأَيُّ الْمُدَّتَيْنِ غَلَبَتْ عَلَى الْأُخْرَى غَلَبَتْ عَلَيْهِ«

(Hearts are of four kinds: the heart that is clear like a shining lamp; the heart that is covered and tied up; the heart that is upside-down; and the heart that is clad in armor. As for the clear heart, it is the heart of the believer in which is a lamp filled with light; as for the covered heart, this is the heart of the disbeliever; as for the upside-down heart, this is the heart of the hypocrite, who recognizes then denies; as for the armor-clad heart, this is the heart in which there is both faith and hypocrisy. The parable of the faith in it is that of legume, a sprout that is irrigated with good water, and the likeness of the hypocrisy in it is that of sores that are fed by blood and pus. Whichever of the two prevails is the characteristic that will dominate.) Its chain of narrators is good (Jayyid) although they (Al-Bukhari and Muslim) did not record it.

Surah: 24 Ayah: 36, Ayah: 37 & Ayah: 38

فِى بُيُوتٍ أَذِنَ ٱللَّهُ أَن تُرْفَعَ وَيُذْكَرَ فِيهَا ٱسْمُهُ يُسَبِّحُ لَهُۥ فِيهَا بِٱلْغُدُوِّ وَٱلْـَٔاصَالِ ﴿٣٦﴾

36. In houses (mosques), which Allâh has ordered to be raised (to be cleaned, and to be honored), in them His Name is remembered (i.e. Adhan, Iqamah, Salât (prayers), invocations, recitation of the Qur'ân etc.) Therein glorify Him (Allâh) in the mornings and in the afternoons or the evenings,

رِجَالٌ لَّا تُلْهِيهِمْ تِجَٰرَةٌ وَلَا بَيْعٌ عَن ذِكْرِ ٱللَّهِ وَإِقَامِ ٱلصَّلَوٰةِ وَإِيتَآءِ ٱلزَّكَوٰةِ يَخَافُونَ يَوْمًا تَتَقَلَّبُ فِيهِ ٱلْقُلُوبُ وَٱلْأَبْصَٰرُ ﴿٣٧﴾

37. Men whom neither trade nor sale (business) diverts them from the Remembrance of Allâh (with heart and tongue), nor from performing As-Salât (Iqâmat-as-Salât), nor from giving the Zakât. They fear a Day when hearts and eyes will be overturned (out of the horror of the torment of the Day of Resurrection).

لِيَجْزِيَهُمُ ٱللَّهُ أَحْسَنَ مَا عَمِلُوا۟ وَيَزِيدَهُم مِّن فَضْلِهِۦ ۗ وَٱللَّهُ يَرْزُقُ مَن يَشَآءُ بِغَيْرِ حِسَابٍ ﴿٣٨﴾

38. That Allâh may reward them according to the best of their deeds, and add even more for them out of His Grace. And Allâh provides without measure to whom He wills.

Transliteration

36. Fee buyootin athina Allahu an turfaAAa wayuthkara feeha ismuhu yusabbihu lahu feeha bialghuduwwi waal-asali 37. Rijalun la tulheehim tijaratun wala bayAAun AAan thikri Allahi wa-iqami alssalati wa-eeta-i alzzakati yakhafoona yawman taqallabu feehi alquloobu waal-absaru 38. Liyajziyahumu Allahu ahsana ma AAamiloo wayazeedahum min fadlihi waAllahu yarzuqu man yashao bighayri hisabin

Tafsir Ibn Kathir

The Virtues of the Masjids, the Correct Etiquette, and the Virtues of Those who take care of them

Having likened the heart of the believer and what it contains of guidance and knowledge to a lamp lit with good oil shining in a clear glass, Allah then states where it belongs, which is in the Masjids, the places on earth that are most beloved to Allah. The Masjids are His houses where He Alone is worshipped. So Allah says:

(In houses which Allah has ordered to be raised,) meaning, Allah has commanded that they be established and that they be kept clean of any filth, idle talk or words or

Chapter 24: An-Noor (The Light), Verses 001-064

deeds that are inappropriate. `Ali bin Abi Talhah reported from Ibn `Abbas concerning this Ayah:

(In houses which Allah has ordered to be raised,) he said; "Allah forbade idle talk in them." This was also the view of `Ikrimah, Abu Salih, Ad-Dahhak, Nafi` bin Jubayr, Abu Bakr bin Sulayman bin Abi Hathamah, Sufyan bin Husayn and others among the scholars of Tafsir. Many Hadiths have been narrated concerning the construction of Masjids, honoring them, respecting them, and perfuming them with incense etc. This has been discussed in more detail elsewhere, and I have written a book dealing with this topic on its own, praise and blessings be to Allah. With Allah's help we will mention here a few of these Hadiths, if Allah wills. In Allah we put our trust and reliance. `Uthman bin `Affan, the Commander of the faithful, may Allah be pleased with him, said; "I heard the Messenger of Allah say:

《مَنْ بَنَى مَسْجِدًا يَبْتَغِي بِهِ وَجْهَ اللهِ بَنَى اللهُ لَهُ مِثْلَهُ فِي الْجَنَّةِ》

(Whoever builds a Masjid seeking the Face of Allah, Allah will build for him something similar to it in Paradise.) It was narrated in the Two Sahihs. Ibn Majah narrated that `Umar bin Al-Khattab, may Allah be pleased with him, said; "The Messenger of Allah said:

《مَنْ بَنَى مَسْجِدًا يُذْكَرُ فِيهِ اسْمُ اللهِ بَنَى اللهُ لَهُ بَيْتًا فِي الْجَنَّةِ》

(Whoever builds a Masjid in which the Name of Allah is remembered, Allah will build for him a house in Paradise.) An-Nasa'i mentioned something similar. There are very many Hadiths which say this. `A'ishah, may Allah be pleased with her, said: "The Messenger of Allah commanded us to build Masjids among the houses, and to clean them and perfume them." This was recorded by Ahmad and the Sunan compilers with the exception of An-Nasa'i. Ahmad and Abu Dawud recorded a similar report from Samurah bin Jundub. Al-Bukhari said: "`Umar said: `Build for the people a place to worship Allah, and beware of using red or yellow for adornment and decoration and distracting the people thereby.'" Abu Dawud narrated that Ibn `Abbas said, "The Messenger of Allah said:

《مَا أُمِرْتُ بِتَشْيِيدِ الْمَسَاجِدِ》

(I was not commanded to Tashyid the Masjids.) Ibn `Abbas said, "Decorating them as the Jews and Christians did." Anas, may Allah be pleased with him, said, "The Messenger of Allah said:

《لَا تَقُومُ السَّاعَةُ حَتَّى يَتَبَاهَى النَّاسُ فِي الْمَسَاجِدِ》

(The Hour will not come until people show off in building Masjids.) It was recorded by Ahmad and the compilers of the Sunan, with the exception of At-Tirmidhi. Buraydah narrated that a man called out in the Masjid and said, "Has any body said anything about a red camel" The Prophet said:

«لَا، وَجَدْتَ، إِنَّمَا بُنِيَتِ الْمَسَاجِدُ لِمَا بُنِيَتْ لَهُ»

(May you never find it! The Masjids were built only for what they were built for.) This was narrated by Muslim. Abu Hurayrah, may Allah be pleased with him, narrated that the Messenger of Allah said:

«إِذَا رَأَيْتُمْ مَنْ يَبِيعُ أَوْ يَبْتَاعُ فِي الْمَسْجِدِ، فَقُولُوا: لَا أَرْبَحَ اللهُ تِجَارَتَكَ، وَإِذَا رَأَيْتُمْ مَنْ يَنْشُدُ ضَالَّةً فِي الْمَسْجِدِ فَقُولُوا: لَا رَدَّهَا اللهُ عَلَيْكَ»

(If you see someone buying or selling in the Masjid, say to him, "May Allah never make your business profitable!" And if you see someone calling out about lost property, say, "May Allah never return it to you!") This was recorded by At-Tirmidhi, who said: "Hasan Gharib." Al-Bukhari recorded that As-Sa'ib bin Yazid Al-Kindi said, "I was standing in the Masjid and a man threw pebbles at me, so I looked and saw `Umar bin Al-Khattab who said, `Go and bring me these two men.' I went and brought them to him, and he said, `Who are you' Or, `Where do you come from' They said, `We are from At-Ta'if.' `Umar said, `If you had been from this town I would have hit you, for you are raising your voices in the Masjid of the Messenger of Allah .'" An-Nasa'i recorded that Ibrahim bin `Abdur-Rahman bin `Awf said: "`Umar heard the voice of a man in the Masjid and said: `Do you know where you are'" This is also Sahih. Al-Hafiz Abu Ya`la Al-Musili recorded from Ibn `Umar that `Umar used to burn incense in the Masjid of the Messenger of Allah every Friday. Its chain of narration is Hasan and there is nothing wrong with it, Allah knows best. It is confirmed in the Two Sahihs that the Messenger of Allah said:

«صَلَاةُ الرَّجُلِ فِي الْجَمَاعَةِ تُضَعَّفُ عَلَى صَلَاتِهِ فِي بَيْتِهِ وَفِي سُوقِهِ خَمْسًا وَعِشْرِينَ ضِعْفًا وَذَلِكَ أَنَّهُ إِذَا تَوَضَّأَ فَأَحْسَنَ وُضُوءَهُ ثُمَّ خَرَجَ إِلَى الْمَسْجِدِ لَا يُخْرِجُهُ إِلَّا الصَّلَاةُ لَمْ يَخْطُ خَطْوَةً إِلَّا بِهَا دَرَجَةٌ وَحُطَّ عَنْهُ بِهَا خَطِيئَةٌ. فَإِذَا صَلَّى لَمْ تَزَلِ الْمَلَائِكَةُ تُصَلِّي عَلَيْهِ مَا دَامَ فِي مُصَلَّاهُ: اللَّهُمَّ صَلِّ عَلَيْهِ، اللَّهُمَّ ارْحَمْهُ. وَلَا يَزَالُ فِي صَلَاةٍ مَا انْتَظَرَ الصَّلَاةَ»

(A man's prayer in congregation is twenty-five times better than his prayer in his house or the marketplace. That is because if he performs Wudu' and does it well, then he goes out to go to the Masjid, and for no other purpose than to pray, he does not take one step but he increases in one level in status and one sin is removed. When he prays, the angels continue sending blessings on him as long as he is in the place where he prays, (they say), "O Allah, send blessings on him, O Allah, have mercy on him." And he will remain in a state of prayer as long as he is waiting for the prayer.) The following is recorded in the Sunan:

«بَشِّرِ الْمَشَّائِينَ إِلَى الْمَسَاجِدِ فِي الظُّلَمِ بِالنُّورِ التَّامِّ يَوْمَ الْقِيَامَةِ»

(Those who walk to the Masjids when it is dark, give them the glad tidings of complete Light on the Day of Resurrection.) When entering the Masjid, it is recommended to enter with one's right foot, and to say the supplication recorded in Sahih Al-Bukhari, where it is narrated from `Abdullah bin `Amr that the Messenger of Allah used to say, when he entered the Masjid:

«أَعُوذُ بِاللهِ الْعَظِيمِ وَبِوَجْهِهِ الْكَرِيمِ، وَسُلْطَانِهِ الْقَدِيمِ، مِنَ الشَّيْطَانِ الرَّجِيمِ»

(I seek refuge with Allah Almighty and with His Noble Face, and with His Eternal Domain, from the accursed Shaytan.) (He (one of the narrators) asked, `Is that all' He answered, `Yes'). If he says this, the Shaytan says: "He will be protected from me all day long." Muslim recorded that Abu Humayd or Abu Usayd said: The Messenger of Allah said:

«إِذَا دَخَلَ أَحَدُكُمُ الْمَسْجِدَ فَلْيَقُلْ: اللَّهُمَّ افْتَحْ لِي أَبْوَابَ رَحْمَتِكَ. وَإِذَا خَرَجَ فَلْيَقُلْ: اللَّهُمَّ إِنِّي أَسْأَلُكَ مِنْ فَضْلِكَ»

(When anyone of you enters the Masjid, let him say: "O Allah, open the gates of Your mercy for me. And when he comes out, let him say: "O Allah, I ask You of Your bounty.") An-Nasa'i also recorded this from them from the Prophet . Abu Hurayrah, may Allah be pleased with him, said: The Messenger of Allah said:

«إِذَا دَخَلَ أَحَدُكُمُ الْمَسْجِدَ فَلْيُسَلِّمْ عَلَى النَّبِيِّ. وَلْيَقُلْ: اللَّهُمَّ افْتَحْ لِي أَبْوَابَ رَحْمَتِكَ، وَإِذَا خَرَجَ فَلْيُسَلِّمْ عَلَى النَّبِيِّ وَلْيَقُلْ: اللَّهُمَّ اعْصِمْنِي مِنَ الشَّيْطَانِ الرَّجِيمِ»

(When anyone of you enters the Masjid, let him invoke blessings on the Prophet then let him say: "O Allah, open the gates of Your mercy for me." When he comes out, let him invoke blessings on the Prophet and say, "O Allah, protect me from the accursed Shaytan.") This was also recorded by Ibn Majah, as well as Ibn Khuzaymah and Ibn Hibban in their Sahihs.

(in them His Name is remembered.) meaning, the Name of Allah. This is like the Ayat:

(O Children of Adam! Take your adornment to every Masjid...) (7:31)

(and you should face (Him only) in each and every Masjid, and invoke Him only making your religion sincere to Him) (7:29).

(And the Masjids are for Allah) (72:18).

(in them His Name is remembered.) Ibn `Abbas said, "This means that His Book is recited therein."

(Therein glorify Him in the mornings and in the evenings.)

(Men whom neither trade nor business diverts from the remembrance of Allah) This is like the Ayat:

(O you who believe! Let not your properties or your children divert you from the remembrance of Allah.) (63:9)

(O you who believe! When the call is proclaimed for the Salah on Friday, hasten earnestly to the remembrance of Allah and leave off business.) (62:9) Allah says that this world and its adornments, attractions and marketplaces should not distract them from remembering their Lord Who created them and sustains them, those who know that what is with Him is better for them than what they themselves possess, because what they have is transient but that which is with Allah is eternal. Allah says:

(Men whom neither trade nor business diverts from the remembrance of Allah nor from performing the Salah nor from giving the Zakah). meaning, they give priority to obeying Allah and doing what He wants and what pleases Him over doing what they want and what pleases them. It was reported from Salim from `Abdullah bin `Umar that he was in the marketplace when the Iqamah for prayer was called, so they closed their stores and entered the Masjid. Ibn `Umar said: "Concerning them the Ayah was revealed:

(Men whom neither trade nor business diverts from the remembrance of Allah)." This was recorded by Ibn Abi Hatim and Ibn Jarir.

(Men whom neither trade nor business diverts from the remembrance of Allah). `Ali bin Abi Talhah reported that Ibn `Abbas said, "This meant from the prescribed prayers." This was also the view of Muqatil bin Hayyan and Ar-Rabi` bin Anas. As-Suddi said: "From prayer in congregation." Muqatil bin Hayyan said, "That does not distract them from attending the prayer and establishing it as Allah commanded them, and from doing the prayers at the prescribed times and doing all that Allah has enjoined upon them in the prayer."

(They fear a Day when hearts and eyes will be overturned.) means, the Day of Resurrection when people's hearts and eyes will be overturned, because of the intensity of the fear and terror of that Day. This is like the Ayah:

Chapter 24: An-Noor (The Light), Verses 001-064

(And warn them of the Day that is drawing near...) (40:18),

(but He gives them respite up to a Day when the eyes will stare in horror) (14:42).

(And they give food, inspite of their love for it, to the poor, the orphan, and the captive, (saying:) "We feed you seeking Allah's Face only. We wish for no reward, nor thanks from you. Verily, We fear from our Lord a Day, hard and distressful, that will make the faces look horrible." So Allah saved them from the evil of that Day, and gave them a light of beauty and joy. And their recompense shall be Paradise, and silken garments, because they were patient) (76:8-12). And Allah says here:

(That Allah may reward them according to the best of their deeds,) meaning, "They are those from whom We shall accept the best of their deeds and overlook their evil deeds."

(and add even more for them out of His grace.) means, He will accept their good deeds and multiply them for them, as Allah says:

(Surely, Allah wrongs not even of the weight of a speck of dust.) (4:40)

(Whoever brings a good deed shall have ten times the like thereof to his credit.) (6:160)

(Who is he that will lend to Allah a goodly loan.) (2:245)

(Allah gives manifold increase to whom He wills.) (2:261) And Allah says here:

(And Allah provides without measure to whom He wills.)

Surah: 24 Ayah: 39 & Ayah: 40

وَٱلَّذِينَ كَفَرُوٓا۟ أَعْمَٰلُهُمْ كَسَرَابٍۭ بِقِيعَةٍ يَحْسَبُهُ ٱلظَّمْـَٔانُ مَآءً حَتَّىٰٓ إِذَا جَآءَهُۥ لَمْ يَجِدْهُ شَيْـًٔا وَوَجَدَ ٱللَّهَ عِندَهُۥ فَوَفَّىٰهُ حِسَابَهُۥ ۗ وَٱللَّهُ سَرِيعُ ٱلْحِسَابِ ۝

39. As for those who disbelieve, their deeds are like a mirage in a desert. The thirsty one thinks it to be water, until he comes up to it, he finds it to be nothing, but he finds Allâh with him, Who will pay him his due (Hell). And Allâh is Swift in taking account.

أَوْ كَظُلُمَٰتٍ فِى بَحْرٍ لُّجِّىٍّ يَغْشَىٰهُ مَوْجٌ مِّن فَوْقِهِۦ مَوْجٌ مِّن فَوْقِهِۦ سَحَابٌ ۚ ظُلُمَٰتٌۢ بَعْضُهَا فَوْقَ بَعْضٍ إِذَآ أَخْرَجَ يَدَهُۥ لَمْ يَكَدْ يَرَىٰهَا ۗ وَمَن لَّمْ يَجْعَلِ ٱللَّهُ لَهُۥ نُورًا فَمَا لَهُۥ مِن نُّورٍ ۝

40. Or (the state of a disbeliever) is like the darkness in a vast deep sea, overwhelmed with waves topped by waves, topped by dark clouds, (layers of)

darkness upon darkness: if a man stretches out his hand, he can hardly see it! And he for whom Allâh has not appointed light, for him there is no light.

Transliteration

39. Waallatheena kafaroo aAAmaluhum kasarabin biqeeAAatin yahsabuhu alththamanu maan hatta itha jaahu lam yajidhu shay-an wawajada Allaha AAindahu fawaffahu hisabahu waAllahu sareeAAu alhisabi 40. Aw kathulumatin fee bahrin lujjiyyin yaghshahu mawjun min fawqihi mawjun min fawqihi sahabun thulumatun baAAduha fawqa baAAdin itha akhraja yadahu lam yakad yaraha waman lam yajAAali Allahu lahu nooran fama lahu min noorin

Tafsir Ibn Kathir

Two Examples of two kinds of Disbelievers

These are two examples which Allah sets forth of two kinds of disbelievers. Similarly He sets forth two parables of the hypocrites at the beginning of Surat Al-Baqarah: one involving fire and the other involving water. Similarly, in Surat Ar-Ra`d He gives two parables of the guidance and knowledge that are instilled in the heart, again involving fire and water; we have discussed each of them in the appropriate place and there is no need to repeat it here, praise be to Allah. The first of these two examples is that of the disbelievers who call others to their disbelief, thinking that they have good actions and beliefs, when this is not in fact the case. Their likeness is that of a mirage which is seen in a desert plain, looking from a distance as if it is a deep sea. The word Qi`ah refers to a vast, flat, level area of land in which the mirage may appear. There are different kinds of mirage, one which appears after midday, and another which appears in the morning and looks like water between heaven and earth. If a person who is in need of water sees the mirage, he thinks that it is water so he heads towards it in order to drink from it, but when he reaches it,

(he finds it to be nothing.); Similarly the disbeliever thinks that he is doing something good and that he has achieved something, but when Allah judges him on the Day of Resurrection, and brings him to account and examines his deeds, he will find that nothing has been accepted at all, either because of a lack of sincere belief or because he did not follow the proper ways of the Shari`ah. As Allah says:

(And We shall turn to whatever deeds they did, and We shall make such deeds as scattered floating particles of dust.) (25:23). And He says here:

(but he finds Allah with him, who will pay him his due. And Allah is swift in taking account.) A similar view was also narrated from Ubayy bin Ka`b, Ibn `Abbas, Mujahid, Qatadah and others. In the Two Sahihs, it is reported that on the Day of Resurrection it will be said to the Jews, "What did you used to worship" They will say, "We used to worship `Uzayr the son of Allah." It will be said to them, "You have lied. Allah has not begotten a son. What do you want" They will say, "O Lord, we are thirsty, give us something to drink." It will be said to them, "Do you not see" Then Hell will be shown to them as if it is a mirage, parts of it consuming other parts, and they will go and fall into it. This is the parable of one whose ignorance is deep and advanced. As for those whose ignorance is simple, those who are uneducated and foolish and blindly follow the leaders of disbelief, knowing and understanding nothing, their parable is as Allah says: d

(Or like the darkness in a vast deep sea, overwhelmed with waves topped by waves, topped by dark clouds, darkness upon darkness: if a man stretches out his hand, he can hardly see it!) meaning, he can hardly see it because it is so intensely dark. This is the parable of the heart of the disbeliever whose ignorance is simple, who merely follows and does not know the true nature of the one whom he follows or where he is going. He is like the ignorant man in the parable who was asked, "Where are you going" He said, "With them." He was asked, "Where are they going" He said, "I do not know."

(darkness upon darkness) Ubayy bin Ka`b said: "He is enveloped in five types of darkness: his speech is darkness, his deeds are darkness, his coming in is darkness, his going out is darkness and his destiny on the Day of Resurrection will be darkness in the fire of Hell." As-Suddi and Ar-Rabi` bin Anas also said something similar.

(And he for whom Allah has not appointed light, for him there is no light.) One whom Allah does not guide is ignorant and doomed, an utter loser and disbeliever. This is like the Ayah:

(Whomsoever Allah sends astray, none can guide him) (7:186) This is in contrast to what Allah says about the believers:

(Allah guides to His Light whom He wills.) (24:35) We ask Allah the Almighty to put light in our hearts and give us light on our right and on our left, and to increase us in light.

Surah: 24 Ayah: 41 & Ayah: 42

أَلَمْ تَرَ أَنَّ ٱللَّهَ يُسَبِّحُ لَهُۥ مَن فِى ٱلسَّمَـٰوَٰتِ وَٱلْأَرْضِ وَٱلطَّيْرُ صَـٰٓفَّـٰتٍۢ ۖ كُلٌّۭ قَدْ عَلِمَ صَلَاتَهُۥ وَتَسْبِيحَهُۥ ۗ وَٱللَّهُ عَلِيمٌۢ بِمَا يَفْعَلُونَ ۝

41. See you not (O Muhammad (peace be upon him)) that Allâh, He it is Whom glorify whosoever is in the heavens and the earth, and the birds with wings outspread (in their flight). Of each one He (Allâh) knows indeed his Salât (prayer) and his glorification, (or everyone knows his Salât (prayer) and his glorification), and Allâh is All-Aware of what they do.

وَلِلَّهِ مُلْكُ ٱلسَّمَـٰوَٰتِ وَٱلْأَرْضِ ۖ وَإِلَى ٱللَّهِ ٱلْمَصِيرُ ۝

42. And to Allâh belongs the sovereignty of the heavens and the earth, and to Allâh is the return (of all).

Transliteration

41. Alam tara anna Allaha yusabbihu lahu man fee alssamawati waal-ardi waalttayru saffatin kullun qad AAalima salatahu watasbeehahu waAllahu AAaleemun bima yafAAaloona 42. Walillahi mulku alssamawati waal-ardi wa-ila Allahi almaseeru

Tafsir Ibn Kathir

Everything glorifies Allah, may He be exalted, and to Him belongs the Sovereignty

Allah tells us that whosoever is in the heavens and on the earth, i.e., the angels, mankind, Jinn, animals and even inanimate objects, all glorify Him. This is like the Ayah:

(The seven heavens and the earth and all that is therein, glorify Him) (17:44),

(and the birds with wings outspread) means, while they are flying they glorify their Lord and worship Him with the glorification with which they are inspired and to which they are guided. Allah knows what they are doing, and so He says:

(Of each one He knows indeed his Salah and his glorification;) meaning, He has guided every creature to its own way of worshipping Allah, may He be glorified. Then Allah tells us that He knows all of that and nothing at all is hidden from Him. He says:

(and Allah is All-Aware of what they do.) Then Allah tells us that to Him belongs the sovereignty of heaven and earth, and that He is the Ruler and Controller, the God Who is worshipped and besides Whom none other is to be worshipped, and there is none to put back His judgement.

(and to Allah is the return) means, on the Day of Resurrection, when He will judge as He wills,

(that He may requite those who do evil with that which they have done...) (53:31) He is the Creator and Sovereign, and His is indeed the Authority in this world and the next. To Him be praise at the beginning and in the end.

Surah: 24 Ayah: 43 & Ayah: 44

أَلَمْ تَرَ أَنَّ ٱللَّهَ يُزْجِى سَحَابًا ثُمَّ يُؤَلِّفُ بَيْنَهُۥ ثُمَّ يَجْعَلُهُۥ رُكَامًا فَتَرَى ٱلْوَدْقَ يَخْرُجُ مِنْ خِلَٰلِهِۦ وَيُنَزِّلُ مِنَ ٱلسَّمَآءِ مِن جِبَالٍ فِيهَا مِنْ بَرَدٍ فَيُصِيبُ بِهِۦ مَن يَشَآءُ وَيَصْرِفُهُۥ عَن مَّن يَشَآءُ يَكَادُ سَنَا بَرْقِهِۦ يَذْهَبُ بِٱلْأَبْصَٰرِ ۝

43. See you not that Allâh drives the clouds gently, then joins them together, then makes them into a heap of layers, and you see the rain comes forth from between them. And He sends down from the sky hail (like) mountains, (or there are in the heaven mountains of hail from where He sends down hail), and strike

therewith whom He will, and averts it from whom He wills. The vivid flash of its (clouds) lightning nearly blinds the sight. (Tafsir At-Tabarî).

$$\text{يُقَلِّبُ ٱللَّهُ ٱلَّيْلَ وَٱلنَّهَارَ إِنَّ فِى ذَٰلِكَ لَعِبْرَةً لِّأُوْلِى ٱلْأَبْصَٰرِ}$$

44. Allâh causes the night and the day to succeed each other (i.e. if the day is gone, the night comes, and if the night is gone, the day comes, and so on). Truly, in these things is indeed a lesson for those who have nsight.

Transliteration

43. Alam tara anna Allaha yuzjee sahaban thumma yu-allifu baynahu thumma yajAAaluhu rukaman fatara alwadqa yakhruju min khilalihi wayunazzilu mina alssama-i min jibalin feeha min baradin fayuseebu bihi man yashao wayasrifuhu AAan man yashao yakadu sana barqihi yathhabu bial-absari 44. Yuqallibu Allahu allayla waalnnahara inna fee thalika laAAibratan li-olee al-absari

Tafsir Ibn Kathir

The Power of Allah to create the Clouds and that which comes from Them

Allah tells us that He drives the clouds from the beginning, when they are formed and are still weak. This is the "Gentle driving."

(then joins them together,) means, He brings them together after they have been scattered.

(then makes them into a heap of layers,) means, He piles them up on top of one another.

(and you see the Wadq) meaning the rain,

(come forth from between them;) means, from the gaps between them. This is how it was understood by Ibn `Abbas and Ad-Dahhak. `Ubayd bin `Umayr Al-Laythi said: "Allah sends the scatterer (wind), which stirs up that which is on the surface of the earth. Then he sends the generator (wind), which forms the clouds. Then He sends the joiner (wind) which brings them together. Then He sends the fertilizer (wind) which fertilizes or `seeds' the clouds." This was recorded by Ibn Abi Hatim and Ibn Jarir.

(and He sends down from (Min) the sky, from (Min) mountains in it of (Min) ice,) Some of the grammarians said that the first Min describes the place from which it is coming, the second specifies from which part of the sky it comes, and the third means some kind of mountains. This is based on the view of those scholars of Tafsir who say that,

(from (Min) mountains in it of (Min) ice) means that there are mountains of hail in the sky from which Allah sends down ice. As for those who say that "mountains" here is used as a metaphor for clouds, they think that the second Min is also used to describe the place from which the ice is coming, and is thus interchangeable with the first. And Allah knows best.

(and strikes therewith whom He wills, and averts it from whom He wills.) It may be that the phrase

(and strikes therewith) means, with what He sends down from the sky of different kinds of rain and hail. So then the phrase

(and strikes therewith whom He wills) means, by His mercy towards them, and

(and averts it from whom He wills.) means, He withholds rain from them. Or it may be that

(and strikes therewith) means, with hail, as a punishment towards whomever He wills, striking their fruits and destroying their crops and trees. And He averts it from whomever He wills as a mercy towards them.

(The vivid flash of its lightning nearly blinds the sight.) the brightness of its lightning almost takes away their sight if the eyes follow it and try to look at it.

(Allah causes the night and the day to succeed each other.) He is controlling them, so that He takes something from the length of one and adds it to the other, which is short, until they become equal, then He does the opposite so that the one which was short becomes long and vice versa. Allah is the One Who is controlling that by His command, power, might and knowledge.

(Truly, in this is indeed a lesson for those who have insight.) means, this is an indication of His greatness, may He be exalted. This is like the Ayah:

(Verily, in the creation of the heavens and the earth, and in the alternation of night and day, there are indeed signs for men of understanding.) (3:190) and thereafter.

Surah: 24 Ayah: 45

وَٱللَّهُ خَلَقَ كُلَّ دَآبَّةٍ مِّن مَّآءٍ فَمِنْهُم مَّن يَمْشِى عَلَىٰ بَطْنِهِۦ وَمِنْهُم مَّن يَمْشِى عَلَىٰ رِجْلَيْنِ وَمِنْهُم مَّن يَمْشِى عَلَىٰٓ أَرْبَعٍ يَخْلُقُ ٱللَّهُ مَا يَشَآءُ إِنَّ ٱللَّهَ عَلَىٰ كُلِّ شَىْءٍ قَدِيرٌ ۞

45. Allâh has created every moving (living) creature from water. Of them there are some that creep on their bellies, some that walk on two legs, and some that walk on four. Allâh creates what He wills. Verily! Allâh is Able to do all things.

Transliteration

45. WaAllahu khalaqa kulla dabbatin min ma-in faminhum man yamshee AAala batnihi waminhum man yamshee AAala rijlayni waminhum man yamshee AAala arbaAAin yakhluqu Allahu ma yashao inna Allaha AAala kulli shay-in qadeerun

Chapter 24: An-Noor (The Light), Verses 001-064

Tafsir Ibn Kathir

Allah's Power in His creation of the Animals

Allah mentions His complete and almighty power to create all the different kinds of animals with their various forms, colors and ways of moving and stopping, from one kind of water.

(Of them there are some that creep on their bellies,) like snakes and so on;

(and some that walk on two legs,) like humans and birds;

(and some that walk on four,) like cattle and all kinds of animals. Allah says:

(Allah creates what He wills.) meaning by His power, because what He wills happens and what He does not will does not happen. So he says:

(Verily, Allah is able to do all things.)

Surah: 24 Ayah: 46

لَّقَدْ أَنزَلْنَآ ءَايَـٰتٍ مُّبَيِّنَـٰتٍ ۚ وَٱللَّهُ يَهْدِى مَن يَشَآءُ إِلَىٰ صِرَٰطٍ مُّسْتَقِيمٍ ۝

46. We have indeed sent down (in this Qur'ân) manifest Ayât (proofs, evidences, verses, lessons, signs, revelations, lawful and unlawful things, and the set boundaries of Islâmic religion, etc. that make things clear showing the Right Path of Allâh). And Allâh guides whom He wills to a Straight Path (i.e. to Allâh's religion of Islâmic Monotheism).

Transliteration

46. Laqad anzalna ayatin mubayyinatin waAllahu yahdee man yashao ila siratin mustaqeemin

Tafsir Ibn Kathir

Allah states that in this Qur'an He has revealed many clear and unambiguous rulings, words of wisdom and parables, and that He guides people of understanding, insight and intellect to ponder and understand them. He says:

(And Allah guides whom He wills to the Straight Path.)

Surah: 24 Ayah: 47, Ayah: 48, Ayah: 49, Ayah: 50, Ayah: 51 & Ayah: 52

وَيَقُولُونَ ءَامَنَّا بِٱللَّهِ وَبِٱلرَّسُولِ وَأَطَعْنَا ثُمَّ يَتَوَلَّىٰ فَرِيقٌ مِّنْهُم مِّنۢ بَعْدِ ذَٰلِكَ ۚ وَمَآ أُوْلَـٰٓئِكَ بِٱلْمُؤْمِنِينَ ۝

47. They (hypocrites) say: "We have believed in Allâh and in the Messenger (Muhammad (peace be upon him)) and we obey," then a party of them turn away thereafter, such are not believers.

وَإِذَا دُعُوٓاْ إِلَى ٱللَّهِ وَرَسُولِهِۦ لِيَحْكُمَ بَيْنَهُمْ إِذَا فَرِيقٌ مِّنْهُم مُّعْرِضُونَ ۝

48. And when they are called to Allâh (i.e. His Words, the Qur'ân) and His Messenger (peace be upon him), to judge between them, lo! a party of them refuse (to come) and turn away.

وَإِن يَكُن لَّهُمُ ٱلْحَقُّ يَأْتُوٓاْ إِلَيْهِ مُذْعِنِينَ ۝

49. But if the right is with them, they come to him willingly with submission.

أَفِى قُلُوبِهِم مَّرَضٌ أَمِ ٱرْتَابُوٓاْ أَمْ يَخَافُونَ أَن يَحِيفَ ٱللَّهُ عَلَيْهِمْ وَرَسُولُهُۥ ۚ بَلْ أُوْلَٰٓئِكَ هُمُ ٱلظَّٰلِمُونَ ۝

50. Is there a disease in their hearts? Or do they doubt or fear lest Allâh and His Messenger (peace be upon him) should wrong them in judgement. Nay, it is they themselves who are the Zâlimûn (polytheists, hypocrites and wrong-doers, etc.).

إِنَّمَا كَانَ قَوْلَ ٱلْمُؤْمِنِينَ إِذَا دُعُوٓاْ إِلَى ٱللَّهِ وَرَسُولِهِۦ لِيَحْكُمَ بَيْنَهُمْ أَن يَقُولُواْ سَمِعْنَا وَأَطَعْنَا ۚ وَأُوْلَٰٓئِكَ هُمُ ٱلْمُفْلِحُونَ ۝

51. The only saying of the faithful believers, when they are called to Allâh (His Words, the Qur'ân) and His Messenger (Peace be upon him), to judge between them, is that they say: "We hear and we obey." And such are the prosperous ones (who will live forever in Paradise).

وَمَن يُطِعِ ٱللَّهَ وَرَسُولَهُۥ وَيَخْشَ ٱللَّهَ وَيَتَّقْهِ فَأُوْلَٰٓئِكَ هُمُ ٱلْفَآئِزُونَ ۝

52. And whosoever obeys Allâh and His Messenger (peace be upon him), fears Allâh, and keeps his duty (to Him), such are the successful ones.

Transliteration

47. Wayaqooloona amanna biAllahi wabialrrasooli waataAAna thumma yatawalla fareequn minhum min baAAdi thalika wama ola-ika bialmu/mineena 48. Wa-itha duAAoo ila Allahi warasoolihi liyahkuma baynahum itha fareequn minhum muAAridoona 49. Wa-in yakun lahumu alhaqqu ya/too ilayhi muthAAineena 50. Afee quloobihim maradun ami irtaboo am yakhafoona an yaheefa Allahu AAalayhim warasooluhu bal ola-ika humu alththalimoona 51. Innama kana qawla almu/mineena itha duAAoo ila Allahi warasoolihi liyahkuma baynahum an yaqooloo samiAAna waataAAna waola-ika humu almuflihoona 52. Waman yutiAAi Allaha warasoolahu wayakhsha Allaha wayattaqhi faola-ika humu alfa-izoona

Tafsir Ibn Kathir

The Treachery of the Hypocrites and the Attitude of the Believers

Allah tells us about the characteristics of the hypocrites who show one thing while hiding another, and who say with their tongues,

("We have believed in Allah and in the Messenger, and we obey," then a party of them turn away thereafter,) meaning, their actions contradict their deeds, and they say that which they do not do. Allah says:

(such are not believers.)

(And when they are called to Allah and His Messenger, to judge between them...) means, when they are asked to follow the guidance which Allah has revealed to His Messenger, they turn away and are too arrogantly proud of themselves to follow him. This is like the Ayah:

(Have you not seen those who claim that they believe in that which has been sent down to you, and that which was sent down before you.) until His saying:

(you see the hypocrites turn away from you with aversion) (4: 60-61).

(But if the truth is on their side, they come to him willingly with submission.) means, if the ruling will be in their favor and not against them, then they will come and will listen and obey, which is what is meant by the phrase

(willingly with submission.) But if the ruling will go against him, he turns away and demands something that goes against the truth, and he prefers to refer for judgement to someone other than the Prophet so that his false claims may prevail. His acceptance in the beginning was not because he believed that it was the truth, but because it happened to be in accordance with his desires. So when the truth went against what he was hoping for, he turned away from it. Allah said:

(Is there a disease in their hearts...) meaning, their situation cannot be anything else, they must necessarily have a disease in their hearts, or else they have some doubts about the religion, or they are afraid that Allah and His Messenger will be unjust in their ruling against them. Whichever it is, it is pure disbelief, and Allah knows which of these characteristics each one of them has. d

(Nay, it is they themselves who are the wrongdoers.) means, they are the evildoers who commit immoral actions, and Allah and His Messenger are innocent of the injustice and unfairness that they imagine; exalted be Allah and His Messenger above such a thing. Then Allah tells us about the attributes of the believers who respond to Allah and His Messenger and who seek no other way apart from the Book of Allah and the Sunnah of His Messenger. Allah says:

(The only saying of the faithful believers, when they are called to Allah and His Messenger, to judge between them, is that they say: "We hear and we obey".)

meaning, to hear to obey. Allah describes them as having attained success, which is achieving what one wants and being saved from what one fears. So Allah says:

(And such are the successful.) Concerning the Ayah:

(they say: "We hear and we obey".), Qatadah said: "We were told that when `Ubadah bin As-Samit, who had been present at Al-`Aqabah and at Badr, and was one of the leaders of the Ansar, was dying, he said to his nephew Junadah bin Abi Umayyah: `Shall I not tell you what you must do and what is your due' He said, `Yes.' He said: `You have to listen and obey when times are easy and when they are hard, when you feel energetic and when you do not want to, and when you feel selfish. You have to train your tongue to speak the truth. Do not go against those who are in authority, unless they openly command you to commit acts of disobedience to Allah. Whenever you are commanded to do something that goes against the Book of Allah, then follow the Book of Allah.'" Qatadah said: We were told that Abu Ad-Darda' said, "There is no Islam except through obedience to Allah, and no goodness except in Jama`ah. Sincerity is to Allah and His Messenger, and to the Khalifah and all the believers." He said: "And we were told that `Umar bin Al-Khattab, may Allah be pleased with him, used to say; `The bonds of Islam are La ilaha illallah, establishing prayer, paying Zakah and obeying those whom Allah has given authority over the affairs of the Muslims.'" This was recorded by Ibn Abi Hatim. There are very many Hadiths and reports which state that it is obligatory to obey the Book of Allah, the Sunnah of His Messenger, the Rightly-Guided Khalifahs and the Imams when they command us to obey Allah; there are too many of these reports to quote them all here.

(And whosoever obeys Allah and His Messenger,) in what he is commanded with, and avoid what he is forbidden,

(fears Allah,) means, for his past sins,

(and has Taqwa of Him,) regarding sins he may commit in the future.

(such are the successful.) means, those who will attain all goodness and be saved from all evil in this world and the Hereafter.

Surah: 24 Ayah: 53 & Ayah: 54

﴿ وَأَقْسَمُواْ بِٱللَّهِ جَهْدَ أَيْمَٰنِهِمْ لَئِنْ أَمَرْتَهُمْ لَيَخْرُجُنَّ قُل لَّا تُقْسِمُواْ طَاعَةٌ مَّعْرُوفَةٌ إِنَّ ٱللَّهَ خَبِيرٌۢ بِمَا تَعْمَلُونَ ۝

53. They swear by Allâh their strongest oaths, that if only you would order them, they would leave (their homes for fighting in Allâh's Cause). Say: "Swear you not; (this) obedience (of yours) is known (to be false). Verily, Allâh knows well what you do."

Chapter 24: An-Noor (The Light), Verses 001-064

قُلْ أَطِيعُوا۟ ٱللَّهَ وَأَطِيعُوا۟ ٱلرَّسُولَ ۖ فَإِن تَوَلَّوْا۟ فَإِنَّمَا عَلَيْهِ مَا حُمِّلَ وَعَلَيْكُم مَّا حُمِّلْتُمْ ۖ وَإِن تُطِيعُوهُ تَهْتَدُوا۟ ۚ وَمَا عَلَى ٱلرَّسُولِ إِلَّا ٱلْبَلَٰغُ ٱلْمُبِينُ ۝

54. Say: "Obey Allâh and obey the Messenger, but if you turn away, he (Messenger Muhammad (peace be upon him)) is only responsible for the duty placed on him (i.e. to convey Allâh's Message) and you for that placed on you. If you obey him, you shall be on the right guidance. The Messenger's duty is only to convey (the message) in a clear way (i.e. to preach in a plain way)."

Transliteration

53. Waaqsamoo biAllahi jahda aymanihim la-in amartahum layakhrujunna qul la tuqsimoo taAAatun maAAroofatun inna Allaha khabeerun bima taAAmaloona 54. Qul ateeAAoo Allaha waateeAAoo alrrasoola fa-in tawallaw fa-innama AAalayhi ma hummila waAAalaykum ma hummiltum wa-in tuteeAAoohu tahtadoo wama AAala alrrasooli illa albalaghu almubeena

Tafsir Ibn Kathir

Allah says about the hypocrites who had promised the Messenger and sworn that if he were to command them to go out for battle, they would go:

(Say: "Swear you not...") meaning, do not swear this oath.

(obedience is known.) It was said that the meaning is, your obedience is known, i.e., it is known that your obedience is merely verbal and is not accompanied by action. Every time you swear an oath you lie. This is like the Ayah:

(They swear to you that you may be pleased with them...) (9:96) And Allah says:

(They have made their oaths a screen (for their evil actions).) (58:16) It is part of their nature to tell lies, even in the issues they choose, as Allah says:

(Have you not observed the hypocrites who say to their friends among the people of the Scripture who disbelieve: "If you are expelled, we indeed will go out with you, and we shall never obey any one against you; and if you are attacked, we shall indeed help you." But Allah is Witness that they verily are liars. Surely, if they are expelled, never will they go out with them; and if they are attacked, they will never help them. And if they do help them, they will turn their backs, and they will not be victorious.) (59:11-12) Then Allah says:

(Say: "Obey Allah and obey the Messenger...) meaning, follow the Book of Allah and the Sunnah of His Messenger .

(but if you turn away,) if you ignore what he has brought to you,

(he is only responsible for the duty placed on him), conveying the Message and fulfilling the trust.

(and you for that placed on you.) accepting that, and venerating it and doing as it commanded.

(If you obey him, you shall be on the right guidance.) because he calls to the straight path,

(The path of Allah to Whom belongs all that is in the heavens and all that is in the earth. ..) (42:53)

(The Messenger's duty is only to convey in a clear way.) This is like the Ayat:

(your duty is only to convey and on Us is the reckoning.) (13:40)

(So remind them -- you are only one who reminds. You are not a dictator over them.) (88:21-22)

Surah: 24 Ayah: 55

وَعَدَ ٱللَّهُ ٱلَّذِينَ ءَامَنُوا۟ مِنكُمْ وَعَمِلُوا۟ ٱلصَّٰلِحَٰتِ لَيَسْتَخْلِفَنَّهُمْ فِى ٱلْأَرْضِ كَمَا ٱسْتَخْلَفَ ٱلَّذِينَ مِن قَبْلِهِمْ وَلَيُمَكِّنَنَّ لَهُمْ دِينَهُمُ ٱلَّذِى ٱرْتَضَىٰ لَهُمْ وَلَيُبَدِّلَنَّهُم مِّنۢ بَعْدِ خَوْفِهِمْ أَمْنًا يَعْبُدُونَنِى لَا يُشْرِكُونَ بِى شَيْـًٔا ۚ وَمَن كَفَرَ بَعْدَ ذَٰلِكَ فَأُو۟لَٰٓئِكَ هُمُ ٱلْفَٰسِقُونَ ۝

55. Allâh has promised those among you who believe, and do righteous good deeds, that He will certainly grant them succession to (the present rulers) in the earth, as He granted it to those before them, and that He will grant them the authority to practice their religion, that which He has chosen for them (i.e. Islâm). And He will surely give them in exchange a safe security after their fear (provided) they (believers) worship Me and do not associate anything (in worship) with Me. But whoever disbelieved after this, they are the Fâsiqûn (rebellious, disobedient to Allâh).

Transliteration

55. WaAAada Allahu allatheena amanoo minkum waAAamiloo alssalihati layastakhlifannahum fee alardi kama istakhlafa allatheena min qablihim walayumakkinanna lahum deenahumu allathee irtada lahum walayubaddilannahum min baAAdi khawfihim amnan yaAAbudoonanee la yushrikoona bee shay-an waman kafara baAAda thalika faola-ika humu alfasiqoona

Tafsir Ibn Kathir

Allah's Promise to the Believers that He would grant them Succession

This is a promise from Allah to His Messenger that He would cause his Ummah to become successors on earth, i.e., they would become the leaders and rulers of mankind, through whom He would reform the world and to whom people would submit, so that they would have in exchange a safe security after their fear. This is what Allah did indeed do, may He be glorified and exalted, and to Him be praise and blessings. For He did not cause His Messenger to die until He had given him victory over Makkah, Khaybar, Bahrayn, all of the Arabian Peninsula and Yemen; and he took Jizyah from the Zoroastrians of Hajar and from some of the border lands of Syria; and he exchanged gifts with Heraclius the ruler of Byzantium, the ruler of Egypt and Alexandria, the Muqawqis, the kings of Oman and An-Najashi of Abyssinia, who had become king after Ashamah, may Allah have mercy on him and grant him honor. Then when the Messenger died, his successor (Khalifah) Abu Bakr As-Siddiq took over the reins of power and united the Ummah, preventing its disintegration. He took control of the entire Arabian Peninsula, and he sent the Islamic armies to the land of Persia, under the leadership of Khalid bin Al-Walid, may Allah be pleased with him, who conquered a part of it and killed some of its people. He sent another army under the leadership of Abu `Ubaydah, may Allah be pleased with him, and the other commanders who came after him in the lands of Syria. He sent a third army under the leadership of `Amr bin Al-`As, may Allah be pleased with him, to Egypt. Allah enabled the army sent to Syria to conquer Busra and Damascus and their provinces the land of Hawran and its environs. Then Allah chose for Abu Bakr to honor him with Him and he died. The people of Islam were blessed that As-Siddiq was inspired to appoint `Umar Al-Faruq as his successor, so he took the reins of power after him and did a perfect job. After the Prophets, the world never saw anyone like `Umar in excellence of conduct and perfect justice. During his time, the rest of Syria and Egypt, and most of Persia, was conquered. Kisra was defeated and utterly humiliated, and he retreated to the furthest point of his kingdom. Mighty Caesar was brought low, his rule over Syria was overthrown, and he retreated to Constantinople. Their wealth was spent for the sake of Allah, as the Messenger of Allah had foretold and promised. May Allah's perfect peace and purest blessing be upon him. During the rule of `Uthman, the Islamic domains spread to the furthest points of the earth, east and west. The lands of the west were conquered as far as Cyprus and Andalusia, Kairouan and Sebta which adjoins the Atlantic Ocean. Towards the east, the conquests extended as far as China. Kisra was killed, his kingdom was utterly destroyed and the cities of Iraq, Khurasan and Al-Ahwaz were conquered. The Muslims killed a great number of Turks and Allah humiliated their great king Khaqan. Taxes were collected from the east and the west, and brought to the Commander of the faithful `Uthman bin `Affan, may Allah be pleased with him. This was a blessing brought by his recitation and study of the Qur'an, and his bringing the Ummah together to preserve and protect it. In the Sahih it was recorded that the Messenger of Allah said:

«إِنَّ اللهَ زَوَى لِيَ الْأَرْضَ فَرَأَيْتُ مَشَارِقَهَا وَمَغَارِبَهَا، وَسَيَبْلُغُ مُلْكُ أُمَّتِي مَا زُوِيَ لِي مِنْهَا»

(Allah showed me the earth and I looked at the east and the west. The dominion of my Ummah will reach everywhere I was shown.) And now we are enjoying that which Allah and His Messenger promised us, for Allah and His Messenger spoke the truth.

We ask Allah to give us faith in Him and His Messenger, and to help us to give thanks to Him in a manner that will earn us His pleasure.

(Allah has promised those among you who believe and do righteous good deeds, that He will certainly grant them succession in the land, as He granted it to those before them, and that He will grant them the authority to practise their religion which He has chosen for them. And He will surely, give them in exchange a safe security after their fear...) Ar-Rabi` bin Anas narrated that Abu Al-`Aliyah said, "The Prophet and his Companions were in Makkah for nearly ten years, calling people in secret to worship Allah Alone with no partner or associate. They were in a state of fear and were not instructed to fight until after they were commanded to migrate to Al-Madinah. When they came to Al-Madinah, then Allah instructed them to fight. In Al-Madinah they were afraid and they carried their weapons morning and evening. This is how they remained for as long as Allah willed..." Then Allah revealed this Ayah. He caused His Prophet to prevail over the Arabian Peninsula, and then they felt safe and put down their weapons. Then Allah took His Prophet and they remained safe throughout the time of Abu Bakr, `Umar and `Uthman, until what happened happened, and fear again prevailed over them, so they instituted a police force and guards. They changed, so their situation changed. One of the Salaf said, "The Khilafah of Abu Bakr and `Umar was true and adhered to the Book of Allah. Then he recited this Ayah." Al-Bara' bin `Azib said, "This Ayah was revealed when we were in a state of extreme fear." This Ayah is like the Ayah:

(And remember when you were few and were reckoned weak in the land) Until His statement:

(so that you might be grateful) (8:26).

(as He granted succession to those before them,) This is like the Ayah where Allah tells us that Musa said to his people:

("It may be that your Lord will destroy your enemy and make you successors on the earth...") (7:129) And Allah says:

(And We wished to do a favor to those who were weak in the land,) until the two Ayat there after. (28: 5-6)

(and that He will grant them the authority to practise their religion which He has chosen for them...) vAs the Messenger of Allah said to `Adiyy bin Hatim when he came to him in a delegation:

»أَتَعْرِفُ الْحِيرَةَ؟«

(Do you know Al-Hirah) He said, "I do not know it, but I have heard of it." The Messenger of Allah said:

»فَوَالَّذِي نَفْسِي بِيَدِهِ لَيُتِمَّنَّ اللهُ هَذَا الْأَمْرَ حَتَّى تَخْرُجَ الظَّعِينَةُ مِنَ الْحِيرَةِ حَتَّى

Chapter 24: An-Noor (The Light), Verses 001-064

تَطُوفَ بِالْبَيْتِ فِي غَيْرِ جِوَارِ أَحَدٍ، وَلَتَفْتَحُنَّ كُنُوزَ كِسْرَى بْنِ هُرْمُزَ»

(By the One in Whose Hand is my soul, Allah will make this matter (i.e., Islam) prevail until a woman riding a camel will come from Al-Hirah and perform Tawaf around the House without needing the protection of anybody, and the treasures of Kisra the son of Hurmuz will be opened.) He said, "Kisra the son of Hurmuz" He said,

«نَعَمْ، كِسْرَى بْنُ هُرْمُزَ، وَلَيُبْذَلَنَّ الْمَالُ حَتَّى لَا يَقْبَلَهُ أَحَدٌ»

(Yes, Kisra the son of Hurmuz, and wealth will be given until there will be no one who will accept it.) `Adiyy bin Hatim said: "Now it is happening that a woman riding a camel comes from Al-Hirah and performs Tawaf around the House without needing the protection of anybody, and I was among those who opened the treasure of Kisra the son of Hurmuz. By the One in Whose Hand is my soul, the third thing will also come to pass, because the Messenger of Allah said it."

(if they worship Me and do not associate anything with Me.) Imam Ahmad recorded from Anas that Mu`adh bin Jabal told him, "While I was riding behind the Prophet on a donkey, with nothing between me and him but the back of his saddle, he said,

«يَا مُعَاذُ بْنَ جَبَلٍ»

(O Mu`adh bin Jabal.) I said, `Here I am at your service, O Messenger of Allah.' Then a while passed, then he said,

«يَا مُعَاذُ بْنَ جَبَلٍ»

(O Mu`adh bin Jabal.) I said, `Here I am at your service, O Messenger of Allah.' Then a while passed, then he said,

«يَا مُعَاذُ بْنَ جَبَلٍ»

(O Mu`adh bin Jabal.) I said, `Here I am at your service, O Messenger of Allah.' He said,

«هَلْ تَدْرِي مَا حَقُّ اللهِ عَلَى الْعِبَادِ؟»

(Do you know the rights that Allah has over His servants) I said, `Allah and His Messenger know best.' He said,

«فَإِنَّ حَقَّ اللهِ عَلَى الْعِبَادِ أَنْ يَعْبُدُوهُ وَلَا يُشْرِكُوا بِهِ شَيْئًا»

(The rights that Allah has over His servants are that they should worship Him and not associate anything with Him.) Then a while passed, then he said,

«يَا مُعَاذُ بْنَ جَبَلٍ»

(O Mu`adh bin Jabal.) I said, `Here I am at your service, O Messenger of Allah.' He said,

«فَهَلْ تَدْرِي مَا حَقُّ الْعِبَادِ عَلَى اللهِ إِذَا فَعَلُوا ذَلِكَ؟»

(Do you know the rights that people have over Allah if they do that) I said, `Allah and His Messenger know best.' He said,

«فَإِنَّ حَقَّ الْعِبَادِ عَلَى اللهِ أَنْ لَا يُعَذِّبَهُمْ»

(The rights that people have over Allah is that He will not punish them.)" This was also recorded in the Two Sahihs.

(But whoever disbelieved after this, they are the rebellious.) means, `whoever then stops obeying Me after that, has stopped obeying the command of his Lord, and that is a great sin.' The Companions -- may Allah be pleased with them -- were the most committed of people after the Prophet to the commands of Allah and the most obedient to Allah. Their victories were in accordance with their level of commitment. They caused the Word of Allah to prevail in the east and the west, and Allah supported them so much that they governed all the people and all the lands. When the people subsequently fell short in their commitment to some of the commandments, their strength and victory fell short accordingly, but it is confirmed through more than one route in the Two Sahihs that the Messenger of Allah said:

«لَا تَزَالُ طَائِفَةٌ مِنْ أُمَّتِي ظَاهِرِينَ عَلَى الْحَقِّ، لَا يَضُرُّهُمْ مَنْ خَذَلَهُمْ وَلَا مَنْ خَالَفَهُمْ إِلَى يَوْمِ الْقِيَامَةِ»

(There will remain a group of my Ummah adhering to the truth, and those who forsake them or oppose them will not harm them until the Day of Resurrection.) According to another report:

«حَتَّى يَأْتِيَ أَمْرُ اللهِ وَهُمْ كَذَلِكَ»

Chapter 24: An-Noor (The Light), Verses 001-064

(.. until the command of Allah comes to pass and they are like that.) According to another report:

«حَتَّى يُقَاتِلُوا الدَّجَّالَ»

(... until they fight the Dajjal.) According to another report:

«حَتَّى يَنْزِلَ عِيسَى ابْنُ مَرْيَمَ وَهُمْ ظَاهِرُونَ»

(... until `Isa bin Maryam comes down and they are prevailing.) All of these reports are Sahih, and there is no contradiction between them.

Surah: 24 Ayah: 56 & Ayah: 57

وَأَقِيمُوا۟ ٱلصَّلَوٰةَ وَءَاتُوا۟ ٱلزَّكَوٰةَ وَأَطِيعُوا۟ ٱلرَّسُولَ لَعَلَّكُمْ تُرْحَمُونَ ۝

56. And perform As-Salât (Iqâmat-as-Salât), and give Zakât and obey the Messenger (Muhammad (peace be upon him)) that you may receive mercy (from Allâh).

لَا تَحْسَبَنَّ ٱلَّذِينَ كَفَرُوا۟ مُعْجِزِينَ فِى ٱلْأَرْضِ ۚ وَمَأْوَىٰهُمُ ٱلنَّارُ ۖ وَلَبِئْسَ ٱلْمَصِيرُ

57. Consider not that the disbelievers can escape in the land. Their abode shall be the Fire, and worst indeed is that destination.

Transliteration

56. Waaqeemoo alssalata waatoo alzzakata waateeAAoo alrrasoola laAAallakum turhamoona 57. La tahsabanna allatheena kafaroo muAAjizeena fee al-ardi wama/wahumu alnnaru walabi/sa almaseeru

Tafsir Ibn Kathir

The Command to pray, give the Zakah and obey the Messenger ; the inability of the Disbelievers to escape, and the ultimate Destiny

Allah commands His believing servants to establish prayer, which means worshipping Allah Alone with no partner or associate; to pay the Zakah, which is an act of kindness towards His poor and weak creatures; and by doing so to obey the Messenger of Allah , i.e., to do as he commands them and to avoid what he forbids them, so that Allah will have mercy on them for that. No doubt, whoever does that, Allah will have mercy on him, as Allah says in another Ayah:

(Allah will have His mercy on them) (9:71)

(Consider not) means, `do not think, O Muhammad,' that:

(the disbelievers) meaning, those who opposed and denied you,

(can escape in the land.) means, that they can flee from Allah. No, Allah is able to deal with them and He will punish them most severely for that. Allah says:

(Their abode) meaning, in the Hereafter,

(shall be the Fire -- and worst indeed is that destination.) means, how terrible the consequences will be for the disbelievers, how evil a place to stay in and how awful a place to rest!

Surah: 24 Ayah: 58, Ayah: 59 & Ayah: 60

يَـٰٓأَيُّهَا ٱلَّذِينَ ءَامَنُوا۟ لِيَسْتَـْٔذِنكُمُ ٱلَّذِينَ مَلَكَتْ أَيْمَـٰنُكُمْ وَٱلَّذِينَ لَمْ يَبْلُغُوا۟ ٱلْحُلُمَ مِنكُمْ ثَلَـٰثَ مَرَّٰتٍ مِّن قَبْلِ صَلَوٰةِ ٱلْفَجْرِ وَحِينَ تَضَعُونَ ثِيَابَكُم مِّنَ ٱلظَّهِيرَةِ وَمِنۢ بَعْدِ صَلَوٰةِ ٱلْعِشَآءِ ثَلَـٰثُ عَوْرَٰتٍ لَّكُمْ لَيْسَ عَلَيْكُمْ وَلَا عَلَيْهِمْ جُنَاحٌۢ بَعْدَهُنَّ طَوَّٰفُونَ عَلَيْكُم بَعْضُكُمْ عَلَىٰ بَعْضٍ كَذَٰلِكَ يُبَيِّنُ ٱللَّهُ لَكُمُ ٱلْءَايَـٰتِ وَٱللَّهُ عَلِيمٌ حَكِيمٌ ۝

58. O you who believe! Let your legal slaves and slave-girls, and those among you who have not come to the age of puberty ask your permission (before they come to your presence) on three occasions; before Fajr (morning) prayer, and while you put off your clothes for the noonday (rest), and after the 'Ishâ' (late-night) prayer. (These) three times are of privacy for you, other than these times there is no sin on you or on them to move about, attending (helping) you each other. Thus Allâh makes clear the Ayât (the Verses of this Qur'ân, showing proofs for the legal aspects of permission for visits, etc.) to you. And Allâh is All-Knowing, All-Wise.

وَإِذَا بَلَغَ ٱلْأَطْفَـٰلُ مِنكُمُ ٱلْحُلُمَ فَلْيَسْتَـْٔذِنُوا۟ كَمَا ٱسْتَـْٔذَنَ ٱلَّذِينَ مِن قَبْلِهِمْ كَذَٰلِكَ يُبَيِّنُ ٱللَّهُ لَكُمْ ءَايَـٰتِهِۦ وَٱللَّهُ عَلِيمٌ حَكِيمٌ ۝

59. And when the children among you come to puberty, then let them (also) ask for permission, as those senior to them (in age). Thus Allâh makes clear His Ayât (Commandments and legal obligations) for you. And Allâh is All-Knowing, All-Wise.

Chapter 24: An-Noor (The Light), Verses 001-064

وَٱلْقَوَٰعِدُ مِنَ ٱلنِّسَآءِ ٱلَّٰتِى لَا يَرْجُونَ نِكَاحًا فَلَيْسَ عَلَيْهِنَّ جُنَاحٌ أَن يَضَعْنَ ثِيَابَهُنَّ غَيْرَ مُتَبَرِّجَٰتٍ بِزِينَةٍ ۖ وَأَن يَسْتَعْفِفْنَ خَيْرٌ لَّهُنَّ ۗ وَٱللَّهُ سَمِيعٌ عَلِيمٌ ﴿٦٠﴾

60. And as for women past child-bearing who do not expect wed-lock, it is no sin on them if they discard their (outer) clothing in such a way as not to show their adornment. But to refrain (i.e. not to discard their outer clothing) is better for them. And Allâh is All-Hearer, All-Knower.

Transliteration

58. Ya ayyuha allatheena amanoo liyasta/thinkumu allatheena malakat aymanukum waallatheena lam yablughoo alhuluma minkum thalatha marratin min qabli salati alfajri waheena tadaAAoona thiyabakum mina alththaheerati wamin baAAdi salati alAAisha-i thalathu AAawratin lakum laysa AAalaykum wala AAalayhim junahun baAAdahunna tawwafoona AAalaykum baAAdukum AAala baAAdin kathalika yubayyinu Allahu lakumu al-ayati waAllahu AAaleemun hakeemun 59. Wa-itha balagha al-atfalu minkumu alhuluma falyasta/thinoo kama ista/thana allatheena min qablihim kathalika yubayyinu Allahu lakum ayatihi waAllahu AAaleemun hakeemun 60. WaalqawaAAidu mina alnnisa-i allatee la yarjoona nikahan falaysa AAalayhinna junahun an yadaAAna thiyabahunna ghayra mutabarrijatin bizeenatin waan yastaAAifna khayrun lahunna waAllahu sameeAAun AAaleemun

Tafsir Ibn Kathir

The Times when Servants and Young Children should seek Permission to enter

These Ayat include a discussion of how people who are closely related should seek permission to enter upon one another. What was mentioned earlier in the Surah had to do with how unrelated people should seek permission to enter upon one another. Allah commanded the believers to ensure that their servants and their children who have not yet reached puberty should seek permission at three times: the first is before the Fajr prayer, because people are asleep in their beds at that time.

(and while you put off your clothes during the afternoon,) means, at the time of rest, because a man may be in a state of undress with his wife at that time.

(and after the `Isha' prayer.) because this is the time for sleep. Servants and children are commanded not to enter upon household members at these times, because it is feared that a man may be in an intimate situation with his wife and so on. Allah says:

((These) three (times) are of privacy for you; other than these times there is no sin on you or on them) If they enter at a time other than these, there is no sin on you if you let them enter, and no sin on them if they see something at a time other than these times. They have been given permission to enter suddenly, because they are those who go around in the house, i.e., to serve you etc., and as such they may be forgiven for things that others will not be forgiven. Although this Ayah is quite clear and has not been abrogated, people hardly follow it, and `Abdullah bin `Abbas denounced the people for that. Abu Dawud recorded that Ibn `Abbas said: "Most of the people do not follow it, the Ayah that speaks about asking permission, but I tell my servant woman to seek permission to enter." Abu Dawud said: `Ata' also narrated that Ibn `Abbas commanded this. Ath-Thawri narrated that Musa bin Abi `A'ishah said, "I asked Ash-Sha`bi (about the Ayah):

(Let your slaves and slave-girls ask your permission.) He said, `It has not been abrogated.' I said: `But the people do not do that.' He said, `May Allah help them.'" Then Allah says:

(And when the children among you come to puberty, then let them (also) ask for permission, as those senior to them (in age)) meaning: when the children who used to seek permission at the three times of privacy reach puberty, then they have to seek permission at all times, i.e., with regard to those who are non-relatives, and at times when a man may be in a state of intimacy with his wife, even if it is not one of the three times stated above.

There is no Sin on Elderly Women if They do not wear a Cloak

(And the Qawa`id among women.) Sa`id bin Jubayr, Muqatil bin Hayyan, Ad-Dahhak and Qatadah said that these are the women who no longer think that they can bear children,

(who do not hope for marriage,) meaning, they no longer have any desire for marriage,

(it is no sin on them if they discard their (outer) clothing in such a way as not to show their adornment.) meaning, they do not have to cover themselves in the same way that other women have to. Abu Dawud recorded that Ibn `Abbas said that the Ayah:

(And tell the believing women to lower their gaze) (24:31) was abrogated and an exception was made in the case of:

(the past childbearing among women who do not hope for marriage, .)

(it is no sin on them if they discard their (outer) clothing) Ibn Mas`ud said about (outer) clothing,, "The Jilbab or Rida'." A similar view was also narrated from Ibn `Abbas, Ibn `Umar, Mujahid, Sa`id bin Jubayr, Abu Ash-Sha`tha', Ibrahim An-Nakha`i, Al-Hasan, Qatadah, Az-Zuhri, Al-`Awza`i and others.

(in such a way as not to show their adornment.) Sa`id bin Jubayr said, "They should not make a wanton display of themselves by removing their outer garment so that their adornment may be seen."

(But to refrain is better for them.) means, not removing their outer garment, even though that is permissible for them, is better for them.

(And Allah is All-Hearer, All-Knower.)

Chapter 24: An-Noor (The Light), Verses 001-064

Surah: 24 Ayah: 61

لَّيْسَ عَلَى ٱلْأَعْمَىٰ حَرَجٌ وَلَا عَلَى ٱلْأَعْرَجِ حَرَجٌ وَلَا عَلَى ٱلْمَرِيضِ حَرَجٌ وَلَا عَلَىٰ أَنفُسِكُمْ أَن تَأْكُلُوا۟ مِنۢ بُيُوتِكُمْ أَوْ بُيُوتِ ءَابَآئِكُمْ أَوْ بُيُوتِ أُمَّهَٰتِكُمْ أَوْ بُيُوتِ إِخْوَٰنِكُمْ أَوْ بُيُوتِ أَخَوَٰتِكُمْ أَوْ بُيُوتِ أَعْمَٰمِكُمْ أَوْ بُيُوتِ عَمَّٰتِكُمْ أَوْ بُيُوتِ أَخْوَٰلِكُمْ أَوْ بُيُوتِ خَٰلَٰتِكُمْ أَوْ مَا مَلَكْتُم مَّفَاتِحَهُۥٓ أَوْ صَدِيقِكُمْ ۚ لَيْسَ عَلَيْكُمْ جُنَاحٌ أَن تَأْكُلُوا۟ جَمِيعًا أَوْ أَشْتَاتًا ۚ فَإِذَا دَخَلْتُم بُيُوتًا فَسَلِّمُوا۟ عَلَىٰٓ أَنفُسِكُمْ تَحِيَّةً مِّنْ عِندِ ٱللَّهِ مُبَٰرَكَةً طَيِّبَةً ۚ كَذَٰلِكَ يُبَيِّنُ ٱللَّهُ لَكُمُ ٱلْءَايَٰتِ لَعَلَّكُمْ تَعْقِلُونَ ۝

61. There is no restriction on the blind, nor any restriction on the lame, nor any restriction on the sick, nor on yourselves, if you eat from your houses, or the houses of your fathers, or the houses of your mothers, or the houses of your brothers, or the houses of your sisters, or the houses of your father's brothers, or the houses of your father's sisters, or the houses of your mother's brothers, or the houses of your mother's sisters, or (from that) whereof you hold keys, or (from the house) of a friend. No sin on you whether you eat together or apart. But when you enter the houses, greet one another with a greeting from Allâh (i.e. say: As-Salâmu 'Alaikum - peace be on you) blessed and good. Thus Allâh makes clear the Ayât (these Verses or your religious symbols and signs, etc.) to you that you may understand.

Transliteration

61. Laysa AAala al-aAAma harajun wala AAala al-aAAraji harajun wala AAala almareedi harajun wala AAala anfusikum an ta/kuloo min buyootikum aw buyooti abaikum aw buyooti ommahatikum aw buyooti ikhwanikum aw buyooti akhawatikum aw buyooti aAAmamikum aw buyooti AAammatikum aw buyooti akhwalikum aw buyooti khalatikum aw ma malaktum mafatihahu aw sadeeqikum laysa AAalaykum junahun an ta/kuloo jameeAAan aw ashtatan fa-itha dakhaltum buyootan fasallimoo AAala anfusikum tahiyyatan min AAindi Allahi mubarakatan tayyibatan kathalika yubayyinu Allahu lakumu al-ayati laAAallakum taAAqiloona

Tafsir Ibn Kathir

Eating from One's Relatives' Houses

What is referred to here is the fact that they used to feel too embarrassed to eat with the blind, because they could not see the food or where the best morsels were, so others might take the best pieces before they could. They felt too embarrassed to eat with the lame because they could not sit comfortably, and their companions might take advantage of them, and they felt embarrassed to eat with the sick because they might not eat as much as others. So they were afraid to eat with them lest they were unfair to them in some way. Then Allah revealed this Ayah, granting them a dispensation in this matter. This was the view of Sa`id bin Jubayr and Miqsam. Ad-Dahhak said: "Before the Prophet's Mission, they used to feel too embarrassed and too proud to eat with these people, lest they might have to help them. So Allah revealed this Ayah."

(nor any restriction on the lame,) `Abdur-Razzaq recorded that Mujahid said: "A man would take a blind, lame or sick person to the house of his brother or sister or aunt, and those disabled people would feel ashamed of that and say, `they are taking us to other people's houses.' So this Ayah was revealed granting permission for that." As-Suddi said: "A man would enter the house of his father or brother or son, and the lady of the house would bring him some food, but he would refrain from eating because the master of the house was not there, so Allah revealed:

(There is no restriction on the blind. ..)

(nor on yourselves, if you eat from your houses,) This is stated here although it is obvious, so that from this starting point the houses of others may be mentioned, and to make it clear that the ruling applies equally to what comes after. Sons' houses are included in this even though they are not mentioned by name, and this is used as evidence by those who regard the son's wealth as being like the father's wealth. In the Musnad and the Sunan, it is reported through several routes that the Messenger of Allah said:

«أَنْتَ وَمَالُكَ لِأَبِيكَ»

(You and your wealth belong to your father.)

(or the houses of your fathers, or the houses of your mothers,) until His statement;

(or (from that) whereof you hold keys,) This is obvious, and this is used as evidence by those who think that it is obligatory for relatives to spend on one another.

(or (from that) whereof you hold keys,) Sa`id bin Jubayr and As-Suddi said, "This refers to a people's servants, whether a slave or otherwise. There is nothing wrong with them eating from the food that is stored with them, within reason." Az-Zuhri narrated from `Urwah that `A'isha, may Allah be pleased with her, said, "The Muslims used to go out on military campaigns with the Messenger of Allah and they would give their keys to people they trusted and say, `We permit you to eat whatever you need.' But they would say, `It is not permissible for us to eat, they have given us permission reluctantly and we are only trustees.' Then Allah revealed:

(or (from that) whereof you hold keys)."

(or (from the house) of a friend.) means, there is no sin on you if you eat from their houses, so long as you know that this does not upset them and they do not dislike it.

Chapter 24: An-Noor (The Light), Verses 001-064

(No sin on you whether you eat together or apart.) `Ali bin Abi Talhah reported from Ibn `Abbas concerning this Ayah, "When Allah revealed the Ayah:

(O you who believe! Eat not up your property among yourselves unjustly) (4: 29), the Muslims said, `Allah has forbidden us to eat up our property among ourselves unjustly, and food is the best of property, so it is not permissible for anyone among us to eat at the house of anyone else.' So the people stopped doing that. Then Allah revealed:

(There is no restriction on the blind,) until His statement;

(or (from the house) of a friend.) A man would also feel embarrassed and would refrain from eating alone until someone else came along, but Allah made the matter easier for them and said:

(No sin on you whether you eat together or apart.)" Qatadah said, "This was a clan of Banu Kinanah who during the Jahiliyyah thought that it was a source of shame for one of them to eat alone, to such an extent that a man might keep on driving his laden camel even though he was hungry, until he could find someone to eat and drink with him. Then Allah revealed:

(No sin on you whether you eat together or apart.) So this was a dispensation from Allah, allowing people to eat either alone or with others, even though eating with others is more blessed and is better. Imam Ahmad recorded from Wahshi bin Harb from his father from his grandfather that a man said to the Prophet , "We eat but we do not feel satisfied." He said:

«لَعَلَّكُمْ تَأْكُلُونَ مُتَفَرِّقِينَ، اجْتَمِعُوا عَلَى طَعَامِكُمْ، وَاذْكُرُوا اسْمَ اللهِ، يُبَارَكْ لَكُمْ فِيهِ»

(Perhaps you are eating separately. Eat together and mention the Name of Allah, and He will bless the food for you.) It was also recorded by Abu Dawud and Ibn Majah. Ibn Majah also recorded that Salim reported from his father from `Umar, may Allah be pleased with him, that the Messenger of Allah said:

«كُلُوا جَمِيعًا، وَلَا تَفَرَّقُوا، فَإِنَّ الْبَرَكَةَ مَعَ الْجَمَاعَةِ»

(Eat together and not separately, for the blessing is in being together.)

(But when you enter the houses, greet one another) Sa`id bin Jubayr, Al-Hasan Al-Basri, Qatadah and Az-Zuhri said, "This means greet one another with Salam." Ibn Jurayj said: Abu Az-Zubayr said, "I heard Jabir bin `Abdullah say, `When you enter upon your family, greet them with a greeting from Allah, blessed and good.' He said, `I do not think it is anything but obligatory.'" Ibn Jurayj said: "And Ziyad said that Ibn Tawus used to say: `When any one of you enters his house, let him say Salam.'"

Mujahid said: "And when you enter the Masjid, say: `Peace be upon the Messenger of Allah'; when you enter upon your families, greet them with Salam; and when you enter a house in which there is nobody, say: `As-Salamu `Alayna wa `Ala `Ibad-Allah-is-Salihin (peace be upon us and upon the righteous servants of Allah).' This is what one is commanded to do, and it has been narrated to us that the angels will return his greeting."

(Thus Allah makes clear the Ayat to you that you may understand.) When Allah mentioned what wise rulings and reasonable, well-constructed laws are contained in this Surah, He points out to His servants that He explains the Ayat to them clearly so that they may ponder them and understand their meanings.

Surah: 24 Ayah: 62

إِنَّمَا ٱلْمُؤْمِنُونَ ٱلَّذِينَ ءَامَنُوا۟ بِٱللَّهِ وَرَسُولِهِۦ وَإِذَا كَانُوا۟ مَعَهُۥ عَلَىٰٓ أَمْرٍ جَامِعٍ لَّمْ يَذْهَبُوا۟ حَتَّىٰ يَسْتَـْٔذِنُوهُ إِنَّ ٱلَّذِينَ يَسْتَـْٔذِنُونَكَ أُو۟لَـٰٓئِكَ ٱلَّذِينَ يُؤْمِنُونَ بِٱللَّهِ وَرَسُولِهِۦ فَإِذَا ٱسْتَـْٔذَنُوكَ لِبَعْضِ شَأْنِهِمْ فَأْذَن لِّمَن شِئْتَ مِنْهُمْ وَٱسْتَغْفِرْ لَهُمُ ٱللَّهَ إِنَّ ٱللَّهَ غَفُورٌ رَّحِيمٌ ۝

62. The true believers are only those, who believe in (the Oneness of) Allâh and His Messenger (Muhammad (peace be upon him)) and when they are with him on some common matter, they go not away until they have asked his permission. Verily! Those who ask your permission, those are they who (really) believe in Allâh and His Messenger. So if they ask your permission for some affairs of theirs, give permission to whom you will of them, and ask Allâh for their forgiveness. Truly, Allâh is Oft-Forgiving, Most Merciful.

Transliteration

62. Innama almu/minoona allatheena amanoo biAllahi warasoolihi wa-itha kanoo maAAahu AAala amrin jamiAAin lam yathhaboo hatta yasta/thinoohu inna allatheena yasta/thinoonaka ola-ika allatheena yu/minoona biAllahi warasoolihi fa-itha ista/thanooka libaAAdi sha/nihim fa/than liman shi/ta minhum waistaghfir lahumu Allaha inna Allaha ghafoorun raheemun

Tafsir Ibn Kathir

Asking Permission to leave when They are doing something together

This is another matter of etiquette to which Allah has guided His believing servants. Just as He commanded them to seek permission when entering, He also commanded them to seek permission when leaving, especially when they are doing something together with the Messenger, such as the Friday, `Id, or congregational prayers, or a meeting for the purpose of consultation and so on. Allah commanded them not to leave him in these situations until they had asked his permission. If they did this, then

Chapter 24: An-Noor (The Light), Verses 001-064   143

they were of the true believers. Then Allah commanded His Messenger to give permission when someone asked for it, if he wanted to. He said:

(give permission to whom you will of them, and ask Allah for their forgiveness.) Abu Dawud reported that Abu Hurayrah said, "The Messenger of Allah said:

«إِذَا انْتَهَى أَحَدُكُمْ إِلَى الْمَجْلِسِ فَلْيُسَلِّمْ، فَإِذَا أَرَادَ أَنْ يَقُومَ فَلْيُسَلِّمْ، فَلَيْسَتِ الْأُولَى بِأَحَقَّ مِنَ الْآخِرَةِ»

(When any of you joins a gathering, let him say Salam, and when he wants to leave, let him say Salam. The former is not more important than the latter.) This was also recorded by At-Tirmidhi and An-Nasa'i; At-Tirmidhi said: "It is a Hasan Hadith."

Surah: 24 Ayah: 63

لَّا تَجْعَلُوا دُعَاءَ الرَّسُولِ بَيْنَكُمْ كَدُعَاءِ بَعْضِكُم بَعْضًا قَدْ يَعْلَمُ اللَّهُ الَّذِينَ يَتَسَلَّلُونَ مِنكُمْ لِوَاذًا فَلْيَحْذَرِ الَّذِينَ يُخَالِفُونَ عَنْ أَمْرِهِ أَن تُصِيبَهُمْ فِتْنَةٌ أَوْ يُصِيبَهُمْ عَذَابٌ أَلِيمٌ ۝

63. Make not the calling of the Messenger (Muhammad (peace be upon him)) among you as your calling of one another. Allâh knows those of you who slip away under shelter (of some excuse without taking the permission to leave, from the Messenger (peace be upon him)) And let those who oppose the Messenger's (Muhammad (peace be upon him)) commandment (i.e. his Sunnah legal ways, orders, acts of worship, statements, etc.) (among the sects) beware, lest some Fitnah (disbelief, trials, afflictions, earthquakes, killing, overpowered by a tyrant, etc.) befall them or a painful torment be inflicted on them.

Transliteration

63. La tajAAaloo duAAaa alrrasooli baynakum kaduAAa-i baAAdikum baAAdan qad yaAAlamu Allahu allatheena yatasalaloona minkum liwathan falyahthari allatheena yukhalifoona AAan amrihi an tuseebahum fitnatun aw yuseebahum AAathabun aleemun

Tafsir Ibn Kathir

The Etiquette of addressing the Prophet

Ad-Dahhak said, reporting from Ibn `Abbas: "They used to say, `O Muhammad,' or `O Abu Al-Qasim,' but Allah forbade them to do that, as a sign of respect towards His Prophet , and told them to say, `O Prophet of Allah,' `O Messenger of Allah.'" This was also the view of Mujahid and Sa`id bin Jubayr. Qatadah said: "Allah commanded that His Prophet should be treated with respect and honor, and that he should be a leader." Muqatil said concerning the Ayah:

(Make not the calling of the Messenger among you as your calling one of another.) "When you address him, do not say, `O Muhammad,' or `O son of `Abdullah'; rather honor him and say, `O Prophet of Allah,' or, `O Messenger of Allah.'

(Make not the calling of the Messenger among you as your calling one of another.) A second view concerning the meaning of the Ayah is that it means `do not think that if he prays against you it is like when anyone else prays against you, because his prayers will be answered; so beware lest he prays against you and you will be doomed.' Ibn Abi Hatim recorded this from Ibn `Abbas, Al-Hasan Al-Basri and `Atiyyah Al-`Awfi. And Allah knows best.

(Allah knows those of you who slip away under shelter.) Muqatil bin Hayyan said, "This refers to the hypocrites who used to find it too difficult to listen to the Khutbah on Fridays, so they would hide behind some of the Companions of Muhammad and sneak out of the Masjid. It was not proper for a man to leave on Fridays once the Khutbah began, unless he had permission from the Prophet . If one of them wanted to leave, he would make a gesture to the Prophet with his finger, and the Prophet would give permission without the man speaking. This is because if the Prophet was giving the Khutbah and a man spoke, it would invalidate his Friday prayer." As-Suddi said, "If they were with him for a congregational prayer, they would hide behind one another so that he could not see them."

The Prohibition of going against the Messenger's Commandment

(And let those beware who oppose the Messenger's commandment) This means going against the commandment of the Prophet , which is his way, methodology and Sunnah. All words and deeds will be measured against his words and deeds; those that are in accordance with his words and deeds will be accepted, and whatever does not match up will be rejected, no matter who the person is who said and did them. It was recorded in the Two Sahihs and elsewhere that the Messenger of Allah said:

«مَنْ عَمِلَ عَمَلًا لَيْسَ عَلَيْهِ أَمْرُنَا فَهُوَ رَدٌّ»

(Whoever does a deed that is not in accordance with this matter of ours will have it rejected.) meaning, let those beware who go against the Shari`ah of the Messenger , in secret and in the open,

(lest some Fitnah should befall them), i.e., lest some disbelief or hypocrisy or innovation enter their hearts.

(or a painful torment be inflicted on them.) means in this world afflicting them with capital punishment, or by law of prescribed punishment, or by confinement in prison, or so on. Imam Ahmad recorded that Abu Hurayrah said, "The Messenger of Allah said:

«مَثَلِي وَمَثَلُكُمْ كَمَثَلِ رَجُلٍ اسْتَوْقَدَ نَارًا فَلَمَّا أَضَاءَتْ مَا حَوْلَهَا جَعَلَ الْفَرَاشُ

& Chapter 24: An-Noor (The Light), Verses 001-064   145

وَهَذِهِ الدَّوَابُّ اللَّائِي يَقَعْنَ فِي النَّارِ يَقَعْنَ فِيهَا، وَجَعَلَ يَحْجُزُهُنَّ وَيَغْلِبْنَهُ فَيَقْتَحِمْنَ فِيهَا قَالَ: فَذَلِكَ مَثَلِي وَمَثَلُكُمْ، أَنَا آخِذٌ بِحُجَزِكُمْ عَنِ النَّارِ هَلُمَّ عَنِ النَّارِ، فَتَغْلِبُونِي وَتَقْتَحِمُونَ فِيهَا»

(The parable of me and you is as the example of a man who kindled a fire and when it illuminated all around him, moths and other creatures started falling into the fire, and he was trying to stop them but they overwhelmed him and still kept falling in. This is the parable of me and you. I am trying to restrain you and keep you away from the fire, but you overwhelm me and fall in.) This was also narrated by Al-Bukhari and Muslim.

Surah: 24 Ayah: 64

أَلَا إِنَّ لِلَّهِ مَا فِي السَّمَاوَاتِ وَالْأَرْضِ قَدْ يَعْلَمُ مَا أَنتُمْ عَلَيْهِ وَيَوْمَ يُرْجَعُونَ إِلَيْهِ فَيُنَبِّئُهُم بِمَا عَمِلُوا ۗ وَاللَّهُ بِكُلِّ شَيْءٍ عَلِيمٌ ۝

64. Certainly, to Allâh belongs all that is in the heavens and the earth. Surely, He knows your condition and (He knows) the Day when they will be brought back to Him, then He will inform them of what they did. And Allâh is All-Knower of everything.

Transliteration

64. Ala inna lillahi ma fee alssamawati waal-ardi qad yaAAlamu ma antum AAalayhi wayawma yurjaAAoona ilayhi fayunabbi-ohum bima AAamiloo waAllahu bikulli shay-in AAaleemun

Tafsir Ibn Kathir

Allah knows your Condition

Allah tells us that He is the Sovereign of the heavens and the earth, and He knows the seen and the unseen. He knows what His servants do in secret and in the open. So He says:

(Indeed, He knows your condition) He knows and it is visible to Him, and not one iota is hidden from him. This is like the Ayah:

(And put your trust in the All-Mighty, the Most Merciful,) until His saying;

(Verily, He, only He, is the All-Hearer, the All-Knower) (26:217-220).

(Neither you do any deed nor recite any portion of the Qur'an, nor you do any deed but We are Witness thereof when you are doing it. And nothing is hidden from your

Lord; (even) the weight of a speck of dust on the earth or in the heaven. Not what is less than that or what is greater than that but is in a Clear Record.) (10:61)

(Is then He Who takes charge of every person and knows all that he has earned) (13: 33) He sees all that His servants do, good and evil alike. And Allah says:

(Surely, even when they cover themselves with their garments, He knows what they conceal and what they reveal) (11:5).

(It is the same (to Him) whether any of you conceals his speech or declares it openly) (13:10).

(And no moving creature is there on earth but its provision is due from Allah. And He knows its dwelling place and its deposit. All is in a Clear Book.) (11:6)

(And with Him are the keys of the Unseen, none knows them but He. And He knows whatever there is in the land and in the sea; not a leaf falls, but He knows it. There is not a grain in the darkness of the earth nor anything fresh or dry, but is written in a Clear Record.) (6:59) And there are many Ayat and Hadiths which say similar things.

(the Day when they will be brought back to Him,) means, the day when all creatures will be brought back to Allah, which is the Day of Resurrection.

(then He will inform them of what they did.) means, He will tell them everything they did in this life, major and minor, significant and insignificant. As Allah says:

(On that Day man will be informed of what he sent forward (of deeds), and what he left behind.) (75:13)

(And the Book will be placed, and you will see the criminals, fearful of that which is therein. They will say: "Woe to us! What sort of Book is this that leaves neither a small thing nor a big thing, but has recorded it with numbers!" And they will find all that they did, placed before them, and your Lord treats no one with injustice.) (18:49) Allah says here:

(the Day when they will be brought back to Him, then He will inform them of what they did. And Allah is All-Knower of everything.) Praise be to Allah, the Lord of all that exists, and we ask Him to help us achieve perfection. The end of the Tafsir of Surat An-Nur, to Allah be praise and thanks.

CHAPTER (SURAH) 25: AL-FURQAN (THE CRITERION, THE STANDARD), VERSES 001-020

(بِسْمِ اللَّهِ الرَّحْمَنِ الرَّحِيمِ)

In the Name of Allah, the Most Gracious, the Most Merciful

Chapter 25: Al-Furqan (The Criterion, The Standard), Verses 001-020

Surah: 25 Ayah: 1 & Ayah: 2

تَبَارَكَ ٱلَّذِى نَزَّلَ ٱلْفُرْقَانَ عَلَىٰ عَبْدِهِۦ لِيَكُونَ لِلْعَٰلَمِينَ نَذِيرًا ۝

1. Blessed is He Who sent down the criterion (of right and wrong, i.e. this Qur'ân) to His slave (Muhammad (peace be upon him)) that he may be a warner to the 'Alamîn (mankind and jinn).

ٱلَّذِى لَهُۥ مُلْكُ ٱلسَّمَٰوَٰتِ وَٱلْأَرْضِ وَلَمْ يَتَّخِذْ وَلَدًا وَلَمْ يَكُن لَّهُۥ شَرِيكٌ فِى ٱلْمُلْكِ وَخَلَقَ كُلَّ شَىْءٍ فَقَدَّرَهُۥ تَقْدِيرًا ۝

2. He to Whom belongs the dominion of the heavens and the earth, and Who has begotten no son (children or offspring) and for Whom there is no partner in the dominion. He has created everything, and has measured it exactly according to its due measurements.

Transliteration

1. Tabaraka allathee nazzala alfurqana AAala AAabdihi liyakoona lilAAalameena natheeran 2. Allathee lahu mulku alssamawati waal-ardi walam yattakhith waladan walam yakun lahu shareekun fee almulki wakhalaqa kulla shay-in faqaddarahu taqdeeran

Tafsir Ibn Kathir

Blessed be Allah

Here Allah praises Himself for the Noble Qur'an He has revealed to His noble Messenger. This is like the Ayat:

(All the praises and thanks be to Allah, Who has sent down to His servant the Book, and has not placed therein any crookedness. (He has made it) straight to give warning of a severe punishment from Him, and to give glad tidings to the believers, who do righteous deeds...) (18:1-2) Here Allah says:

(Blessed be He.) The verbal form used here implies an ongoing, permanent, eternal blessing.

(Who sent down the criterion) The verb Nazzala is a form which implies something done a great deal and often. This is like the Ayah:

(And the Book which He (Nazzala) sent down to His Messenger, and the Scripture which He (Anzala) sent down to those before (him)) (4:136). Each of the previous Books was sent down at one time, but the Qur'an was revealed gradually, in stages, Ayat after Ayat, rulings after rulings, Surahs after Surahs. This is more eloquent and indicative of greater care for the one to whom it is revealed, as Allah says later in this Surah:

(And those who disbelieve say: "Why is not the Qur'an revealed to him all at once" Thus, that We may strengthen your heart thereby. And We have revealed it to you gradually, in stages. And no example or similitude do they bring, but We reveal to you the truth, and the better explanation thereof.) (25:32-33) This Surah was named Al-Furqan, because it is the criterion that decides between truth and falsehood, guidance and misguidance, right and wrong, lawful and unlawful.

(to His servant) This description is one of praise and commendation, because here Allah is connecting him to Himself, describing him as His servant. Allah also described him in this manner when referring to the noblest of events, the Night of the Isra', as He said:

(Glorified be He Who took His servant for a journey by night) (17:1). Allah also described him in this way when He described how he stood and called to Him:

(And when the servant of Allah stood up invoking Him in prayer they (the Jinn) just made round him a dense crowd as if sticking one over the other (in order to listen to the Prophet's recitation).) (72:19) This description is also used here when Allah describes how the Book is revealed to him and how the angel comes down to him:

(Blessed be He Who sent down the criterion to His servant that he may be a warner to all nations.)

(that he may be a warner to all nations.) means, he alone has been blessed with this great, detailed, clear Book which,

(Falsehood cannot come to it from before it or behind it, (it is) sent down by the All-Wise, Worthy of all praise (Allah).) (41:42) The One Who made it the mighty criterion, singled him out to convey it to those who seek the shade of trees and to those who live on the land (i.e., to all of mankind, nomad and settled alike), as the Prophet said:

«بُعِثْتُ إِلَى الْأَحْمَرِ وَالْأَسْوَدِ»

(I have been sent to the red and the black.) And he said:

«إِنِّي أُعْطِيتُ خَمْسًا لَمْ يُعْطَهُنَّ أَحَدٌ مِنَ الْأَنْبِيَاءِ قَبْلِي»

(I have been given five things which no Prophet before me was given.) Among them he mentioned:

«كَانَ النَّبِيُّ يُبْعَثُ إِلَى قَوْمِهِ خَاصَّةً وَبُعِثْتُ إِلَى النَّاسِ عَامَّةً»

(Before me) a Prophet was sent only to his own people, but I have been sent to all of mankind.) And Allah says:

Chapter 25: Al-Furqan (The Criterion, The Standard), Verses 001-020

(Say: "O mankind! Verily, I am sent to you all as the Messenger of Allah...") (7:158), meaning, the One Who has sent me is the Sovereign of the heaven and the earth, who merely says to a thing "Be!" and it is. He is the one who gives life and causes death. Allah says here:

(He to Whom belongs the dominion of the heavens and the earth, and Who has begotten no son and for Whom there is no partner in the dominion.) Allah states that He is above having any offspring or partner. Then He tells us:

(He has created everything, and has measured it exactly according to its due measurements.) meaning, everything apart from Him is created and subject to Him. He is the Creator, Lord, Master and God of all things, and everything is subject to His dominion, control and power.

Surah: 25 Ayah: 3

وَٱتَّخَذُواْ مِن دُونِهِۦٓ ءَالِهَةً لَّا يَخْلُقُونَ شَيْـًٔا وَهُمْ يُخْلَقُونَ وَلَا يَمْلِكُونَ لِأَنفُسِهِمْ ضَرًّا وَلَا نَفْعًا وَلَا يَمْلِكُونَ مَوْتًا وَلَا حَيَوٰةً وَلَا نُشُورًا ۝

3. Yet they have taken besides Him other âlihâ (gods) who created nothing but are themselves created, and possess neither hurt nor benefit for themselves, and possess no power (of causing) death, nor (of giving) life, nor of raising the dead.

Transliteration

3. Waittakhathoo min doonihi alihatan la yakhluqoona shay-an wahum yukhlaqoona wala yamlikoona li-anfusihim darran wala nafAAan wala yamlikoona mawtan wala hayatan wala nushooran

Tafsir Ibn Kathir

The Foolishness of the Idolators

Allah tells us of the ignorance of the idolators in taking other gods instead of Allah, the Creator of all things, the One Who controls the affairs of all things; whatever He wills happens and whatever He does not will does not happen. In spite of that, they still worshipped others besides Him, idols who could not even create the wing of a gnat, but were themselves created. They could neither do harm nor bring benefit to themselves, so how could they do anything for their worshippers

(and possess no power (of causing) death, nor (of giving) life, nor of raising the dead.) means, they could not do any of that at all; that power belongs only to Allah, Who is the One Who gives life and death, and is the One Who will bring all people, the first and the last, back to life on the Day of Resurrection.

(The creation of you all and the resurrection of you all are only as (the creation and resurrection of) a single person) (31:28). This is like the Ayat;

(And Our commandment is but one as the twinkling of an eye.) (54:50)

(But it will be only a single Zajrah. When behold, they find themselves on the surface of the earth alive after their death.) (79:13-14)

(It will be a single Zajrah, and behold, they will be staring!) (37:19)

(It will be but a single Sayhah, so behold they will all be brought up before Us!) (36:53). He is Allah besides Whom there is no other God and besides Whom there is no other Lord. No one should be worshipped except Him because whatever He wills happens and whatever he does not will does not happen. He has no offspring nor progenitor, nor equal nor likeness nor rival nor peer. He is the One, the Self-Sufficient Master, Whom all creatures need, He begets not, nor was He begotten, and there is none co-equal or comparable unto Him.

Surah: 25 Ayah: 4, Ayah: 5 & Ayah: 6

وَقَالَ ٱلَّذِينَ كَفَرُوٓاْ إِنْ هَـٰذَآ إِلَّآ إِفْكٌ ٱفْتَرَىٰهُ وَأَعَانَهُۥ عَلَيْهِ قَوْمٌ ءَاخَرُونَ ۖ فَقَدْ جَآءُو ظُلْمًا وَزُورًا ۝

4. Those who disbelieve say: "This (the Qur'ân) is nothing but a lie that he (Muhammad (peace be upon him)) has invented, and others have helped him at it. In fact they have produced an unjust wrong (thing) and a lie."

وَقَالُوٓاْ أَسَـٰطِيرُ ٱلْأَوَّلِينَ ٱكْتَتَبَهَا فَهِىَ تُمْلَىٰ عَلَيْهِ بُكْرَةً وَأَصِيلًا ۝

5. And they say: "Tales of the ancients, which he has written down, and they are dictated to him morning and afternoon."

قُلْ أَنزَلَهُ ٱلَّذِى يَعْلَمُ ٱلسِّرَّ فِى ٱلسَّمَـٰوَٰتِ وَٱلْأَرْضِ ۚ إِنَّهُۥ كَانَ غَفُورًا رَّحِيمًا ۝

6. Say: "It (this Qur'ân) has been sent down by Him (Allâh) (the Real Lord of the heavens and earth) Who knows the secret of the heavens and the earth. Truly, He is Oft-Forgiving, Most Merciful."

Transliteration

4. Waqala allatheena kafaroo in hatha illa ifkun iftarahu waaAAanahu AAalayhi qawmun akharoona faqad jaoo thulman wazooran 5. Waqaloo asateeru al-awwaleena iktatabaha fahiya tumla AAalayhi bukratan waaseelan 6. Qul anzalahu allathee yaAAlamu alssirra fee alssamawati waal-ardi innahu kana ghafooran raheeman

Tafsir Ibn Kathir

What the Disbelievers said about the Qur'an

Allah tells us about the foolishness of the disbelievers' ignorant minds, when they said about the Qur'an:

(This is nothing but a lie), meaning an untruth.

Chapter 25: Al-Furqan (The Criterion, The Standard), Verses 001-020

(that he has invented,) meaning the Prophet .

(and others have helped him in it.) means, he asked other people to help him compile it. So Allah said:

(In fact, they have produced an unjust wrong and a lie.) meaning, they are the ones who are telling a lie, and they know that it is false, for their own souls know that what they are claiming is not true.

(And they say: "Tales of the ancients which he has written down...") meaning, the ancients wrote them down, and he has copied it.

(and they are dictated to him) means, they are read or recited to him.

(morning and afternoon.) at the beginning and end of the day. Because this idea is so foolish and is so patently false, everyone knows that it is not true. It is known through Mutawatir reports and is a common fact that Muhammad the Messenger of Allah never learned to read or write, either at the beginning or the end of his life. He grew up among them for approximately forty years, from the time he was born until the time when his mission began. They knew all about him, and about his honest and sound character and how he would never lie or do anything immoral or bad. They even used to call him Al-Amin (the Trustworthy One) from a young age, until his mission began, because they saw how truthful and honest he was. When Allah honored him with that which He honored him, they declared their enmity towards him and came up with all these accusations which any reasonable person would know he was innocent of. They were not sure what to accuse him of. Sometimes they said that he was a sorcerer, at other times they would say he was a poet, or crazy, or a liar. So Allah said:

(See what examples they have put forward for you. So they have gone astray, and never can they find a way.) (17:48) In response to their stubbornness, Allah says here:

(Say: "It has been sent down by Him Who knows the secret of the heavens and the earth".) meaning, He has revealed the Qur'an which includes true information about the earlier and later generations, information which concurs with the realities of the past and future.

(Who knows the secret) means, Allah is the One Who knows the unseen in the heavens and on the earth; He knows their secrets just as He knows what is visible therein.

(Truly, He is Oft-Forgiving, Most Merciful.) This is an invitation to them to repent and turn back to Allah, telling them that His mercy is vast and His patience is immense. Whoever repents to Him, He accepts his repentance. Despite all their lies, immorality, falsehood, disbelief and stubbornness, and saying what they said about the Messenger and the Qur'an, He still invites them to repent and give up their sin, and to come to Islam and true guidance. This is like the Ayat:

(Surely, disbelievers are those who said: "Allah is the third of the three." But there is no god but One God. And if they cease not from what they say, verily, a painful torment will befall on the disbelievers among them. Will they not turn with repentance to Allah and ask His forgiveness For Allah is Oft-Forgiving, Most Merciful.) (5:73-74)

(Verily, those who put into trial the believing men and believing women, and then do not turn in repentance, then they will have the torment of Hell, and they will have the punishment of the burning Fire.) (85:10) Al-Hasan Al-Basri said: "Look at this kindness and generosity! They killed His friends and He is calling them to repentance and mercy."

Surah: 25 Ayah: 7, Ayah: 8, Ayah: 9, Ayah: 10, Ayah: 11, Ayah: 12, Ayah: 13 & Ayah: 14

وَقَالُوا۟ مَالِ هَـٰذَا ٱلرَّسُولِ يَأْكُلُ ٱلطَّعَامَ وَيَمْشِى فِى ٱلْأَسْوَاقِ لَوْلَآ أُنزِلَ إِلَيْهِ مَلَكٌ فَيَكُونَ مَعَهُۥ نَذِيرًا ۝

7. And they say: "Why does this Messenger (Muhammad (peace be upon him)) eat food, and walk about in the markets (as we)? Why is not an angel sent down to him to be a warner with him?

أَوْ يُلْقَىٰٓ إِلَيْهِ كَنزٌ أَوْ تَكُونُ لَهُۥ جَنَّةٌ يَأْكُلُ مِنْهَا ۚ وَقَالَ ٱلظَّـٰلِمُونَ إِن تَتَّبِعُونَ إِلَّا رَجُلًا مَّسْحُورًا ۝

8. "Or (why) has not a treasure been granted to him, or why has he not a garden whereof he may eat?" And the Zâlimûn (polytheists and wrong-doers) say: "You follow none but a man bewitched."

ٱنظُرْ كَيْفَ ضَرَبُوا۟ لَكَ ٱلْأَمْثَـٰلَ فَضَلُّوا۟ فَلَا يَسْتَطِيعُونَ سَبِيلًا ۝

9. See how they coin similitudes for you, so they have gone astray, and they cannot find a (Right) Path.

تَبَارَكَ ٱلَّذِىٓ إِن شَآءَ جَعَلَ لَكَ خَيْرًا مِّن ذَٰلِكَ جَنَّـٰتٍ تَجْرِى مِن تَحْتِهَا ٱلْأَنْهَـٰرُ وَيَجْعَل لَّكَ قُصُورًا ۝

10. Blessed is He Who, if He wills will assign you better than (all) that - Gardens under which rivers flow (Paradise) and will assign you palaces (i.e. in Paradise).

بَلْ كَذَّبُوا۟ بِٱلسَّاعَةِ ۖ وَأَعْتَدْنَا لِمَن كَذَّبَ بِٱلسَّاعَةِ سَعِيرًا ۝

11. Nay, they deny the Hour (the Day of Resurrection), and for those who deny the Hour, We have prepared a flaming Fire (i.e. Hell).

Chapter 25: Al-Furqan (The Criterion, The Standard), Verses 001-020

$$إِذَا رَأَتْهُم مِّن مَّكَانٍ بَعِيدٍ سَمِعُوا۟ لَهَا تَغَيُّظًا وَزَفِيرًا ۝$$

12. When it (Hell) sees them from a far place, they will hear its raging and its roaring.

$$وَإِذَآ أُلْقُوا۟ مِنْهَا مَكَانًا ضَيِّقًا مُّقَرَّنِينَ دَعَوْا۟ هُنَالِكَ ثُبُورًا ۝$$

13. And when they shall be thrown into a narrow place thereof, chained together, they will exclaim therein for destruction.

$$لَّا تَدْعُوا۟ ٱلْيَوْمَ ثُبُورًا وَٰحِدًا وَٱدْعُوا۟ ثُبُورًا كَثِيرًا ۝$$

14. Exclaim not today for one destruction, but exclaim for many destructions.

Transliteration

7. Waqaloo mali hatha alrrasooli ya/kulu alttaAAama wayamshee fee al-aswaqi lawla onzila ilayhi malakun fayakoona maAAahu natheeran 8. Aw yulqa ilayhi kanzun aw takoonu lahu jannatun ya/kulu minha waqala alththalimoona in tattabiAAoona illa rajulan mashooran 9. Onthur kayfa daraboo laka al-amthala fadalloo fala yastateeAAoona sabeelan 10. Tabaraka allathee in shaa jaAAala laka khayran min thalika jannatin tajree min tahtiha al-anharu wayajAAal laka qusooran 11. Bal kaththaboo bialssaAAati waaAAtadna liman kaththaba bialssaAAati saAAeeran 12. Itha raat-hum min makanin baAAeedin samiAAoo laha taghayyuthan wazafeeran 13. Wa-itha olqoo minha makanan dayyiqan muqarraneena daAAaw hunalika thubooran 14. La tadAAoo alyawma thubooran wahidan waodAAoo thubooran katheeran

Tafsir Ibn Kathir

What the Disbelievers said about the Messenger, refutation of Their Words, and Their ultimate Destiny

Allah tells us about the disbelievers' stubborn resistance to and rejection of the truth, with no proof or evidence for doing so. Their excuse was, as they said:

(Why does this Messenger eat food,) meaning, `as we eat, and why does he need food as we need it'

(and walk about in the markets.) means, he walks around and goes there often seeking to trade and earn a living.

(Why is not an angel sent down to him to be a warner with him) They were saying: why doesn't an angel come down to him from Allah, to be a witness that what he is claiming is true This is like when Fira`wn said:

("Why then are not golden bracelets bestowed on him, or angels sent along with him") (43:53). These people had a similar mentality and said the same kind of thing. They said:

(Or (why) has not a treasure been granted to him) meaning, treasure that he could spend on his needs and wants.

(or why has he not a garden whereof he may eat) meaning, a garden that would go with him wherever he went. All of this is easy for Allah, but He had a reason for not doing any of these things, and with Him is the perfect proof and argument.

(And the wrongdoers say: "You follow none but a man bewitched.") Allah said:

(See how they coin similitudes for you, so they have gone astray,) meaning, they accused you and belied you when they said that you were a sorcerer or bewitched or crazy or a liar or a poet, but all of these are false ideas. Everyone who has the slightest understanding will recognize that they are lying. Allah says:

(so they have gone astray) from the path of guidance.

(and they cannot find a path.) Everyone who steps outside of the way of truth and guidance has gone astray, no matter what direction he takes, because the truth is one and its methodology is unified, parts of it confirming other parts. Then Allah tells His Prophet that if He willed, He could bestow on him in this world something far better than what they were saying. He said:

(Blessed be He Who, if He wills, will assign you better than (all) that...) Mujahid said, "This means in this world." And he said: "The Quraysh used to call every house that was made of stone a `palace', whether it was large or small."

(Nay, they deny the Hour,) means, they say this in stubborn disbelief, not because they are seeking insight and guidance, but because their disbelief in the Day of Resurrection makes them say what they say.

(And We have prepared) means, `We have made ready,'

(for those who deny the Hour, a flaming Fire.) means, an unbearably hot and painful torment in the fire of Hell.

(When it sees them) means, when Hell sees them,

(from a far place,) means from the place of gathering (on the Day of Resurrection),

(they will hear its raging and its roaring.) means, (it will make those sounds) out of hatred towards them. This is like the Ayah,

(When they are cast therein, they will hear the (terrible) drawing in of its breath as it blazes forth. It almost bursts up with fury) (67:7-8), which means that parts of it almost separate from other parts because of its intense hatred towards those who disbelieved in Allah. Imam Abu Ja`far bin Jarir narrated that Ibn `Abbas said: "A man will be dragged towards Hell, which will be expanding and contracting, and Ar-Rahman will say to it: `What is the matter with you' It will say: `He is seeking refuge from me.' So Allah will say, `Let My servant go.' Another man will be dragged towards Hell and he will say, `O Lord, I never expected this from You.' Allah will say, `What

Chapter 25: Al-Furqan (The Criterion, The Standard), Verses 001-020

did you expect' The man will say, `I expected that Your mercy would be great enough to include me.' So Allah will say, `Let My servant go.' Another man will be dragged towards Hell, and Hell will bray at him like a donkey braying at barley. Then it will give a moan that will instill fear in everyone." Its chain of narrators is Sahih.

(they will hear its raging and its roaring.) `Abdur-Razzaq recorded that `Ubayd bin `Umayr said: "Hell will utter a moan such that there will be no angel who is close to Allah and no Prophet sent to mankind, but he will fall on his face, shaking all over. Even Ibrahim, peace be upon him, will fall to his knees and say: `O Lord, I do not ask You for salvation this Day except for myself.'"

(And when they shall be thrown into a narrow place thereof, chained together,) Qatadah narrated from Abu Ayyub that `Abdullah bin `Amr said: "Like the point of a spear, i.e., in its narrowness."

(chained together,) Abu Salih said, "This means, tied from their shoulders."

(they will exclaim therein for destruction.) means, they will utter cries of woe, regret and sorrow.

(Exclaim not today for one destruction...)

Surah: 25 Ayah: 15 & Ayah: 16

قُلْ أَذَٰلِكَ خَيْرٌ أَمْ جَنَّةُ ٱلْخُلْدِ ٱلَّتِى وُعِدَ ٱلْمُتَّقُونَ ۚ كَانَتْ لَهُمْ جَزَآءً وَمَصِيرًا

15. Say: (O Muhammad (peace be upon him)) "Is that (torment) better or the Paradise of Eternity which is promised to the Muttaqûn (the pious and righteous persons - see V.2:2)?" It will be theirs as a reward and as a final destination.

هُمْ فِيهَا مَا يَشَآءُونَ خَٰلِدِينَ ۚ كَانَ عَلَىٰ رَبِّكَ وَعْدًا مَّسْـُٔولًا

16. For them there will be therein all that they desire, and they will abide (there forever). It is a promise binding upon your Lord that must be fulfilled.

Transliteration

15. Qul athalika khayrun am jannatu alkhuldi allatee wuAAida almuttaqoona kanat lahum jazaan wamaseeran 16. Lahum feeha ma yashaoona khalideena kana AAala rabbika waAAdan mas-oolan

Tafsir Ibn Kathir

Is the Fire better, or Paradise

Here Allah says: `O Muhammad, this that We have described to you about the state of those who are doomed, who will be dragged on their faces to Hell, which will receive them with a scowling face, with hatred and moans. There they will be thrown into their constricted spaces, tied up to their shoulders, unable to move or call for help, and unable to escape their plight --- is this better, or the eternal Paradise which Allah has promised to the pious among His servants, which He has prepared for them as a reward and ultimate destiny in return for their obedience to Him in this world'

(For them there will be therein all that they desire,) of delights such as food, drink, clothing, dwellings, means of transportation and scenery, and other things that no eye has seen, no ear has heard, nor the heart of anyone can comprehend. They will abide therein forever; it will never cease or come to an end, and they will never leave it. This is what Allah has promised to those whom He has blessed and to whom He has shown His favor. He says:

(It is a upon your Lord a Wa`dan Mas'ula) meaning, it must inevitably come to pass. Abu Ja`far bin Jarir reported from some of the scholars of the Arabic language that the words

(Wa`dan Mas'ula) mean: a binding pledge. In this Surah Allah mentions Hell, then refers to the situation of the people of Paradise. This is similar to the passage in Surat As-Saffat where Allah mentions the status of the people of Paradise, with its beauty and joy, then He says:

:(Is that better entertainment or the tree of Zaqqum Truly, We have made it a trial for the wrongdoers. Verily, it is a tree that springs out of the bottom of Hellfire, The shoots of its fruit stalks are like the heads of Shayatin. Truly, they will eat thereof and fill their bellies therewith. Then on the top of that they will be given boiling water to drink so that it becomes a mixture. Then thereafter, verily, their return is to the flaming fire of Hell. Verily, they found their fathers on the wrong path. So they hastened in their footsteps!) (37:62-70)

Surah: 25 Ayah: 17, Ayah: 18 & Ayah: 19

وَيَوْمَ يَحْشُرُهُمْ وَمَا يَعْبُدُونَ مِن دُونِ ٱللَّهِ فَيَقُولُ ءَأَنتُمْ أَضْلَلْتُمْ عِبَادِى هَٰٓؤُلَآءِ أَمْ هُمْ ضَلُّوا۟ ٱلسَّبِيلَ ۝

17. And on the Day when He will gather them together and that which they worship besides Allâh (idols, angels, pious men, saints, 'Iesa (Jesus) - son of Maryam (Mary)) He will say: "Was it you who misled these My slaves or did they (themselves) stray from the (Right) Path?"

قَالُوا۟ سُبْحَٰنَكَ مَا كَانَ يَنۢبَغِى لَنَآ أَن نَّتَّخِذَ مِن دُونِكَ مِنْ أَوْلِيَآءَ وَلَٰكِن مَّتَّعْتَهُمْ وَءَابَآءَهُمْ حَتَّىٰ نَسُوا۟ ٱلذِّكْرَ وَكَانُوا۟ قَوْمًۢا بُورًا ۝

18. They will say: "Glorified are You! It was not for us to take any Auliyâ' (Protectors, Helpers) besides You, but You gave them and their fathers comfort till they forgot the warning, and became a lost people (doomed to total loss).

Chapter 25: Al-Furqan (The Criterion, The Standard), Verses 001-020

فَقَدْ كَذَّبُوكُم بِمَا تَقُولُونَ فَمَا تَسْتَطِيعُونَ صَرْفًا وَلَا نَصْرًا وَمَن يَظْلِم مِّنكُمْ نُذِقْهُ عَذَابًا كَبِيرًا ﴿١٩﴾

19. Thus they (false gods - all deities other than Allâh) will belie you (polytheists) regarding what you say (that they are gods besides Allâh): then you can neither avert (the punishment), nor get help. And whoever among you does wrong (i.e. sets up rivals to Allâh), We shall make him taste a great torment.

Transliteration

17. Wayawma yahshuruhum wama yaAAbudoona min dooni Allahi fayaqoolu aantum adlaltum AAibadee haola-i am hum dalloo alssabeela 18. Qaloo subhanaka ma kana yanbaghee lana an nattakhitha min doonika min awliyaa walakin mattaAAtahum waabaahum hatta nasoo alththikra wakanoo qawman booran 19. Faqad kaththabookum bima taqooloona fama tastateeAAoona sarfan wala nasran waman yathlim minkum nuthiqhu AAathaban kabeeran

Tafsir Ibn Kathir

The gods of the Idolators will disown Them on the Day of Resurrection

Allah tells us about what will happen on the Day of Resurrection, when those whom the idolators used to worship instead of Allah, angels and others, will rebuke them. Allah says:

(And on the Day when He will gather them together and that which they worship besides Allah.) Mujahid said, "This means `Isa, `Uzayr and the angels."

(He will say: "Was it you who misled these My servants..") Allah will say to those who were worshipped: `Did you call these people to worship you instead of Me, or was it their own idea to worship you, without any call to that on your part' This is like the Ayah,

(And when Allah will say: "O `Isa, son of Maryam! Did you say unto men: `Worship me and my mother as two gods besides Allah' " He will say: "Glory be to You! It was not for me to say what I had no right (to say). Had I said such a thing, You would surely have known it. You know what is in my innerself though I do not know what is in Yours; truly, You, only You, are the All-Knower of all that is hidden. Never did I say to them aught except what You did command me to say.") (5:116-117) Describing how those who were worshipped will respond on the Day of Resurrection, Allah says:

(They will say: "Glorified be You! It was not for us to take (Nattakhidh) any Awliya' besides You...") Most of the scholars recite a Fathah on the Nun of the word Nattakhidh in His saying:

("...for us to take (Nattakhidh) any Awliya' besides You,") meaning, `it is not right for any created being, neither us nor them, to worship anyone except You; we did not call them to do that, but they did it of their own accord, without us telling them to do it or accepting what they did. We are innocent of them and their worship.' This is like the Ayah,

(And (remember) the Day when He will gather them all together, then He will say to the angels: "Was it you that these people used to worship" They (the angels) will say: "Glorified be You!") (34:40-41) Other scholars understand this phrase to mean: `it is not proper for us to take anyone except You as protectors or helpers (Awliya'), ' meaning, `it is not proper for anyone to worship us, for we are Your servants and in need of You.' This meaning is close to the first.

(but You gave them and their fathers comfort) means, `You made such a long period of time pass that they forgot the Reminder, i.e., they forgot what had been sent down to them through the Messengers, calling them to worship You alone with no partner or associate.'

(and became a lost people.) Ibn `Abbas said, "This means, they were destroyed." Al-Hasan Al-Basri and Malik narrated from Az-Zuhri: "There was no good in them." And Allah says:

(Thus they will deny you because of what you say;) meaning, `those whom you used to worship besides Allah will show you to be liars in your claims that they were your helpers and protectors bringing you closer to Allah.' This is like the Ayat:

(And who is more astray than one who calls on besides Allah, such as will not answer him till the Day of Resurrection, and who are unaware of their calls to them. And when mankind are gathered, they will become their enemies and will deny their worshipping.) (46:5-6)

(then you can neither avert nor find help.) means: they will not be able to avert the punishment from themselves, nor will they be able to help themselves.

(And whoever among you does wrong,) means by associating others in worship with Allah,

(We shall make him taste a great torment.)

Surah: 25 Ayah: 20

وَمَآ أَرْسَلْنَا قَبْلَكَ مِنَ ٱلْمُرْسَلِينَ إِلَّآ إِنَّهُمْ لَيَأْكُلُونَ ٱلطَّعَامَ وَيَمْشُونَ فِى ٱلْأَسْوَاقِ ۗ وَجَعَلْنَا بَعْضَكُمْ لِبَعْضٍ فِتْنَةً أَتَصْبِرُونَ ۗ وَكَانَ رَبُّكَ بَصِيرًا ۝

20. And We never sent before you (O Muhammad (peace be upon him)) any of the Messengers but verily, they ate food and walked in the markets. And We have made some of you as a trial for others: will you have patience? And your Lord is Ever All-Seer (of everything).

Chapter 25: Al-Furqan (The Criterion, The Standard), Verses 001-020

Transliteration

20. Wama arsalna qablaka mina almursaleena illa innahum laya/kuloona alttaAAama wayamshoona fee al-aswaqi wajaAAalna baAAdakum libaAAdin fitnatan atasbiroona wakana rabbuka baseeran

Tafsir Ibn Kathir

All of the Previous Messengers were Human

Allah tells us about the previous Messengers He sent: they all used to eat food needing the nourishment in it. They used to go around in the marketplaces seeking to engage in trade and earn a livelihood. This should not, however, affect their status as Messengers, for Allah gave them good characteristics and caused them to speak fine words and do noble deeds, and gave them miracles and clear proofs, from which any person with sound insight may see the confirmation that what they brought from Allah was true. This Ayah is similar to the Ayat;

(And We sent not before you any but men unto whom We revealed, from among the people of townships) (12:109).

(And We did not create them bodies that ate not food) (21:8).

(And We have made some of you as a trial for others; will you have patience) means, `We test some of you by means of others, so that We may see who will be obedient and who will be disobedient.' Allah says:

(will you have patience And your Lord is Ever All-Seer.) meaning, He knows who deserves to receive revelation, as Allah says elsewhere:

(Allah knows best with whom to place His Message) (6:124). And He knows who deserves to be guided to the Message with which He sent them, and who does not deserve to be guided.

(And We have made some of you as a trial for others. Will you have patience) Muhammad bin Ishaq said: Allah is saying, "If I had willed that the world be such that no one would oppose My Messengers, I could have made it so, but I wanted to test My servants by means of them." In Sahih Muslim it is narrated from `Iyad bin Himar that the Messenger of Allah said:

«يَقُولُ اللهُ تَعَالَى: إِنِّي مُبْتَلِيكَ وَمُبْتَلٍ بِك»

(Allah says: "I will test you and test others by means of you.") In the Sahih it is recorded that he was given the choice between being a Prophet and king, or being a servant and Messenger, and he chose to be a servant and Messenger.

www.ingramcontent.com/pod-product-compliance
Lightning Source LLC
Chambersburg PA
CBHW081110080526
44587CB00021B/3534